TRISTAN TAORMINO'S
True Lust

TRISTAN TAORMINO'S
True Lust

*Adventures in
Sex, Porn, and
Perversion*

CLEIS
PRESS

Published in the United States by Cleis Press Inc., P.O. Box 14684, San Francisco, California 94114.

Printed in the United States.
Cover design: Scott Idleman
Cover photograph: Richard Mitchell
Hair and makeup: Tatijana Suljic-Shoan
Book design: Karen Quigg
Cleis Press logo art: Juana Alicia
First Edition.
10 9 8 7 6 5 4 3 2 1

All the essays first appeared, some in different versions, in *The Village Voice* (1999–2002), and several later appeared in *The Spectator, Clean Sheets, Velvet Park, You Are Being Lied To* edited by Russ Kick (Disinformation Books, 2001), *Faster Pussycats* edited by Trixie (Alyson Publications, 2001), and *Everything You Know Is Wrong* edited by Russ Kick (Disinformation Books, 2002), with the following exceptions: "My Virgin Lap," "Intro to Swingers 101," "I Was a Pro-Dom Virgin," "Sir, Yes Sir!," "Pierced for Pleasure," "The Tourist and the Puppy," "My Date with Betty Dodson," and "I Fucked a Straight Girl" first appeared in *On Our Backs* (1998–2001); "My Date with Howard Stern" first appeared as "Rear Guard" in *The Boston Phoenix* (January 1998); "This Girl Is Different" first appeared in *A Woman Like That: Lesbian and Bisexual Writers Tell Their Coming Out Stories* edited by Joan Larkin (Avon Books, 1999); "The Name of the Rose" first appeared on Nerve.com (February 2001); "Why I Love Porn" first appeared in *Vibe* (July 2002). "My Adventures in Sex, Porn, and Perversion," "My Life as a Feminist Pornographer," "On Being Buttgirl," "Looking for Mommy," and "Stone Femme" © 2002 by Tristan Taormino.

Acknowledgements

Behind every good writer is an even better editor, and I've had the privilege to be edited by some of the finest. First and foremost, my tremendous thanks and gratitude to Doug Simmons, my hands-on editor at *The Village Voice* for two and a half years who taught, encouraged, and challenged me with exceptional generosity. A variety of others have taken my work in their capable hands, among them Diana Cage, Athena Douris, Heather Findlay, Richard Goldstein, Russ Kick, Joan Larkin, Felice Newman, Emily Nussbaum, Ed Park, Susan Ryan-Vollmar, Carla Spartos, Carmen Thompson, Trixie, Layne Winklebleck, and Mark Woodworth. To my agent Andrew Blauner for his quick wit, friendship, and a very long leash. To Frédérique Delacoste, Felice Newman, Don Weise, and everyone at Cleis Press, for one of the best long-term working relationships I've ever had. To Rachel Kramer Bussel and Michelle Cronk for making my life easier and better. To Richard Mitchell for the cover photo and Tatijana Suljic-Shoan for her styling genius.

So many people, places, and things inspired, facilitated, and participated in many of my adventures: Kim Airs, Juli Ashton, Krystal Bennett, Hanne Blank, Kate Bornstein, Fairy Butch, Seymore Butts, Loren Cameron, Trashina Cann, Barbara Carrellas, the cast and crew of my two videos, Chloe, Come As You Are, Community Ties, The Disposable Boy Toys, Betty Dodson, The Dyke Uniform Corps, Eminem, Karen Everett, John Fleuvog, Larry Flynt, Mario Grillo, Judith Halberstam, Bert Herrman, Jim and Glenda, Stan Kent, Joy King, Nan Kinney and Christi Cassidy, Dr. Anne Lawrence, Ron Lieber, FetishDiva Midori, Sir Michael and His pups, Eden Miller, Jack Morin, Joan Nestle, Candice Owen, Eva Pendleton, Professor Claire Potter, Bryn Pryor, the puppy and the tourist, Red, Shar Rednour, Lance Ryan, Michael Selditch, Sherry and Vilma, John Stagliano, Howard Stern, Jackie Strano, Debi Sundahl, Ron Suresha, Matt Bernstein Sycamore, Mistress Sydney and Mistress Maxim, Toys in Babeland, Sir Turino, Del LaGrace Volcano, Deb Wasser, The Water Boys, and Riki Wilchins.

To my mom for religiously reading (and commenting on) my *Village Voice* columns. To my friends and family—Toni Amato, Morgan Dunbar, Nina Hartley, Sarah Lashes, Ira Levine, Stacey Meadow, Audrey Prins-Patt, Julie Levin Russo, and Winston Wilde—for their love and affection. And, finally, to Colten, whose presence in my life is a gift I will always treasure.

Contents

Introduction:
My Adventures in Sex, Porn, and Perversion

Pornography has made me be honest, about myself and some of the most intimate details of my life and my fantasies. I think that's an important part of writing: being able to dare to put oneself on the page. —John Preston, *My Life as a Pornographer and Other Indecent Acts*

I didn't exactly major in feminist sex education and pornography at college. I went to Wesleyan, a private liberal arts college in Connecticut, where I found a politically active community, accessible professors, and plenty of sex. I did my share of rabble-rousing there, mostly in the form of queer and sex-positive activism. Through my activism, I decided that I wanted to go to law school and become a lawyer for the disenfranchised and downtrodden. Ah, youth and idealism! I had the grades, the recommendations, the over-achiever's extracurricular activity list, and some mediocre LSAT scores. Everyone advised me not to worry about the standardized test numbers, so I was shocked to receive ten rejection letters, two "you're on the waiting list" letters, and no acceptance letters. I was devastated. I remember going to my professor and senior thesis advisor, Claire Potter, crying in her office about what to do. Claire said to me in her signature straightforward style:

"Tristan, I don't think you want to go to law school, and I don't think you want to be a lawyer. I think you want to write about sex. I think you're good at it."

Where on earth did that come from? Well, I had worked for a year and a half on my senior thesis, about butch/femme lesbian sexuality, under her guidance. In the two hundred and fifty page project, I talked a lot about lesbian identity, sadomasochism, pornography, and, yes, sex. I even used lesbian porn stories, magazines, and videos as some of my primary source materials. So, while pornography may not have been my major (it was American Studies) or even my concentration (it was Women's Studies), I managed to make it part of my college curriculum. Later, I was taken off the waiting list and accepted to one school. I decided to defer for a year, pursue sex writing, and see what happened. Claire's advice seemed downright scary to me, not part of my original plan. I didn't know quite where to start.

I had written my first piece of erotic fiction, a story called "Bombshell," as a part of the thesis, so I fine-tuned it and submitted it to a few magazines and an anthology. I began to write more, attend readings, and meet other writers whose primary interest was sex. Why sex? For me, sex is the most interesting area of our lives. It is a source of ecstasy, pain, discovery, and inspiration. It's a space where we connect, learn about others and ourselves; where we hope; where we heal. It can be a microcosm of life itself, a minidrama of politics, identity, and power. The bed (literal or symbolic) is where we shed clothes and inhibitions, where we put our bodies on the line, where we show ourselves to others in unique ways. I couldn't think of richer territory to read and write about.

How I Became a Smut Peddler

I became an avid reader of sexy, alternative magazines—like *On Our Backs, Brat Attack, Frighten the Horses,* and *Venus Infers*—that fueled my imagination and my libido. One by one, each ceased publication or went on indefinite hiatus. The more widely read gay and lesbian glossies like *Out, Curve,* and *Girlfriends* didn't focus on erotica or have an edge. There was some renegade, insightful work still being published in underground zines, but they didn't have a big enough circulation to make a critical impact.

I started the pansexual erotic magazine *Pucker Up* with my partner Karen Green in 1995 to fill the void left when some of my favorite pervy magazines disappeared, as well as to showcase the erotic fiction, photography, essays, and creativity of post–sex war sex radicals. Our choice to make *Pucker Up* pansexual was a conscious one. We wanted to include the voices of all sexualities and genders—from lesbian, bisexual, straight, and leather to woman, boy, and butch—to create a complex and meaningful dialogue about sex and gender. We saw *Pucker Up* as an opportunity to pose some new questions: what stories, images, and desires are missing from current representations of erotica? Whose voices haven't we heard? How do we chart the terrain beyond the literal flesh of bodies and sexual acts? *Pucker Up* became a place to explore some answers while unearthing even more questions.

Although publishing transgressive work was easier in the '90s than it was a decade before, it still raised issues. There is an assumed correlation between a reader's identity and her or his tastes in smut: lesbians read only lesbian erotica; straight women read only straight erotica, and so on. But that ignores the possibility that our libidos are a lot more perverse, and I believe they are! In our magazine we attempted to conquer what was then new turf: writing across gender lines, queering heterosexuality, and exploring the multitude of lesbian (and female) genders, from femmes and daddies to girlfags and drag kings. As we incited both desire and debate, we challenged readers to think about their own identities, fantasies, and boundaries. That's a challenge I continue to this day.

Adventure Girl Is Born

When *On Our Backs* was reborn in 1998, the new publisher asked me to write a regular column for the magazine called "Adventure Girl." The premise was that editors would send me on sexual adventures—preferably things I had *not* experienced before—and I would write about them. At first, the concept intimidated me slightly. I mean, I'd *been* writing true stories, disguising characters, combining events, and calling it erotic fiction. If I embraced Adventure Girl, I had to come clean and dive into a new genre: first-person, *non*fiction. I decided to go for it.

The staff of *On Our Backs* brainstormed a preliminary list of possible adventures, which included: have a session with a dominatrix at a professional dungeon; go to sex therapy; visit a sex club; work as a phone sex operator; attend a fetish support group; learn how to female ejaculate; get electrocuted or be set on fire by an S/M expert; attend Ms. Vera's Finishing School for Boys Who Want to Be Girls and learn how to be a girl; participate in a workshop for people who don't like to be touched;

audition for a soft-core porno; have my clit pierced or acquire another piercing; go to a porno theater; get a lap dance; participate in a sex study; audition as a stripper; and consult a sex surrogate. Together, we added to the list: go to a sex magic workshop; visit a nudist colony; train to work at La Nouvelle Justine (a New York City S/M-themed restaurant); visit the set of a *Playboy* shoot; take Diane Torr's Drag King Workshop; get a branding; go to a slave auction; and attend a piercing class.

To complete my first three assigned adventures (get a lap dance at a strip club, go to a swingers party, have a session with a professional dominatrix), I had to navigate a world created primarily by and for heterosexual men. My first realization: the sex industry—from strip clubs and porn to escorts and pro-doms—does not see women as a viable market for any of these services. Women are still not seen as sexual aggressors, predators, or consumers. Because we are not seen as consumers, we often don't see *ourselves* as such. If women are in a public place where sex is being sold, we are the ones doing the selling and not the buying, we are the *consumed*. For example, a woman with a man at a strip club can be read as: dragged there, a little wild, into three-ways, bi-curious. By contrast, a woman with another *woman* at a strip club can be read as: in the industry, wanting to be in the industry, or a lesbian. A woman alone at a strip club is more difficult to read, except by the management; to them, she's there to work (that is, she's a prostitute). Even when we are "misread," when we do pop up in these dens of masculine lust, we definitely disrupt the boys club. What happens when women decide to take the reins, producing as well as partaking in sex work?

After more than a year (and a dozen escapades) as *On Our Back's* Adventure Girl, I began to share my adventures with a larger, more sexually diverse world when I began writing a sex column called "Pucker Up" for *The Village Voice* in New York. Since 1999, I've attended tantric sex workshops and BDSM conferences, met adult film stars and golden shower aficionados, researched swingers and sex reassignment surgery. I claim dildos, dirty videos, bondage seminars, and books like *Deviant Desires* as business expenses on my tax return. The best part? I have permission to delve into unknown territory and to try out everything from anal fisting to human puppy play—because it's my job.

Speaking and acting on our desires and fantasies has a lot to do with permission—the permission society gives (or denies) us to be open about sex as well as the permission we give ourselves to be honest about our sexuality. I hope that my travels into new, unknown, and exciting erotic territory demystify sexual practices and communities and give my readers permission to explore their own undiscovered sexual worlds.

If you don't already know it by now, sexually speaking, I'll try just about anything once. Curiosity, fascination, and my anthropological tendencies will get me past the fear, the absurdity, even the potential disgust I might feel. I am unequivocally interested in gender identities, sexual subcultures, kinks, fetishes, and turn-ons, even when they are not my own. Lucky for me, a lot has changed in the decade since I graduated from college. Many more aspects of sexuality are more available, more accessible, and less taboo than they've ever been.

True Lust is a collection of sixty-eight (sixty-nine including this introduction) of my adventures in sex, porn, and perversion: my Adventure Girl stories, my *Village Voice* columns, and other essays written between 1997 and 2002. I have also included a list of my favorite books, movies, and websites at the end of the book, for those readers interested in further "research." My work has given me the chance to experience things I never thought I would and to share them with all of you. Not only have I learned a great deal about a variety of erotic people, places, and things, but I have engaged these subjects in a very personal, visceral way. In the process, my adventures have pushed me to look deep inside myself—at my own sexual desires, fears, fantasies, and foibles. Imagine if, each time you had a sexual experience, you had to process and analyze it and put it all down on paper for the world to read! Consider this, then, a public journal of my private journey. Of course, this isn't the whole story. There *are* some adventures I am not quite ready to share. Well, not yet, anyway....

Tristan Taormino
New York City, July 2002

The Sexual Is Political

My Date with Howard Stern

"Did you have fun? Were you nervous? Did you mind being called a slut? Would you do it again?" These were the probing questions asked in an e-mail sent by my friend Rich, a reporter for *TV Guide*, the morning after I was on *The Howard Stern Show*.

I had been booked to promote my new book, *The Ultimate Guide to Anal Sex for Women*, a fun, practical self-help guide. Since Howard is very vocal about his obsession with both lesbians and anal sex, everyone thought it was a perfect fit.

Did I have fun?

When I arrived at the studio at 7 A.M., the cameras were rolling. The radio segment is filmed for Stern's nightly cable show on E! Entertainment Television, and the producers like to include clips of guests as they wait beforehand in the green room. As I waited, Gary the Producer and other staff members asked me strange questions, such as: "Would you have anal sex with anyone?" There was a live feed of the show in the room, and I could hear Howard teasing the listeners with my imminent arrival, referring to me as "the anal sex woman," "the anal sex expert," or simply "anal sex girl."

As soon as they opened the door to the studio, I was on the air. Although it was eight o'clock in the morning, it felt strangely like midnight. Wearing his trademark sunglasses, Howard sat directly in the middle of the studio, behind a block of computer screens. Robin was behind glass in her own booth to the left of the guest area. Jackie the Joke Guy and Fred the Engineer were lurking behind stacks of equipment. Gary the Producer, Howard's Assistant, and all the interns were frantically taking orders and hurrying in and out of the studio. It was chaotic, and more than a little difficult to get a word in edgewise.

Was I nervous?

A few weeks before my scheduled appearance, I began listening to Howard's show every morning before work and watching it at night on E!. I wanted to get a better feel for the show. In fact, that made me even more nervous, because each time I heard or saw a show, I thought, "What am I getting myself into?" But I'm glad I arrived with well-researched expectations.

I expected him to try to guess my bra size, though I didn't expect a breast expert to actually guess wrong, erring on the side of voluptuousness. (The feminist in me was horrified at the objectification, while the late-blooming-and-flat-chested-until-I-was-seventeen girl was delighted.) I expected him to tell me to stand up so that he could check me out; I didn't expect him to tell me I had a "hot little body." I expected him to ask personal, rude, and inappropriate questions; I didn't expect him to ask me how many people I had slept with in my entire lifetime. Generally, knowing what to expect made it easier not to make a big deal out of his queries. I simply answered them honestly, and moved on to my book.

What was the biggest surprise? That there was someone else in the studio more nervous than I was: the radio station's general manager. Before I went on, Gary told me the words one cannot say on the air, per FCC regulations: *fuck, shit, piss, cocksucker, motherfucker, cunt, tits.* I was ready for those. What I wasn't ready for was Gary's next set of instructions for keeping the show clean (read: uncensored). "You cannot refer to penetration—vaginal or anal—in any way," he told me. "Nothing can be in anything else—like, no penis in a vagina. Nothing can have been in something—like, 'My finger was in his butt.' You can't describe any act involving penetration."

What? How was I going to discuss my book without referring to penetration?

"Howard will lead you through it," Gary assured me. "You can say things like, 'When you've experienced that type of pleasure,' or 'When I have pleasured someone in that way'—stuff like that."

I didn't know what to make of these supposedly helpful suggestions. I feared I would end up sounding like an uptight sexologist who couldn't even say the words written in her own book. I wanted listeners to know that the way I described things was restricted by the FCC and that I usually talk about sex in an honest, straightforward, accessible way.

Except for one slight screw-up (I said *fuck* without realizing it, and they bleeped me), I thought I was doing pretty well. But then Howard asked me about positions for anal sex. "Can I go through all the positions and their pros and cons?" I asked. "No!" he burst out.

During a break after the segment, I learned that the general manager had been freaking out, panicked that not only would this part of the show be censored, but Howard would be fined by the FCC again (he's already been tagged for over $2 million). I imagine that warnings such as "Get off this positions thing now!" were flashing on Howard's computer screens. I didn't know about any of this scandal as it was happening; I just knew that Howard was being cagey and weird about the question of positions.

This served as a reminder of just how taboo the topic of anal sexuality is. Not only is there still widespread misinformation, misunderstanding, and myth out there, but I'm confronted with silence and censorship everywhere I go to promote my book—even on *The Howard Stern Show*.

Did I mind being called a slut?

Howard can be really mean to his guests, and I knew that going in. I knew I shouldn't take anything he said personally. After all, it's his persona that's offensive and outrageous, not him. He was ultimately fascinated with the topic of my book, and approached me with enthusiasm and, well, respect—insofar as he can respect any guest he has on his show. So I ended up having an even better time than I expected.

Would I do it again?

In a heartbeat. While all this was going on in New York, at the West Coast offices of my publisher, Cleis Press, the staff had arrived at 4:30 A.M. to answer the phones (Howard repeated the toll-free number for ordering the book several times, and Cleis anticipated some calls). They ended up working a fourteen-hour day, taking orders that came in almost faster than they could record them.

So, whatever you think of Howard Stern, I have to give him credit for his huge and loyal following. Keep in mind that the mainstream media—including the national queer media—won't cover this book. Because of the provocative nature of the topic, I have limited outlets to promote the book, and I'll take the exposure where I can get it.

And besides all that, my mother called me from Long Island after the show to tell me that she thought I handled Howard quite well. Who would have thought going on *The Howard Stern Show* to talk about a book I penned on anal sex would make my mother proud?

Sex and Silence in D.C.

Within hours of arriving in our nation's capital, I had a naked nineteen-year-old woman in my hotel room. She seemed so young to have such well-developed exhibitionist tendencies, though she had a hint of shyness as she turned around to reveal two curved cello *S*'s on her back, an homage to Man Ray. She rolled around on the white sheets, her hair morning-messy, her creamy skin flushed with nervousness and excitement. Out of the bed, we put her in a warm bath. We decided against any bubbles so that we could see her body through the water. As she moved the soap between her legs, she arched her neck and tilted her head. "That's perfect!" said the photographer. "Can you move your arm so I can see your pussy?"

Whenever I travel to other cities, I like to squeeze in a little porno to make my trip worthwhile: I set up photo shoots for *On Our Backs,* the lesbian sex magazine, to showcase the, um, local talent. I hadn't come to Washington, D.C., to corrupt just one woman, but this perky, well-poised, freckled wonder happened to be first on my list. And it was a long list of events for the weekend—the Gay and Lesbian Press Summit, a national gay and lesbian leather contest, the Equality Rocks Concert, and the controversial Millennium March on Washington (MMOW). With so many queers descending on the home of the world's most famous blow job, I expected there'd be plenty of sex in the city. I was way more off-base than John Rocker at a PFLAG meeting.

As a sex radical and a leatherdyke, I was supposed to be boycotting the MMOW. In fact, so were plenty of gay people, at the urging of critics who charged that MMOW producers excluded people of color, S/M folk, transgendered people, and many others from the organizing process. Antimarchers accused MMOW of being one big marketing event designed to funnel money and database information into the Human

Rights Campaign (HRC), one of the richest, most conservative, most powerful, and (among many activists) most despised gay and lesbian organizations in the country.

Instead of protesting by staying home, I decided to protest by showing up.

I was invited to address the Gay and Lesbian Press Summit, a conference for members of the queer press. In my keynote, I made sure to say the word *pussy* three times (what other keynoter can claim that?) to remind everyone in the room that I'm not a card-carrying member of the squeaky-clean, nonthreatening, advertiser-friendly gay and lesbian press. Afterward, people applauded me for being so out about my sexuality. One woman commented, "You said *pussy* like it was the greatest word in the English language." Isn't it?

I followed up my speech by driving out of the city to a women's S/M play party in an affluent, suburban neighborhood home that had been converted to a private dungeon. There I saw dykes piercing, paddling, and panting their way to ecstasy. Now that's more like it.

That sacred, sensual energy was missing from the Millennium March—indeed, all the vitality, diversity, and uniqueness of the gay, lesbian, bisexual, and transgender community were eclipsed by corporate sponsorship and preppy, white, middle-class gay men in polo shirts sporting the HRC logo. Surrounded by clean-cut cuteness, you might say I stuck out like a sore fist. Likewise, sexual freedom was absent from all the rhetoric, testimonials, speeches, and even the T-shirts. I searched everywhere for the souvenir for my mom that read: "My anal-sex-expert pornographer daughter and her butch, dildo-wielding dyke girlfriend went to the Millennium March on Washington and all I got was this lousy T-shirt." No luck.

My moment of redemption came when I strutted past the chanting right-wing March protesters holding signs like "AIDS Cures Gays" and "You Are Perverts." With my fierce girlfriend in a leather cowboy hat on one arm and a tranny boy with a mohawk on a leash on the other, I proudly stood before them—wearing a purple PVC push-up bra, matching skintight pants, and the word PERVERT written across my stomach in lipstick. Memo to antigay zealots: Sticks and stones may break my bones, but you need to get some new names to call us.

Surrounded by too many marketing opportunities at the Millennium Festival and still feeling alienated from our supposed tribe, we decided to leave the March early. Only a ten-minute taxi ride away, we descended a staircase into the dark, low-ceilinged Improv club. At the final segment of the two-day American Brotherhood contest, more than a hundred leatherfolk celebrated their sexuality, erotic differences, and visions for the community. All of them boycotted the March. During his speech, one contestant noted that leather groups had been approached by March organizers inviting them to join but requesting that they "tone things down" and not wear chaps, leather vests, and other signs of unconventional sexual lives. Such a request outraged most kinky people—as it should have.

Yet, as American Leatherman, Leatherwoman, and Leatherboy were crowned that night, I couldn't help but wish that the winners, the contestants, and the room full of attendees had marched. A sizable leather contingent, we would have sent a clear message to HRC, the "good gays," and the world at large: S/M people are a vital part of the gay, lesbian, bisexual, and transgender community. We will not go away or be pushed back into the closet. We will not be silenced about the erotic component of our identities.

When we refuse silence and instead are loud, out, and proud of our erotic acts, we make the most basic of political statements about sexual freedom. Such a statement was not on the agenda of the HRC or the MMOW. Like other conservative segments of the gay and lesbian civil rights movement, these groups would have us believe that to achieve equal rights, we need to divorce our sex from our politics. But that denies the power of sex. Whom we have sex with, how we have sex, why we have sex is inherently political. What terrifies the religious right is that we love and fuck people of the same gender. Antigay protesters referenced it in their "Fag Sin" posters, but marchers played it down, down, way down.

Perhaps it was the attempt to sweep sex under the rug that made me so obsessed with it all weekend. Everywhere we went, I wanted to have sex. I had lesbian sex, kinky sex, sadomasochistic sex, public sex, even polyamorous sex (for all of you preppy gays, that means with more than one person at the same time) every chance I got. There in the land of politics, I became a political beast, compelled to make a political statement over and over and over again. And I've got the sore muscles to prove it.

Two's Too Tough

Matrimonial polls reveal that 40 to 60 percent of people cheat on their spouses at least once, and half of all marriages topple. Haven't we learned anything from Monica's mouthwork, Frank Gifford's elevator shenanigans, and all the other scarlet-letter activities? Let's face it, folks: Monogamy is dead.

Maybe not completely dead, but, goddess knows, it's barely breathing. Many couples might benefit from breaking the equation of one-ball-plus-one-chain-equals-love. Look, the hair-pulling caveman is gone, and the Cleavers seem oh-so-retro. When the state of Vermont legalized civil unions (read: gay marriages), that single act struck fear into the hearts of conservatives everywhere and signaled the downfall of the American marriage as we know it. We're all going to hell now anyway, so why not move into the new century and expand the possibilities of our intimate relationships? Let's explore polyamory!

I am not recommending you all go Mormon on me. Some Mormons practice their own brand of polygamy, which involves men marrying multiple women at a very young age, marrying their new wives' relatives, and making way too many babies. So, let's just leave the Mormons out of this discussion.

Polyamory, a catchall term for many different practices, encompasses relationships that fall outside the traditional, sexually faithful, two-person model known as monogamy. Think of it as a postmillennial antidote to chronic serial monogamy, which includes an abundance of cheating, embarrassment, deception, scandal, separation, and divorce. Many polyamorous couples practice nonmonogamy—the partners are emotionally committed to one another, but their relationship isn't sexually exclusive. Some poly people have multiple partners with whom they have both sexual and emotional/love relationships. Some polyamorous couples expand to become a triad or a group.

It may be every red-blooded American man's dream come true (finally, that threesome with your wife and her best friend legitimized!), but that doesn't mean it's a free-for-all. Polyamory for couples requires honesty, communication, boundaries, mutual respect, and rules—rules based on your individual relationship, desires, needs, and goals; rules that everyone can agree on; rules that you need to stick to. You may decide that having the occasional ménage à trois to spice things up is okay by both of you. Or you may allow each other to have fuckbuddies as long as you two remain the primary relationship. Your rules are whatever you need (no sleepovers? no anal sex? no blondes?) to feel secure, sane, and satisfied. One member of a poly dyke couple told me, "Say I am going through this phase where I want to be spanked and tied up, and my lover's not really into it. What about if we just go find someone that I could do that with? It could be safe, fun, and hot. It doesn't mean I am going to go run off and marry that person."

I know one polyamorous couple that comes to the table as a package deal: If you want to get jiggy with him, you have to boink her, too. Another duo bases their sanctioned dalliances on geography; when either or both are out of town, they have free rein to do the nasty with whomever they choose. While in the same zip code, they remain true-blue. A rad bisexual couple works the gender angle. She's allowed to muffdive with other girls, but he's the only XY in her equation. He can suck all the cock he wants, but must remain loyal to one and only one pussy—hers. Two leatherwomen in a Daddy/boy relationship have a rule based on S/M roles: They are allowed to play with other tops and bottoms as long as the boy has only one Daddy and vice versa.

My freaky friends are not the only ones expanding their horizons— there are plenty of people doing it, trust me. If you're looking for them, a good place to start is a magazine called *Loving More*, which has a wealth of information on the subject and celebrates alternative arrangements of all kinds. At the risk of sounding like my fellow *Village Voice* columnist Michael Musto, I have it on good authority that a certain married couple of actors who starred in a late-'80s drama has a three-way marriage with another woman; they all live and have tantric sex together in Northern California. Dude, everything's way cooler on the West Coast.

While it may seem reminiscent of '70s free love without the drugs, polyamory today encompasses a greater consciousness of safer sex and everyone's feelings and boundaries than it did in the days of wife swapping and key parties. It's a surefire way to challenge your sexual and emotional boundaries and explore your feelings about jealousy and possessiveness. If you were allowed to stray within the confines of your relationship—the illicit naughtiness of an affair no longer present—would it still be desirable? Could you live with the knowledge that your partner was fucking someone else but still loved you? Polyamory is not a tool to avoid issues in your marriage, not an excuse to act out irresponsibly, and not for everyone. It takes just as much work as monogamy, and probably more honesty. The sneers *slut, swinger,* and *sex addict* may be vaulted your way by others, but check the source—they're probably just jealous. Who says there can't be a president, two First Husbands, and a First Girlfriend in the White House?

Dallas Dildo Defiance

I've been on sixteen planes since September 11, from Ohio to Oregon, and my carry-on luggage has been searched nearly every time I've walked through the metal detector. There were the nail clippers at JFK, a shiny knife pendant at LAX, and a silver lock dangling from the ring of a leather collar in Chicago. In Columbus, after my personal belongings took their trip down the conveyor belt, a security guard asked me to step out of line for a bag check. Since all three of the aforementioned items were safely packed in my checked suitcase, I wondered what could have possibly triggered suspicion. He led me to a long table off to the side, where the bags of two other passengers were being checked. He rooted around in my backpack until he found what had alerted the person at the X-ray machine: my portable and innocuous-looking vibrator. Known to many as the "pocket rocket," this little buzzer is barely bigger than a lipstick and wouldn't intimidate even preppie Charlotte from *Sex and the City*.

"What's this?" he asked.

"It's a vibrator," I said. Sure, I could have gone the easy route, claiming my right to carry a personal shoulder massager on board, but what about the next girl who's got a glow-in-the-dark cock, circumcised head and all? I wanted the security folks to get hip to how some of us relax on a long flight.

"What do you mean?" he said.

"What do you mean 'What do I mean?'" I replied. "Would you like me to show you how it works?"

The guys on either side of me blushed and chortled respectively, then the man repacked my bag and let me go on my way.

As I travel, I continue to put as many whips, riding crops, and sharp objects as I can in my checked luggage, but I was especially nervous when I recently booked a flight to Dallas–Fort Worth International Airport.

I'd heard that it's illegal to sell dildos in the state of Texas. Worse yet, rumor had it that having more than six dildos constitutes the intent to distribute them, so zealous dong ownership alone is against the law.

In case my luggage was X-rayed and I was plucked from the boarding line once again, I wanted to be prepared. I decided that honesty was my best defense: I would have only two dildos with me—the other fifteen would actually be vibrators and butt plugs. (You may think it's overkill to pack so many, but a girl's gotta be prepared.) Well, after doing a little homework, I learned that it's not just dildos that are illegal, but all things "obscene," which Texas law defines as dildos, artificial vaginas, or any device "designed or marketed as useful primarily for the stimulation of human genital organs." In my house, we call that *sexual pleasure,* and in the land of the free, some states regulate how you get yours.

Dallas Cowboy cheerleaders who want to play bury-the-bone are not alone: There are similar laws on the books in Georgia, Louisiana, Mississippi, Kansas, Colorado, and Alabama. Since the majority of people who use dildos, vibrators, and other insertable sex toys are women, making them contraband is another institutionalized form of controlling female sexuality. There's also an insidious double standard at play: A much higher percentage of men than women can masturbate to orgasm with their own hands.

Vibrators deliver consistent, powerful stimulation unparalleled by any human being. The first time I ever used a vibrator, all I could think was, Wow, now I know what all the fuss is about! Actually, I couldn't really think at first, since I was too busy reeling from the amazing orgasm. Vibes aren't just for solo missions anymore. Let's face it: Even the most ambitious lover can get a stiff neck, repetitive stress injury, or just plain exhaustion from going that extra mile to make you squeal. A person who whips out a vibrator in the bedroom says to me, "I am sexually confident, adventurous, and dedicated to your pleasure." And I don't want any state legislature telling me how I can or cannot come.

Although I wasn't in Dallas for a silicone-sausage shopping spree, I wondered, What do Texans do when they want to fill a hungry hole or stuff a slippery slit? What if a girl wants to celebrate Masturbation Month (which is May, by the way) in the Lone Star State? Could Debbie do Dallas without any dildo diddling?

Some stores, like Austin's women-owned Forbidden Fruit, require customers to sign a release form declaring that they are purchasing toys for educational purposes only. While there isn't a Commission to Crack Down on Dildo Distribution (well, none that we know of), Forbidden Fruit's diligence is a result of being raided and shut down in the '90s. Incidentally, the store carries copies of a new amateur, authentic lesbian porn flick called *Home Cookin'*, which was filmed in Texas. Trust me, if the hotties in this vid were performing for educational purposes, then remind me to apply to the University of Texas pronto.

Other shops don't openly display plastic phalluses, but if you ask and they know you're not a cop, they might show you something on the Q.T. Once again, sexuality is shrouded in mystery, hidden behind the counter, relegated to the back room, available only to those who know the secret password. Ironically, S/M gear is perfectly acceptable (signs posted say it's sold for costume use only), so I could buy all the leather chastity belts, bondage gear, and ball gags I wanted at local fetish shops Leather by Boots and Shades of Gray. Plus, there are plastic penis swizzle sticks aplenty at novelty shops. Just those pesky jerk-off tools are off-limits.

This, from the state where not only are guns legal and easily available, but concealed firearms are A-OK as long as you have a license. Hey, I'm all for a sex-toy licensing program if it makes motorized muff-movers lawful. Imagine what the test would be like to carry a concealed dildo. I can see it now: Lea Delaria as the hard-nosed instructor and Drew Barrymore, with a strap-on beneath her silk dress, as the nervous first-time driver. Excuse me while I grab my pocket rocket and whack off to that image. After all, it's my right under New York State law.

Eminem Is My Bitch

I don't know what it is about Los Angeles, but whenever I go there, strange desires surface. Maybe it's all those bright, sunny days with a thick layer of smog looming above my head. Maybe the number of cell phones in use per square inch is fucking with my brain waves.

I arrived in L.A. just in time to witness the best pairing since Sonny and Cher: Eminem and Elton John singing together at the Grammys. Considering how they were hyped and protested to the hilt, I was slightly disappointed by their low-key rendition of "Stan." You see, in my fantasy, Elton actually raps the controversial lyrics of "The Way I Am," Eminem is strung up in full bondage, and Dido (whose song was sampled in their performance) is there dressed as a dominatrix. Oh, forget Dido. *I* am the dominatrix, and Eminem is my bottom, on his knees and at my mercy. Don't get me wrong—I would never humiliate, beat, or torture Eminem without his consent. I just happen to think he'd enjoy himself: He definitely has a masochistic streak. I want Eminem to be my bitch.

Does my urge make me as depraved as he's supposed to be? (My bitch says, "I am whatever you say I am.")

I am embarrassed to say that, like many of Eminem's antifans, I bought into all the rhetoric about him—you know, I'm queer, and queers should hate him—before even listening to his music. My gay leatherdaddy, whom I was staying with in Los Angeles, happens to dig the dude, so he played every track from *The Marshall Mathers LP* for me. I must say that his stuff is a lot more complicated than the Gay and Lesbian Alliance Against Defamation press releases would have me believe. Is Eminem truly evil, or is he simply saying what America is thinking? Nearly half of the country elected a drunk-driving, double-talking idiot and a conservative politician who adamantly supports anti-gay legislation even though his own daughter is an out lesbian. Eminem's lips may be the ones that are moving, but he's not the only one with homophobia and misogyny on his mind.

The porn phenomenon known as bukkake shoots homophobia and misogyny right on your face. The concept of this particular peckerfest began in Japan (where its depiction is illegal): A group of men stand around, yank their chains, and ejaculate all over a woman's kisser. Although this is a supposedly "straight" sexual exchange intended to turn on hetero men, many watchers can't help but notice that lots of naked men are standing near one another, holding their own hard-ons, and jerking off. The fact that there is some submissive slut who wants their spooge all over her face seems as inconsequential as a girlfriend for Ricky Martin. Gee, sounds a lot like a gay circle-jerk to me. A researcher from Playboy TV's *Sexcetera* told me about his visit to the set of a bukkake video that took this sperm-o-rama to its highest homoerotic level. Eighty-nine men masturbated and came on this girl (who, incidentally, was wearing an E-collar, the white plastic lamp shade you put on a recently neutered puppy to keep it from licking its stitches). When number ninety stepped up to the plate, he popped, then proceeded to lap all the cum off her like a rabid dog. The cum of eighty-nine men. If that's not gay, I don't know what is. (Note to my bitch: This material is ripe for your next album. Say, "Thank you, Ma'am.")

Since the gay leatherdaddy and the straight fetish master have joint custody of me whenever I am in town, I've gotta say, "Thank you, Sir" to my other host, a dear friend and kinky top who generously opened his world-renowned S/M dungeon to me (it happens to double as guest quarters). It's always a fairly surreal experience when I stay with him; as I climb into bed, I am surrounded by rows of menacing whips, shiny silver clips and clamps, and tray after tray of medical implements. The walls are covered with eclectic sadomasochistic art, mostly of men dominating women, his particular bent. (This guy's fantasies would scare the living daylights out of Eminem.) When I wake up in the morning, I sometimes forget where I am. I shuffle to the bathroom, where I am greeted by a wall of enema bags, rubber tubing curled around hooks, forty different enema nozzles, and a black latex apron hanging on the back of the door. Sometimes a girl just wants to pee without being bombarded by someone else's enema fetish. And sometimes I don't want a toilet there. I want my bitch underneath me. Eminem: Forget about washing your mouth out with soap. I've got a better idea.

I am ultimately always thankful for Mr. Top's enema fetish, and I was especially grateful on this trip, since I found myself in a photo shoot for Hustler's *Taboo* magazine. I think I am the first *Taboo* columnist—I'm the Anal Advisor—to put my pen down and my pussy forward for a hardcore pictorial. For me, it was an excuse to get my hands on my favorite adult star in the world, Chloe, who just signed an exclusive contract to direct and perform for VCA Pictures. After sticking a purple Japanese eggplant up my ass (the photographer's idea), Chloe tortured my pussy with clamps and weights, gave me a faux enema, and dominated me in various ways. I was Chloe's bitch. Well, sometimes you just gotta turn those tables.

Someone else with a passion for turning tables is Larry Flynt, and I love to visit his retail venture, Hustler Hollywood, when I am in town. The store takes the whole notion of the sleazy adult bookstore on the wrong side of town and turns it upside down. The Flynt empire created a brightly lit adult emporium smack in the middle of West Hollywood amid all the trendy hotels and clubs. At Hustler Hollywood, you can buy a pink velvety pillow with the words *Barely Legal* embossed on it, a realistic replica of porn star Janine's pussy (it vibrates!), a supersized bottle of lube or massage oil, and even a handcrafted glass dildo created by local company Heart On. I picked one up as a special gift for Eminem. If that bitch only knew how he has inspired me.

The Name of the Rose

"How many vaginas are in the house?"

When was the last time you heard someone shout that from the Madison Square Garden stage? No, not even a Spice Girls reunion concert or Lesbian Day at the WNBA could prompt such a question. And it wasn't so much a question as a call to arms when it came from the mouth of Eve Ensler, creator of *The Vagina Monologues,* at V-Day, a Valentine's Day benefit staging of the play. Eve had some help from a cast of over seventy actors, musicians, performers, and activists, including such fabulous divas as Oprah, Carol Kane, Isabella Rossellini, and Rosie Perez—all deliciously decked out in fiery-red satin, fuzzy pink sweaters, wine-colored velvet, and fuchsia feather boas and aptly named "The Vulva Choir." They talked about their vaginas, um, I mean they read from the play, to speak out against violence against women around the world. Talk about pussy power.

Although I had been told repeatedly on the phone there would be no celebrity access, I found myself on the press list at the post-performance celebration at the Hammerstein Ballroom. There I was, surrounded by ladies in red, and I didn't even have a tape recorder! While reporters from *People* and *Marie Claire* buzzed around them asking thoughtful questions about feminism and reclaiming women's bodies, I pondered my strategy as I fished for a small pink Hello Kitty notebook stashed in my purse. If I could ask all these powerful, sassy women just one question, here on V-Day, what would it be?

"What is your favorite word for vagina and why?"

I looked Swoosie Kurtz squarely in the eyes, hoping she wouldn't roll hers and have security remove me from the building.

"Twat."

"Twat?" I repeated, a little surprised I admit, but suddenly excited I had asked.

"Twat. Because I can finally say it. I mean, in grade school, I thought that was one of the worst words you could ever say, and now I am not only saying *twat,* I am saying it on stage. A friend said to me, 'You know, Swoosie, you've done *The Vagina Monologues* so many times, you should change your name to Twatsie.'"

"And you liked that, didn't you?" I probed, suddenly feeling brave.

"I did," she said with a giddy smile on her face.

When I posed the question to Ann Magnuson, who was appearing in *The Vagina Monologues* off Broadway, she said, "China. Because I couldn't pronounce the word *vagina* when my mother first said it to me, so I called it *china.* It seems appropriate since it's halfway around the world."

"I thought it appropriate too, but in a different way," I said. "It's delicate, yet resilient, and sometimes you want to put it on a pedestal with its own spotlight. And men, with their groping ways, can be bulls in china shops, get it?"

"Oh, I get it," she winked.

Once the better half of Superman and now a supermom, Teri Hatcher told me, "I am teaching my three-year-old daughter the word *vagina.* We were at a restaurant one night, in the bathroom, in stalls right next to each other. She asked me, 'Mommy, why do you have a hairy vagina?' I called over the wall of the stall separating us, 'Because when women get older and mature, they get hair on their vaginas.' Well, actually it's the vulva and pubic mound, but close enough," Teri said to me as if we were cramming for a test on *Our Bodies, Ourselves,* then continued, "I told her, 'You'll have hair there too one day.' When we came out of the stalls, a line of women had formed in the bathroom, and I just smiled at all of them...."

Since her monologue that night was the infamous "Reclaiming CUNT," where she said the word so many times with such love and conviction I swear I peed my pants, I paused before I approached Glenn Close.

"I am asking everyone the same question tonight, but for you, considering your monologue, it may be redundant: What is your favorite word for *vagina* and why?"

"I'd have to say *cunt* because I can say it. I'm not afraid of it anymore. I don't feel shame about it anymore. When Eve first asked me, I didn't think I could do it. I didn't think I could say it. But now I feel totally comfortable saying it." Trust me, folks, *cunt* rolls off her tongue as naturally as it does off mine.

And so it went all night:

Marisa Tomei: *"Coochie,* because it's cute." I am sure it is, honey.

Kathy Najimy: *"Woodle.* It just happened one night, and now that's my word."

Lesbian comic Kate Clinton: *"Puffy Gyn*—it's so soft you just dive right in."

Law and Order: Special Victims Unit star Mariska Hargitay (who wasn't actually in the performance, but I spotted her at the party, and was on a roll): "I've got so many, it depends on what mood I'm in." Every girl should be so lucky.

When I finally caught up with feminist legend Gloria Steinem, her answer was: *"Vagina* is still my favorite word for *vagina.* Do you know that *60 Minutes* wouldn't cover this event because they didn't want to say *'vagina'* on the air? Because it's still a word that is difficult to print, to publish, to get the media to even say out loud, it's still important to remain my favorite."

"Oh, that's easy. It's very politically incorrect," said Jane Fonda, as if she was going to say she liked an Eminem record. "But it's *pussy.*" Jane Fonda said *pussy* to me!

"That's her favorite word too," said a familiar voice from behind me. It was my girlfriend, who'd quietly been observing my celebrity chats all evening without saying a word. Jane turned to her and smiled, and I quickly explained who she was.

"Pussy—such a great word. Definitely my favorite," Jane repeated, then another reporter snagged her for a photo.

I slept soundly that night, dreaming of Jane's scarlet power suit crumpled on my bedroom floor.

My Life as a Feminist Pornographer

My mom is the first feminist I ever knew. But I didn't know then that she was a feminist. I just knew she wasn't like the other moms in my homogenous suburban community. She didn't wear a bra, which always embarrassed and horrified me as a child trying to fit in. It's not as if she had enormous breasts or wore extremely tight shirts; neither was the case, but that didn't matter to my nine-year-old brain.

"Why don't you wear a bra?" I asked her one day. She said she was a feminist, and it was her decision. My parents were divorced, and my mother raised me alone. She refused to take child or spousal support from my father. So, as a kid, I thought being a feminist was about going braless and being broke all the time.

As I studied feminism in college, I gained new respect for my mother and the sacrifices she made to juggle a career and be an involved, available parent to me. She showed me independence, strength, and the will to survive. She taught me that I could be anything I wanted to, that there were no limits I couldn't overcome. I also began to connect her experiences with the theories of feminist thinkers and realized that feminism was about the value of choices and freedom of expression. My mom *chose* not to wear a bra as a symbol of the Women's Movement. My mom *chose* to raise me and support us financially by herself.

In many circles today, *feminist* is a bad word, and it saddens me that many of the young women whom I consider to be on "my team"—zinestresses; reproductive rights activists; women furthering the dialogue on issues like body image and sexuality—refuse to identify themselves as feminist. Frankly, a riot grrrl's choice not to call herself by the "f" word is a legacy of feminism. We've come a long way, baby, so far that now you can enjoy all the progress of the Equal Rights Movement and the luxury of declaring yourself *not* a feminist.

I am not afraid to use the "f" word. I think it's important and necessary to keep feminism alive and kicking. Besides, without feminism, I
wouldn't have a career. Without feminism, I wouldn't be a pornographer.
Sound like a paradox? The arguments of antiporn feminists never res-
onated with me; they reduce all pornography to an objectifying, violent
tool of the patriarchy. I believe that feminism and pornography can rub
up against one another, make sparks fly, respect and empower women.

When I came out in college in the early '90s, one of the first lesbian
magazines I ever read was *On Our Backs* (my girlfriend subscribed to it),
and it was very significant in the development of my lesbian identity—it
was a source of validation, information, and entertainment. The magazine offered plenty of visual and written smut that inspired actual sex acts.
I became a reader, a fan, then a contributor. And, a decade later, I became
the editor. So you see, as much as it sounds like a sentimental greeting
card, lesbian porn changed my life. Which is a convoluted way of saying
that porn is a medium that's not only valid, but significant, powerful, and
political as well.

When *On Our Backs* first hit the stands in the '80s (with the tag line
"entertainment for the adventurous lesbian"), its mere existence in the
lesbian community was radical in and of itself; it was a document of a new
sexual revolution spawned by the Lesbian Sex Wars. By 1998, the magazine changed ownership twice, went on hiatus, and relaunched itself as
"the best of lesbian sex." By then, sex-positive lesbians had won the Sex
Wars, and had made tremendous strides in the process. A new challenge
emerged with the magazine's rebirth: Its presence alone was no longer
enough. What was the significance of a lesbian porn mag when we were
no longer arguing about whether porn was good or bad?

As editor, my daily tasks consisted of writing dirty words and looking at dirty pictures. Sounds like a typical pornographer's job, with one
important difference: All of our pin-ups were amateurs, many of them
real-life couples, with little or no modeling experience. Unlike mainstream mags that usually assign photographers a scenario ("we'd like a
doctor/patient scene") then find models to plug into the picture, *On Our*

Backs approached the women we featured very differently. We wanted to know what turned them on, what they did with each other in bed, what they wanted to see in the magazine, how they wanted to be represented. Our goal was to capture a moment of their real sexual lives on film. The models were as much a part of the process of creating the photos as the editor and photographer, which put a new spin on objectification—what happened when the object willingly and enthusiastically participated in the creation of her own image? For one thing, we learned you *can* create sexual images without stripping away someone's entire identity.

Sometimes, I found myself with a totally new spin on the old bra-issue: Does she brandish it, burn it, or forego it altogether? (Her choice, of course.) Mainstream media has long equated porn with images of naked people fucking. Sounds simple, but in the case of lesbian pornography, that definition doesn't always translate. For queers, what we put on (or leave on) for sex is as important as what we take off. This is especially true when it comes to showing the sexuality of butch women, boydykes, and others who embody female masculinity. Men's suits, 501s, chaps, boxers, and briefs can become erotically charged costumes in the bedroom. They can also be necessary components of a person's sexual identity. One of the challenges I constantly faced as editor was: How do we represent the butch body in porn without completely undressing it?

On Our Backs was and is a unique porn magazine because it puts pleasure and politics on the same page. We relied on our readers and the queer women in our community to share their ideas, their fantasies, and their sex lives with us; you wouldn't find airbrushed Barbie dolls with mainstream "perfect" bodies that aspired to traditional notions of beauty. We prided ourselves on representing women of all shapes and sizes, races and ethnicities, different turn-ons, kinks, and fetishes. A commitment to diversity was a tall order, since lesbian sex is not just one thing. Nor is it ten or fifty things. With such a wide variety of gender and sexual expression among queer women, I found I was precariously juggling the vanilla with the BDSM, the butch/femme with the andro-girls, the romantic with the anonymous, the fuckbuddies with the married couples, the separatists with the trannies, the vulva lovin' with the cock suckin'. There are plenty of people and stories that don't describe themselves with these hard-and-fast labels or defy such falsely stable categories—they're both, they're neither, they're something altogether different. *On Our Backs* taught me that it's impossible to fully represent lesbian sexuality in forty-eight pages six times a year!

On Our Backs puts the theory of feminist pornography into action. Its mission, longevity, and evolution illustrates that porn can be an important tool for empowerment—to build community, reinforce identity, incite debate, and create a forum for dialogue.

True Lust Adventures

Intro to Swingers 101

"Do you want to go to a swingers party with me?" she asked. I had just landed at Michelle's place, weary from my grueling book tour. I was looking forward to a good night's sleep on her futon to prepare for several events the next day.

"A swinger's party?"

"Yeah, I know it's kinda strange, but I go every once in a while, and I'm seeing this guy right now, and we're going together tonight."

First of all, people actually still call themselves swingers? *Swingers* seems like such a retro-phenomenon from the '70s, reminiscent of wife-swapping, bong-smoking orgy-goers, and key parties. I saw that dismal key party in *The Ice Storm*—no, thank you. Plus, it's 1998—don't you think there should at least be some new term coined? I'd go with something like S.A.S.H.—Sexually Adventurous Suburban Heterosexuals.

I didn't know that swingers parties still happened, and I certainly didn't know anyone who went to them. But I thought this might be my one and only opportunity to check out how the other half plays, so I decided to go. Before we left, Michelle gave us her version of an "Introduction to Swingers" orientation.

About a half hour outside the city in an industrial park off the highway, we drove past rows of identical, nondescript low-rise buildings. We were in the middle of nowhere. We looked for the only office with lights on, and a modest sign greeted us at the door: "Computer Users Group Annual Spring Meeting—Time to Clean Your Hard Drives!" (Michelle's Intro to Swingers Lesson 1: To rent its meeting space with discretion, the swingers group calls itself a computer group.)

Each office in the typical corporate space had been converted into a playspace; inside a door or behind a makeshift curtain was a dimly lit room with one or more mattresses on the floor. The main common area looked like the all-purpose rec room of a suburban condominium complex: a modern bar, couches, big-screen TV, and, in the middle, gray carpet leading to a wood parquet dance floor. You know, swingers party tonight, George and Ida's twenty-fifth anniversary party tomorrow, and Adam's bar mitzvah on Saturday. Not exactly sexy, warm, or inviting.

The majority of the people there were white, professional married couples in their forties. It didn't seem very promising to this dyke. But I came all the way to a swingers party, and I wasn't going to just stand around. I made eye contact several times with one guy until he came over and introduced himself. His name was Dave. He was vaguely handsome, well-built, told me he was a TV producer. After we chatted for a while, he said he really wanted me to meet his girlfriend, Lynn. (Intro to Swingers Lesson 2: Many of the women identify as "bi-curious, so there can be girl-on-girl action, but there is absolutely no boy-on-boy anything.)

Lynn was dressed in a pastel-colored business suit. She had frosted blonde hair cut in a neat, chin-length bob. Stiff and nervous, she looked absolutely terrified to be there.

"This is my first time at one of these things," she said. She had a nice smile.

Straight girls and femmes usually aren't my thing, so I was a little skeptical.

Since I was an out-of-towner, I was planning to remain anonymous at the party; unfortunately, someone recognized me from a recent local event and word quickly spread that I was the girl who wrote a book on anal sex. About that time, a line formed. One by one, men approached me and told me they wanted to have anal sex with me. (Lesson 3: The scene is pretty heterosexist and usually revolves around men—they're the ones who make the moves.)

After a particularly sketchy proposition from an overgrown frat boy and his drunk, reluctant wife, I decided that Dave and Lynn were definitely my best bet. (Lesson 4: There are three kinds of rooms. 1) Private: The door can be shut and locked. If unlocked, people can come in and watch if they first ask permission, but they can't join in. 2) Semi-Private: There is a curtain instead of a door. People come and go and watch; they

can join in if they ask permission. 3) Anything Goes: Self-explanatory.)
Dave and Lynn wanted a private room.

They were both cautious, and wanted me to take the lead. I took
condoms, gloves, lube, and a butt plug out of my little backpack. (Lesson 5:
Unlike the sex parties I've been to with safer sex rules and supplies everywhere, swingers rarely practice safer sex, so you have to be adamant about
it.) I was still wary about just how bi Lynn really was, so I was pleasantly
surprised when she was eager and enthusiastic. She licked her fingers and
took my nipples between the slick tips. I kissed her as I unhooked her bra.
The white lace revealed soft, full breasts and raspberry-red nipples. Her
body was curvaceous, big hips, a dreamy round ass—the way I always
imagined Joan Nestle looked from her erotic stories.

Lynn was really in touch with her body, confident and sexy, and she
proved it wasn't her first time with another girl when she went down on
me. Dave was gentle and sweet. He touched us both with reverent hands.
He stayed back for the most part, but not in that gross I-wanna-watch-
and-jerk-off way. It was never about his pleasure. The focus shifted to
Dave and me teaming up to make Lynn come, and we took turns pleasing her with our mouths and tongues and fingers, until she let out a high-
pitched scream and collapsed. Her skin was glowing, and we stroked her,
kissed her cheeks. Then we talked for a long time, probably longer than
our sexual encounter.

I don't think I'm ready to become a regular in the swingers scene.
But it was nice to dip my foot in a pool of foreign water, see how the
water looked, smelled, felt. See the different creatures and their distinc-
tive world. A world very different from my own. But for one night, I could
be a visitor in that world, and the visit was memorable. I still believe they
need a new name, but I've got to give them credit for creating a community where they can explore their desires. On that we can agree.

The Tourist and the Puppy

The tranny boy was flagging a yellow hanky on the right. In a hotel full of kinky girls there for a conference, that's what caught my eye. Because you see plenty of heavy S/M black and fisting red and Daddy dark-green, but a bright canary-yellow hanky—the color of golden showers—is a rarity. And I was in the mood for a good pissing scene.

Sir Turino orchestrated the whole thing: Four of us would all co-top the boy and his femme girlfriend. Each top had various plans for the willing duo. Madame picked out a suitable pair of thigh-high red vinyl boots she wanted the boy to polish with his tongue. Sir Turino busied herself with selecting various floggers, canes, and other torture devices with which to beat the two. Sir Red pushed her big black dick into her tight briefs. I poured myself a nice cool glass of water.

When I opened the door, they were in the hallway on their knees each with packs of cigarettes in their mouths for Sir Turino. The boy had obviously not had time to change clothes before the scene, and he was wearing corduroy shorts and a plaid shirt. He looked fresh off the bus, as if a camera belonged around his neck, so we decided to call him The Tourist. The girl had her long shiny blond hair in two pony tails and a rhinestone collar around her neck like a Lhapsa apso might have. We decided she was The Puppy.

The Tourist and the Puppy were told to address the two ladies in the room as Madame (as in *Muh-dahm*) and Mistress Tristan (because it's so hard to say). I asked him to spell my name, and when he struggled with my last name, I didn't want him to forget it. I grabbed Madame's dark plum lipstick, and told the Tourist to spread his legs. On his right thigh, I wrote the correct spelling; on his left thigh, I wrote it phonetically: TARA-MEAN-O. But as we teased and tormented him, the Tourist repeatedly confused me and Madame. That just would not do. The difference between Madame and Mistress Tristan was cleared up with a little breast worship and some smothering—Madame is a double D and I'm a B.

I sat back—drinking lots of water—and watched as Madame gave the Puppy a tail, a leash, and a bone. Every so often throughout the scene, I would exclaim loudly, "I am so thirsty!" and the other three tops would giggle and cackle. The Puppy and the Tourist both got spanked, paddled, flogged, and caned by Sir Turino and Sir Red. Sir Red also got her dick sucked by the Tourist, and, at my suggestion, both Sirs put their dicks in the Tourist's mouth at once. The Tourist was quite an accomplished cocksucker.

Of course there was more beating and teasing, but after a few hours I was antsy. Finally, we brought the Tourist into the bathroom, told him to strip to just his boots, and lie in the tub. Sir Red balanced herself on the edges of one end of the tub, Sir Turino did the same on the other end. I stood in the tub directly over the Tourist. The deal was, I got the first shot. My bladder was about to burst at that point from all the water.

This was the moment I had been waiting for, to have a willing boy beneath my feet ready for me to pee on him. I told the Tourist to ask me for it. He said, "Please, Mistress Tristan, spill your golden nectar on me." I spread my lips and just let go. The urine spilled and splashed over his hungry body as he writhed and moaned. Sir Red and Sir Turino joined in, each holding her dick and peeing on the boy. Madame snapped a few shots with her camera for posterity.

I find peeing so erotic because, for one, having a full bladder feels arousing and makes my clit hard. Being able to release that feeling of pressure is orgasmic in its own way. Spilling and sharing that bodily fluid with a lover is intense and intimate. When I can just let go of my inhibitions and anxieties and do something you're not supposed to do with another person, the taboo and the forbidden are made exciting and sexy. Peeing on someone can also be eroticized as act of dominance, and that's what made it hot for me with the Tourist. It was a way of marking him like a dog marks her territory. Because the Tourist was so into it, so willing to surrender, it was twice as hot to be above him giving him exactly what he craved.

While the Puppy helped the Tourist shower and clean up, Sir Red fucked me on the bed, and Sir Turino fucked Madame right alongside us. When the two emerged from the bathroom, we positioned the Tourist underneath me, and Sir Red fucked me some more from behind. Then Sir Red fucked the Tourist. We all switched then—I crawled underneath Madame while Sir Turino fucked her, and Sir Red fucked the Puppy, who was on top of the Tourist. We were a pile of intertwined legs and arms and cunts and mouths and cocks and clits and tongues. We strapped the biggest dick we had—it's called "Man o' War"—to the Puppy and she plowed Madame with it. At one point, I turned my head toward Madame, who was moaning, "Oh, yeah. That's. A. Good. Puppy." Madame was so breathy and sexy, I could have come just from hearing her say it. A good Puppy, and a good Tourist indeed.

My Date with Betty Dodson

I was so excited about this adventure I nearly peed my pants. Imagine having your own private one-on-one session with the author of the groundbreaking, critically acclaimed *Self Loving* and *Sex for One*, with the woman credited as the "Mother of Masturbation." I was going to touch myself for Dr. Betty Dodson. When I arrived at her swank Madison Avenue apartment, I was immediately struck by two things: Betty conducts her sessions and runs her office where she lives, and she has an amazing living space. Plus, the masturbation goddess herself has celebrated her seventieth year on the planet, and yet she does not look a day over fifty. (And, no, folks, she has not had any plastic surgery.) I told her, "I pray I can look like you and live like this when I'm your age!" And she owes it all to masturbation. It's obviously the key to a long, healthy, happy life.

Our session began with Betty asking me questions about my sexuality, my masturbation practices, and my orgasm experiences. Usually, clients come to her with a specific problem or issue they want to work on. Some have never masturbated before, some are having a sexual problem, and others have never had an orgasm. I've been jerking off since I was four years old, so I was pretty comfortable with it, but I still believed that I could benefit from Betty's knowledge and expertise. You can never be too rich or too sexually skilled.

I felt ready to come out to Betty and to all my readers about an important fact that impacts my sex life: Adventure Girl is a member of Prozac Nation. (Did you think I was this fun and charming naturally?) Since I've been taking antidepressants, my orgasmic ability had radically changed. There was a time when I could come at the drop of a hat. Nowadays, it takes a lot more patience and finesse. Some people on antidepressants cannot have an orgasm at all, but for me it's just a more difficult task. Tricks that used to work no longer do, and sometimes I have to get pretty creative. I've resorted to some of my old ways, which means that it is much easier for me to come on my stomach than on my back. So, Betty and I decided that we would work on coming on my back.

We started with a standard from the days of feminist consciousness-raising: looking at my pussy in the mirror. Betty encouraged me to look closely at my cunt, find and identify the important parts, stroke it, rub it, play with it. She commended me on my pussy hair shaving job, and told me that women who shave/groom often have a better relationship with their pussies as a result of looking at and fussing over them on a regular basis. I was glad to discover that my love of shaving my twat was considered healthy by someone with a Ph.D.!

When we got down to the meat of the session, Betty told me to start masturbating and talked to me while I was touching myself. I told her that I was really into having a lot of pressure on my clit, rather than light flicks of the tongue or little circles with a finger. And when I say pressure, I mean stack a ton of bricks on me and I am pleased as punch. She pointed out that relying on the pressure to get off was limiting and that if I trained myself to come from other kinds of stimulation, I would be a more versatile lover. Betty hit on it right there: I love a challenge, and I love learning new stuff that makes me a better lover. Then I got to stick various things in my pussy, like the Crystal Wand, a Lucite S-shaped dildo designed to hit your G-spot and a barbell that resembles the Kegelcisor but that Betty designed herself and had specially made. I had a one-of-a-kind piece of Betty Dodson sculpture in my pussy *and* in my ass! That was enough to make me come on the spot. But I was on my back, remember, so it took a little more work and the help of the Queen of All Vibrators, the Hitachi Magic Wand. I did eventually get there, and once Betty was satisfied that I had worked for it, she let me turn over on my stomach and ride the magic wand to another rousing climax.

I joked to my friends later about the session: "You jerk off in front of Betty, and she tells you what you're doing wrong." Actually, it's more like she grades you in different areas: how you work your clit, what kind of G-spot stimulation you like, vaginal stimulation/penetration, anal stimulation/penetration, pelvic rocking and thrusting, PC muscle contractions, breathing, and making noise. I scored very high in pelvic thrusting and PC muscles (she says mine are very strong) and had the poorest performance in the breathing category. I tend to hold my breath a lot while I jerk off, or take very shallow breaths since I get a kind of head rush that way. Betty reminded me that while the light-headed feeling is nice, it's temporary. Taking really deep breaths while jerking off gets your blood pumping to all the right places, thereby encouraging your clit and pussy to become engorged and increasing stimulation and pleasure. So many lessons to learn for this smarty pants.

Betty also helped me remember something I knew, but sometimes tend to forget, especially when having really good sex with an amazing lover: The one person who holds the key to my pleasure is me. We tend to rely on others to get us off, and get lazy about self-love. The more you get in touch with your own body, what you like and dislike, your personal hot spots, and what gets you off, the better lover you will ultimately be. The more you practice receiving pleasure, test your own responsiveness, and really work at your orgasms, the better sex you'll have alone and then with others. Thanks to Betty, I had a back-to-school experience that left me educated, motivated, stimulated, and satiated. I'm waiting patiently for my next homework assignment, Dr. Dodson.

Going for the Gold in Michigan

I was afraid that I wouldn't be let into the Michigan Womyn's Music Festival. This annual estrogen celebration (which turned twenty-five in 2000) has a reputation for being a bastion of '70s feminism. So I was picturing a bunch of topless, hairy-armpitted, hippie, camping lesbians dining on tofu, drumming in goddess circles, and humming along to Cris Williamson. Don't get me wrong—I love tofu, but I have my own reputation: I'm a push-up-bra, shaved-all-over femme dyke; editor of a pro-S/M smut rag; a known man-fucker; and a wannabe porn star. I'm a radical lesbian feminist separatist's worst nightmare. But I couldn't resist the idea of a giant, girls-only slumber party in the woods for a week. I wanted to know if the festival, at its quarter-century anniversary, was still strumming that same old tune. Was separatism alive on a secluded plot of land near Hart, Michigan? Was there room on 640 acres of wooded womyn-born womyn-identified womyn space for me and my kind?

Politics aside, I was impressed by the sheer scope of the festival: Over 650 women (including 400 volunteers) erected a self-contained village providing child and health care, three meals a day, disability resources, even designated areas (quiet, clean and sober, rowdy, or kid-friendly) to accommodate all 6,500 campers. Women come from all over North America (and pay $290 to $340 for six days) to enjoy several hundred workshops and more than a hundred performers.

I anticipated that going might be like walking back in time to a world of separatism, but I can't deny that being at a chicks-only camp was pretty cool. Determined to be myself and not change my gender presentation to suit the masses (well, isn't that what feminism's all about?), I wore my best "tool of the patriarchy" purple marabou sex-kitten teddy. I walked around in my knee-high these-boots-weren't-made-for-hikin' platforms. I shaved my pussy in the communal outdoor showers as a political statement.

There were enough glares and criticism from some of my sisters to tell me I didn't have the votes to become festival prom queen, but the spectrum of women on stage and on line for the "Porta-Janes" gave me hope. Boydykes, butches, and other fine specimens of female masculinity moved proudly through womyn space, casually grabbing the packages in their pants. Girly girls posed and strutted in the first-ever Femme Parade, reminding us (again!) that we can be feminists and still wear makeup. Once known as strongly anti-S/M, the festival had enough leatherwomen hanging slings between trees to make me wanna go back. Old-school favorites like Holly Near and Ferron shared the stage with riot grrrls the Butchies. You know something's shifted when Tribe 8, with its raunchy stage show, headlines a women's music festival.

Just being on the same property with Lynn Breedlove made my girlfriend, Red, and me less nervous about teaching our series of sexuality workshops, including "The Ultimate Guide to Lesbian Sex," which seemed to stick out among offerings like "Healing Through the Voice of the Mother" and "Completing the Soul's Journey." (Organizers told us that this was the first year that so many sex-related workshops were offered.) We were shocked when over four hundred women came to our first class. After I lectured about sex toys, strap-ons, and female ejaculation, women lined up for the interactive section. I introduced a few brave girls to the world of anal pleasure, and Red located the G-spots of some thirty women! Once we realized how popular our workshops were, we wanted to take full advantage of our unique surroundings. Where else could we do so much hands-on teaching about sex than in an all-women, clothing-optional campsite? It was *Our Bodies, Ourselves*-style consciousness-raising for the new millennium!

To go out with a bang, we decided to follow our final workshop, "How to Ejaculate," with the First Annual Ejaculation Contest. Armed with more than one hundred latex gloves, plenty of lube, absorbent pads, and a big blue tarp (remember, we're in the woods!), we signed up sixteen women to compete in four categories (you could enter alone or with a partner, or request a partner whom we would provide). We began with the speed category. A judge yelled "Go!" and, at the first sign of ejaculatory fluid, screamed "Stop!" to the woman with the stopwatch. Two contest-ants didn't shoot before the three-minute limit; one made herself squirt in an impressive eighteen seconds. A shy, silver-haired fiftysomething butch prefaced her performance with: "I only began ejaculating after I turned forty. I don't know what's going to happen, but I'm gonna give it a try." Paired with a complete stranger (one of our generous "volunteer ejacula-tion helpers"), she squirted her way to the championship in two—that's right, two—seconds. The crowd went wild.

Next up was distance. Red assisted a hot femme wearing false eye-lashes to beat out two others with her winning spurt of twenty-seven inches on the tape measure. As you can imagine, the quantity category was more difficult to gauge. We decided to have contestants ejaculate on an absorbent pad laid on top of the tarp (which of course would be wiped dry between contestants). After each gal gave it her best shot, judges would inspect the pad, the tarp, as well as other areas—the helper's shoes or arm, for example—and rate the quantity from one to ten. Scoring a perfect ten was a young, gorgeous, leggy redhead who gushed so much fluid, she probably soaked the ground.

The final category, "Best Single-Handed Job," required women to make themselves come by their own hand or a favorite toy without the assistance of a partner; judges rated technique and style. The four lined up and went at it simultaneously. As the contestant on the far right was coming like a banshee (but not actually ejaculating!), the quiet brunette on the left stole the show when she inserted a clear acrylic dildo in her pussy and practically splashed the first two rows of the audience with her fantastic flow.

There were oohs and aahs galore, cheering and moaning; I know that after the prizes and sashes were given out, more than one pair snuck off to their tent for an instant replay. Later that night, I saw the second-place finisher in the quantity category and her girlfriend. "When we get home, we're going to start training for distance," she told me with an Olympian spirit that made me proud. I could see the gleam of gold in her eyes.

My Throbbing Mouse

Experts say that the majority of the most heavily trafficked sites on the Web—and the ones making loads of cash—are those devoted to sex. Pornography does appear to rule the Internet, giddy in its ability to show anything and everything. Its print and video counterparts are subject to obscenity laws and community standards, which hold them back from getting really raunchy. But in the dot-com world, golden showers, enemas, bestiality, and other bizarre sex acts are par for the course. In addition to downloading pictures, reading stories, watching streaming video, and, for big bucks, interacting with a real live girl online, people are meeting each other in cyberspace. Sure, there are AA support groups and chat rooms to sound off on political issues, but most of the people communicating online are not exactly exchanging recipes. I know plenty of people taking full advantage of this carnal free-for-all, but I admit that I was until recently a cybersex virgin.

As you may know by now, I tend to like my bump-and-grind in the flesh. But in the interest of adventure and satisfying my own curiosity, I decided to fire up the modem and see if I could get laid. I don't have America Online, the service with by far the most chat rooms (they call them "communities"), so I had to go to my girlfriend's house for my experiment. I probably would have gone there anyway, since I have an old Mac that runs Netscape 3.0 (how '90s of me!), which crashes at the mere mention of a Java application or anything else worth running while you surf.

At her place while she was at work, I signed on and jumped into the AOL chat rooms. I decided to go anywhere that sounded like a dungeon or S/M space. In one room, I "listened" as several tops bullied willing bottoms, and all I could think was: I'd rather be stuck in traffic on the Brooklyn Bridge. A few people sent me instant messages with really bad come-ons, which I ignored. I decided quickly that America Online does not hold the key to my orgasm.

I surfed over to a new website that calls itself "the spot for female sexuality." Libida.com offers users erotica, an online sex-toy store, and features on everything from a six-hundred-man porn gang bang to the effects of antidepressants on your sex drive. After answering a few brief questions, you can even calculate the exact time of the month when you are most in the mood. What bizarrely organized computer horndog wrote that program? I also checked out the "How To" section, but the only information available was how to give a great blow job. Not exactly one of my most pressing concerns at the moment. Plus, in the "Advanced Tips," it offered these mind-blowing lessons: "Use your hand around the base of his penis to control how deep he goes into your mouth. You can start a blowjob when your partner's penis is flaccid and stimulate him to erection. Run your hands over his inner thighs as your mouth moves on his shaft. Keep your teeth away from his penis, or very, very lightly rub them against him while sucking." Duh—I am a dyke and even I know that. I finally registered to chat, but, sadly, there was no one in any of the rooms of the Libida Lounge.

Dejected, I moved on to Nerve.com, which promised me a "community of thoughtful hedonists" in the Nerve Center. I signed up and picked a user name announcing my intentions: "buttgirl," of course. After the marketing hedonists probed me for details about my tax bracket and other demographic possibilities, I clicked Enter and the screen announced: "Play ball, buttgirl!" This seemed very promising, and I even felt a little twitch between my legs. I headed to the most crowded chat room, the Bar; when I got there, I immediately caught the attention of Fred, who proclaimed, "She backs that thing up in a single bound!" Now that's a good opening line. Everyone in the Bar was talking about tea—I kid you not, different kinds of tea, because one of them had a sore throat. Where were all the thoughtful hedonists? Fred seemed like my best and only chance to get some, so I convinced him to follow me into an "empty" room. Then I made my move.

I started by telling him I wanted to have sex, and he seemed quite agreeable. He said he was a guy, but I just pretended he was a butch dyke. We did some back-and-forth flirting. I told him I was a leggy redhead with a tattoo on my inner thigh. He told me he was getting hard. Geez, guys are so easy. He interrupted our dialogue with "Do you want to do this on the phone?" I wanted to say, "Fred, I am trying to have cybersex as an experiment, and I am going to write about it in *The Village Voice*, so having phone sex with you would defeat the whole purpose. Besides, if you would just play along and fuck me online, I can make you famous!" Instead, I simply responded, "No, Fred, I am happy just where we are." I told him to get on his knees while I undressed for him. Whenever he seemed a little too pushy, I told him that either he was going to be a good boy and shut up, or I was leaving. He agreed and promised he would be good. I can spot a submissive man a mile away, and, apparently, even down the information superhighway. I continued to tease him as quickly as I could type, which isn't as fast as I think.

Then my cell phone rang, and I had to pick it up because I was actually expecting an important call. It turned out to be my girlfriend, who must have intuited that I was having, or trying to have, sex with someone else. And on her computer no less.

"Where are you?"

"At your place."

"What are you doing at my house? I thought you were working on a column."

"Um, I am, honey. Can I call you back?"

Meanwhile, Fred was getting antsy, and asked me two more times, "Are you absolutely sure that you do not want to do this on the phone?"

"I'm sure, Fred, I am sure." I tried to get back on track, but after a few lines, Fred said, "buttgirl, this isn't really working for me. I am going back to the bar. Bye." But Fred! I am buttgirl, and I am here to play ball! Unfortunately, no one would play with me. My eyes were glazing over from staring at the computer screen for so long, and I was sick of typing. Alone in my girlfriend's house, I decided to hunt for a vibrator and wait for her to get home from work.

Cruising for Girls

I will never forget the first blow job I ever gave: It was in the woods during the summer, and I was being mercilessly bitten by mosquitoes as I attempted to fit a boy's cock in my mouth. It was less than ideal, but somehow still exciting because we could have been caught at any moment. Since then, some of the best sex I've ever had has been in public places. I've trolled around in various locales, from the awkward to the ironic, including cars, restrooms, movie theaters, hotel pools, beaches, parking garages, and crowded bars and clubs—I even did it once in bustling Grand Central Station. Public sex is cut-to-the-chase copulation: It can be fevered and frenetic, naughty and exhibitionistic, slightly risky or downright dangerous. For some people, sex with a complete stranger can be equally hot and forbidden. No small talk, no romance, no baggage, no emotions—just raw, unadulterated pleasure.

I've always believed that gay men have the market cornered on getting some anonymously and out in the open, and the website I've recently been turned on to, squirt.org, confirms it. In New York City alone, there are more than eighty-five gay cruising areas listed, including bathrooms in hotels, department stores, restaurants, bookstores, and airports, as well as gyms, video arcades, parks, theaters, and even subways: "The last car of the 2 train is infamous! Heading uptown through the Bronx toward 241st. After rush hour. Or midday when kids are in school and adults are at work. Just rub your dick and look for others doing the same. Make eye contact and go from there." My first impression of Squirt was that fags are so organized! You can go to any major city almost anywhere in the world and know exactly where to go to cruise other men; with a little effort, you can probably have anonymous, semi-public sex while you are there. Not to mention all the gay bathhouses and sex clubs.

The closest spurting equivalent for queer women I found on the Web is a lesbian personals site called womanline.com, where there is actually an "intimate encounters" section for women who are just looking for sex. A sample of the offerings: "Little Squirter says: Lipstick will spread for you! Let's chat about my talent." It's not exactly the infamous tone of the gay personals—"eat my 10 inches of man meat"—but it's a start. Beyond the virtual world, there are few, if any, cruising spots for dykes. Why not? Women don't have public sex with women very often, women cruise other women even less often, and women rarely have anonymous sex with each other. No, I don't really have the data on this phenomenon. (Somehow, no one has funded a grant to study the public sex practices of lesbians—shocking.)

We have many of the same opportunities as the boys: rest stop areas, gym locker rooms, AA and Al-Anon meetings. We even have a few of our own: Prospect Park's Nethermead during dog off-leash hours, the bathrooms during WNBA games and Indigo Girls concerts, post–Dyke March gatherings, and the Michigan Womyn's Music Festival. So why aren't we doing it like the boys? First of all, guys have a much easier time having sex standing up; public encounters often involve mutual masturbation where they whip it out, jerk it off, and go. Chicks can't whip out their clits in quite the same way, and we often prefer to lie back and spread our legs, which is not easy to do in, say, a bathroom stall. Plus, when you're in the great outdoors, there's rarely a reliable electrical outlet for the Hitachi Magic Wand when you really need one. There are also safety issues with a woman alone walking down by the pier after midnight. Most dolls won't take the chance just for a quickie muffdive.

Like it or not, there are some marked differences between girls and boys when it comes to scoring. I hate to essentialize sex based on gender, and I don't necessarily want to debate nature versus nurture, but many women seem to be wired differently from men when it comes to sex, and, for the most part, we are socialized to get to know our partners. We are a lot pickier than guys. For many women, it's not so much about the fix of sex and the come. We like to cultivate the emotional part of a physical relationship; our feelings contextualize, enhance, and fuel our sexual desires. On top of all that, dykes have an uncanny desire for a lot of information from their sex partners. And I mean name, address, occupation, eating habits, pets' names, and names of last three lovers. We're looking for a Scorpio with Cancer rising, we're looking for Prince Charming, we're looking for the mother of our children. Seldom are we looking for a good hot fuck (or if we are, we are hard-pressed to admit it to anyone, including ourselves). But some of us wouldn't mind if, every once in a while, we ran into a randy woman in a bathroom ready to hike up her skirt for a good time.

Cruising, anonymous sex, and public sex are certainly part of the fantasy lives of my sapphic sisters; I've read countless erotic tales of seeing a stranger on the subway and following her home or meeting a sexy tourist at the local bar and showing her the sights in your bedroom. Don't get me wrong, I have seen women have sex on the spot without knowing a thing about each other. Throb, the monthly sex party for women that my girlfriend produces, creates a sex-club environment, the kind gay men take for granted. What could be safer and more conducive to raunchy girl–girl public action than a dark back room at a sex club and safer-sex supplies in plenitude? It warms my heart and pussy when girls who don't know each other get down at Throb. But more than once, after they've done the deed, one asks for the other's name or e-mail address. Dykes can't resist bonding; they just can't walk away. A friend of mine recently came to Throb on her birthday and wanted a face train, where women sat on her face, one after another, and she serviced them. She told me later, "I don't know why, but a lot of them wanted foreplay. What part of 'face train' didn't they get?"

Lusting for Lingerie

"This is only their third time making an appearance in public—aren't they divine?" my friend gushed as he wrapped his arm around his fiancée's tiny waist. She lifted her dress up, way above the knee, to reveal luxurious, black silk stockings. They stopped at the top of her shapely thighs, met by the straps of a satin garter belt. The fasteners clasped the stocking tops with deliberate, almost forceful affection, like Bogie grabbing Bacall for a passionate kiss. I admired the seamed hose and commended my pal on his taste. He nodded, gave me a knowing glance, and said with quiet assurance, "Agent Provocateur."

The bawdy brainchild of Joseph Corre (son of world-famous fashionista Vivienne Westwood and former Sex Pistols manager Malcolm McLaren) and his wife, Serena Rees, Agent Provocateur is a lingerie company like no other. The twosome opened the flagship store in London in 1994, a mail-order business in 1996, a second London location in 1997, and their first American sister in Los Angeles in 2000. (Rumor has it New York is next!) They've made quite a splash in London with explicitly erotic window displays, naughty promotional events, and eye-catching slogans like "A gentleman is expected to rise when a lady enters the room."

Erection-hunting entrepreneurs Corre and Rees have even loftier goals for their bras and panties, namely to "provide inspiration for desires that have been repressed by years of white-cotton conservatism." The store's philosophy is so British in concept, clearly flying in the face of English puritanical ideas about sexuality. While remnants of sexual repression are alive and well in America, can Agent Provocateur carve out a place for itself in a country with a Victoria's Secret in every mall? And especially in Los Angeles, home of infamous places like Frederick's of Hollywood, Trashy Lingerie, and the best stripperwear stores in the world?

An unabashed lingerie junkie, I had fingered Agent Provocateur's decadent catalog (which comes in the form of pinup playing cards) and cruised its website, but never saw the store in the flesh. When I drove by the Melrose Avenue shop and saw a parking spot right in front, it seemed like fate. To the naked eye, the display window looks like any other lingerie peddler (what was risqué in London wouldn't cause the same stir in this sin city), but step inside and you are in for a wholly unique trip. Since I hadn't planned to visit Agent Provocateur (I would have gotten a manicure and wax at the very least), I arrived feeling way too underdressed in my undercover reporter outfit—Old Navy sweatpants and a "Kiss My Ass" T-shirt.

Despite my attire, when I walked in, I was greeted like Julia Roberts on a shopping spree. Two gorgeous saleswomen completely focused on me, and they were wearing high heels, seamed stockings, and Agent Provocateur's trademark pink dresses—haute couture versions of '50s pink waitress uniforms—designed by Vivienne Westwood (thanks, Mom!). Their uniforms were unbuttoned to reveal the merchandise (of the store, that is), and each woman was, well, showing the undergarments at their best.

I fondled a few pieces of underwear, pausing over a black bustier with purple accents, but it was out of my reach at more than $350. (That's in the midrange.) On the opposite wall there seemed to be more affordable treats: a $95 bra, $55 panties. In addition to expensive undergarments, there was an entire display of top-of-the-line jewelry not-so-subtly inspired by dominance and submission: matching sets of cufflike bracelets (really wrist restraints) and choker necklaces (aka collars) complete with rhinestone-studded locks, and handcrafted chains to clip them together. Some were made of Swarovski crystal, and all were priced at the equivalent of people's monthly salaries. There were even diamanté-handled riding crops—kink couture at its very best.

I chose a French red tulle push-up bra with black embroidery and satin bows, matching thong, and garter belt, and one of the blondes quickly leaped to find my size. She led me to the dressing room, a silk-curtained boudoir with velvet couches. When she popped her head in moments later, she looked quite pleased at my selection. She adjusted the straps, apologizing for making them so snug: "I am used to wearing my bra straps extremely tight for maximum cleavage." But I already knew that. She moved down to the garter belt, wanting to slide it from my waist lower down to my hips, but I realized I was not wearing any underwear, so I scrunched down my sweats trying not to blush. She suggested a pair of stockings (naturally), and in her hands, there they were, the stockings I saw on my friend, yet they looked so innocent without legs to fill them.

"I have something that I think will really work for you," she said and darted off. She returned with a sheer black demi-cup bra, and I slipped it on, but my breasts were popping out in all the wrong places.

"You're full all around; it's made for someone with a more teardrop shape. But that's OK, because sugar looks really good on you," she reassured.

Sugar must be the name of the red bra I chose. The way "sugar looks good on you" rolled off her tongue, though, made me want to dip her and kiss her passionately, then fuck her on the dressing room's lavishly carpeted floor. And I am not usually into blonde-bombshell types, but the store—its goodies, its girls, its ambiance—does what its owners say it will: It inspires.

She wrapped "sugar" and my other purchases in a signature pink box with black ribbon. I managed to leave having spent just under $300, which I think is definitely an accomplishment for such a pricey place. (I briefly toyed with the idea of sending the receipts to my *Voice* editor, requesting reimbursement for research costs.) About two weeks later, I received a pink envelope in the mail with a Los Angeles return address. Inside, a scented, handwritten note from the saleswoman who helped me read: "I hope that you had a nice time the other day when you stopped by. It was so nice to meet you. The next time you're in town, do stop by!" The businesswoman in me recognized a smart marketing move that conveys personal attention, the epitome of impeccable customer service. The girl who was waited on, pampered, and treated like a princess just smiled as she plotted her next shopping trip.

Sex Outside the City

It's really a challenge for this city girl to leave the comforts of the Gap, Starbucks, and my DSL line to take a vacation. When my girlfriend, Red, and I were invited to a friend's wedding in Aspen, we decided to take a road trip afterward to San Francisco, along the way exploring the great American West. We skipped Salt Lake City and Reno and dove into places whose names you have to squint at to read on the map. In Unionville, Nevada, we planned to stay at a place I read about called the Old Pioneer Garden Country Inn. The travel-book writer said it was "off the beaten path," which is exactly what I wanted—to spend some time in a simpler, quieter, slower place than the one to which I am accustomed. The book said that the place had enjoyed some famous visitors, including America's runner-up sweetheart (next to Julia Roberts), the charmingly bland Sandra Bullock.

"Well, if Sandra Bullock stays there, then it's probably pretty nice," said my girlfriend, trying to reassure herself that we weren't going to be roughing it too much. "Yeah, either that or Sandra Bullock is a total freak with bad taste in country inns," I replied. She was not amused.

It was already dark when we turned off Interstate 80 and drove about twenty miles south on a road dotted with a trailer here and a ranch there, but was otherwise pretty much desolate. Then we turned onto a dirt road to drive three more miles into, well, the middle of nowhere. It was pitch black. We pulled over when we saw a farmhouse with a light on. A pickup truck drove toward us. I approached it, and the window was rolled down. There was a friendly fortysomething couple inside. "Are you looking for the B and B?" the woman asked. Why else would we be here at night several miles down a dirt road leading to nothing? "Um, yes," I replied. "We left the lights on and the door open. Just make yourselves comfortable, and we'll see you in the morning." Breakfast would be at 8:30, we were told. With that, they drove off. We both giggled. I thought our hosts lived in the house.

We were amazed to discover that this small farmhouse dating from 1864 was full of bedroom after bedroom; from the outside, it looked tiny. There were exquisite antique chairs, armoires, beds, claw-foot tubs, and a majestic grandfather clock. I slept pretty soundly, except for the bizarre dream I had about dozing on the floor with a wet blanket in the quaint room, until being awakened by an intruder standing above me, who looked like an oiled, muscled Latino porn star. In the dream, I was terrified, so much so that I screamed and woke my girlfriend up. I am still not sure what terrified me so much—that I was sleeping in the middle of nowhere or that a porn star might be trying to have his way with me.

I so looked forward to waking up in the country. No car alarms, no horns from the local car service, no neighbors blasting their stereos, just peaceful tranquility. Promptly at 4:30 A.M. I heard a rooster crow. The rooster was followed by the sounds of goats, sheep, geese, and all the other animals that were presumably sleeping when we arrived the night before. It was a veritable chorus of farm friends. So much for peace and quiet. I got out of bed, looked out the window, expecting to see them right outside. They were actually down the road. Sound carries differently in the country.

Since it was the crack of dawn, four hours before breakfast, I decided to wake up my sweetie with some morning nooky, her absolute favorite. I climbed over the wooden footboard and gently pounced on top of her. As I felt my naked body make contact with hers, I also felt the bed crash down under us. She said that I had a priceless "uh-oh, I fucked up" look on my face. I broke the antique bed, I thought; how will we ever explain this to the folks who run the place? We both climbed out of the bed to assess the damage. She concluded that the slats had simply fallen out of their grooves, and we could put them back. That involved taking the mattress and the box spring off. Thank God I have a butch, weightlifter girlfriend, or I don't know what I would have done. She tossed the mattress aside like Superman, then proceeded to lift the box spring, while I had to adjust all the slats that had, in fact, come off the bed frame and were lying on the floor. This whole thing took about half an hour, but my desire had not waned one bit, especially after seeing my buff girl-friend flex her muscles to fix the bed that I "broke." We crawled back into the bed gingerly and started kissing, but as things heated up, she started moving around a lot, naturally. "Stay still," I said. "We are not going to break the bed again." She smiled and did what I told her. Since she is a notorious ejaculator, I knew we had another problem as well. "Do not, under any circumstances, squirt on these antique linens!" She smiled. I said, "When you're ready to come, tell me, and we shall relocate to the claw-foot tub."

She nodded in agreement as she moaned gently. Then it was a test of her will, to see how long she could hold out until we had to get up. The goats were making a racket outside as the sun blazed stronger through the window. Finally, she had that look on her face, and I knew it was time. We ever so carefully got out of bed and walked to the bathroom, where I lay in the tub and she stood above me. I made her come like a banshee, all over my chest, and I was thankful we hadn't disturbed anything else in the process.

We showered and dressed for breakfast, then walked over to the main house, on the way meeting all the boisterous animals. Our hosts greeted us, inquiring, "Did you city folks sleep well?"

"We had quite a wake-up call," I grinned.

"Between the rooster and the goats, you must have just jumped out of bed," said the man we saw the night before.

"We jumped, all right," Red said, and then we sat down for a good old-fashioned country breakfast.

Kinky Summer Camp

Did you go to summer camp when you were a kid? I got my first standard-issue blue T-shirt with the camp logo on it when I was eight years old, when I rode a horse for the first time ever. The moment I mounted a cream-colored quarter horse named Coffeemate, I fell in love, and it was the beginning of an eight-year career in equestrian competition. I also had a raging crush on a counselor-in-training named Tommy; he was blond and freckled, and for as long as I rode horses, I carried a torch for him. My virgin experience of unrequited love was for someone older, in a position above me, thus ushering in my taste for the eroticism of power dynamics—and it was only day camp!

My friends who went to sleep-away camp made it sound even better, filled with parent-free days of woodsy wonder and nights of sneaking out of cabins to kiss summer loves. After I saw teenagers Tatum O'Neal and Kristy McNichol in *Little Darlings* (the perfect butch–femme dyke couple), I couldn't wait to go—not to lose my virginity to Matt Dillon, but to have a sexy slumber party with those two cuties. Well, I got my wish, and I didn't even have to get a permission slip from my parents. Since I didn't get to go to sleep-away camp when I was a child, I decided to make up for it as an adult. I didn't choose an ordinary camp full of go-carts, archery, and arts and crafts; I went for an adults-only five-day retreat. So gather round the campfire, boys and girls, gulp down the last of that fluorescent red "bug juice," and listen to my tale of kinky summer camp.

It may not have been surrounded by water, but my kinky summer camp was definitely the closest thing to Fantasy Island I've experienced, with 450 S/M folks gathered for fetishes and fun. The organizers have produced the event for five years, and there were so many activities you couldn't possibly do them all, from clothing-optional swimming to Japanese rope bondage workshops to massages in the Pamporium (which

I mistakenly thought was a special hangout for diaper fetishists). At a large auction people bid on service-oriented submissives, pain sluts, and gentle sadists. There were a BDSM state fair with pony rides and tug-of-war games, a campfire with s'mores for the (adult) kids, and yummy midnight snacks. For campers caught up in all the authentic fire-toasted marshmallows, reminders were everywhere that we were not at a 4-H event, with bondage crosses carefully placed on grassy knolls, suspension systems rigged from thick oak trees, and leather slings hung in every available gazebo.

In addition to these naughty nature nooks, three large, fully equipped dungeons (aptly named Heaven, Hell, and Purgatory) were open around the clock for disciplinary canes and polishing Mary Janes, single-tail whippings and hot-wax drippings. Campers had the opportunity to use equipment you don't usually see at your local dungeon, like exquisite bondage benches and a system that could suspend five women at once.

It was a bizarrely perfect mix of simplicity and sophistication: the bunk-bed giddiness of flirting and staying up past your bedtime plus a no-holds-barred atmosphere of intricate, mind-blowing S/M scenes. Adult supervision may not have been an issue at this camp, but that didn't mean there were no rules whatsoever. We had to abide by several guidelines—for example, no tossing cigarette butts on the ground (flesh butts OK), no sex in the pool or the dining hall, and "no nonhuman pets allowed." When was the last time you heard that phrase?

The meals were definitely reminiscent of real summer camp, but the announcements while we munched down room-temp pancakes and melted ice cream were decidedly unique. Over the PA system, we heard things like:

"The fire demonstration will be tonight at 8 P.M. We still need volunteers for the human zipper; if you love clothespins, please sign up!"

"Remember, the Portable Clit Washer, or PCW, is located near the tennis courts, and it does shoot hot water. Just turn the dial to the right, but please do not touch the big box."

"I want to remind everyone that there is no group sex in Heaven. If you've planned an orgy, go to Hell."

"If you put in an application to be kidnapped, your liaison or Top or Master must come to the kidnapping office to touch base with us and review your file as soon as possible. Keep in mind that the red hood is the official kidnapping hood, so if you see someone struggling with this on, please do not interrupt the scene. Not all kidnappings will use this hood; keep in mind there are also privately arranged ones."

That's one of the beauties of kinky summer camp: You can have elaborate fantasies come to life—like being captured by five strangers, dragged off into the woods, and taken against your will—all meticulously arranged in advance by you, the victim, and executed in a safe, sane, and consensual environment. While they may go to other events for educational seminars or community-activism workshops, people definitely come to camp to play, and many set up dates way in advance. Trainers prepare their human ponies for months to compete in the annual equestrian classic, which broke a world record this year with twenty-three ponies competing. While I wasn't quite ready to re-create my horse-show days with a two-legged creature, I anally fisted another virgin (which makes four for four—I am on a roll!), did temporary piercing in the middle of the woods, and had my pussy shaved with a straight razor. I didn't have time to redo *Little Darlings* with a hot lesbian three-way, but I did orchestrate another classic camp fantasy.

I asked the lucky boy who accompanied me there if he'd ever been to sleep-away camp before.

"Yes," he said.

"Did you have a crush on any of your counselors?"

"Yes," he said.

"Did you get to fuck any of them?"

"No," he giggled and blushed.

Well, this year, he finally got his chance.

Fuck Your Gender

Of Butches, Kings, and Masculinity

Straight men (my friends included) can and have been friendly to my lovers, but they're often uncomfortable when they're butches. Part of their discomfort is that butches are inherently threatening to most men. Men sense that a butch's masculinity is more appealing to me than theirs, and if she's packin' heat (wielding a dildo), which you know they imagine she is, well, there you have it. My girlfriend, Red, is a better man than most men.

At my cousin's wedding a few weeks back in upstate New York, Red and I were (surprise, surprise) the only lesbians. We were seated at a table with all my cousin's friends—married yuppies. The husbands were totally fascinated by Red. One in particular wanted to know where she got her hair cut, and he admired her flattop repeatedly, saying he wished his looked so good. This experience at the wedding has actually been happening a lot lately, and other butches I know report similar situations. I'm still mystified when straight men seem drawn to Red, but I have a few theories. In some cases, I think that men feel they can have a safe gay interaction with her; they can flirt and be playful (and even talk interior decorating) as if she were another guy because they know she's really a woman. Sometimes men actually identify with her as one of the guys, automatically admitting her into that fraternal order. But when they admire her suit, her wingtips, her hair, they seem to be learning from her what it's like to be a good man. She embodies a study of ideal masculinity, which is all in the details.

I recently told some of my stories to butch scholar and gender theorist Judith "Jack" Halberstam. She is the author of the ball-busting book *Female Masculinity*, so you could imagine she had a lot to say on the subject of butches. Here's how she read the phenomenon of my butch girlfriend as a straight-man magnet: "These men who are drawn to your girlfriend recognize the effort that goes into producing masculinity. Masculinity becomes visible when it's on a body that's not male." To Halberstam and others, masculinity (like femininity) is ultimately artificial, a performance, something you create and re-create through clothing, style, gestures, and body language.

Halberstam's latest project, *The Drag King Book*, is a collaboration with photographer Del LaGrace Volcano on the world of drag kings, particularly documenting drag king scenes in New York, San Francisco, and London. Halberstam's text, which includes interviews and analysis, is full of rich imagery, penetrating insight, and striking personalities (including her own). Volcano is the photographer formerly known as Della Grace, now a transman and hermaphrodyke. His photos of drag kings are not mere snapshots or *National Geographic* anthropological wonders; they are probing portraits, interpretive pictures, alluring images of those at the forefront of gender performance. This treasure is both a document of alternative culture and a coffee-table book for the new millennium—just don't assume you know what's in the coffee.

One subject in *The Drag King Book* is Mo B. Dick, creator-producer of the famed but now defunct Club Casanova, who has been a king among kings. Her club was the center of the thriving New York drag king scene, and made it possible for this new art form to grow and show-case itself to the world. The alter ego of a girl named Mo, Mo B. Dick is a sleazy, lounge-lizardy guy with sideburns, a pompadour, and plenty of attitude. Mo's persona is a parody of one type of masculinity, and she plays it to the hilt. Dréd, another New York subject of the book, is in a league all her own. She chooses from a diverse bunch of African-American masculinities, from a super-fly Isaac Hayes to a badass rapper to the andro king himself, The Artist (Prince). Her performances are sharp, thoughtful, and sexy. When drag kings are good, they're very good.

When drag kings are bad...well, I've seen performances that are so sloppy and haphazard that they're reminiscent of unrehearsed high school talent shows. Halberstam says when she goes to a bad drag king performance, it's usually too long and feels as if the same one joke is being played over and over and over. But she reminds me that performing in male drag is a very young, growing art form, and we have yet to see the potential reached for performances that go beyond simple parody, that are complex, nuanced, funny, and seductive; I'd like to see drag kings make sport of not only male icons (like Elvis, the Bee Gees, the Village People) but also archetypes. Drag king Murray Hill is leading that front, with her performance of a middle-aged, overweight guy who could be a used-car salesman who's running for office. The BackDoor Boys, a takeoff of the insidiously cute Backstreet Boys, go for all the fag subtext of these homoerotic boy bands, exploring their interpretation of the real meaning of the hit song "I Want It That Way"—it's all about butt fucking. This drag king act is refreshing and right up my alley. That would be the alley of fetishizing and celebrating too-well-groomed gay men, cheesy dance moves, and, of course, anal sex. Hey, boys, butches, and drag kings: I want it that way too.

Trouble in Utopia

The Michigan Womyn's Music Festival seems quite comfortable on its 640 acres of secluded land near Hart, Michigan. From security and shuttles to signage and sanitation, more than 650 women (including 400 volunteers) worked to put the event in 2000. Nearly 6,500 campers came for six days of music, workshops, performances, and that unique, penis-free, testosterone-free, male-energy-free place called "womenspace."

Like the women's movement, the festival has had its share of controversies, which usually reflect larger sociopolitical issues being debated in feminist and lesbian communities. In 1991, Nancy Jean Burkholder was "outed" as a transsexual woman and ejected from the festival by staff members because she was not a woman-born woman. Two years later, and every year since, transgender activists have hosted Camp Trans just across the street from the festival. Some of these rabble-rousers purchase tickets, attend the festival, and do education and outreach about the exclusion of certain women. In 1999, notable gender activist Riki Wilchins pitched her tent at Camp Trans for the third year, paid her $300 for the Womyn's festival, and presented a gender workshop on the festival grounds; in 2000, she was denied admission because she had openly identified as transsexual the year before.

Although it was the first year that organizers were willing to put their admission policy in writing, that policy still remained unfairly vague. At the front gate, each festival-goer was handed a sheet titled "Festival Affirms Womyn-Born Womyn Space" that explained that it is "an event intended for womyn who were born and who have lived their entire life experience as female—and who currently identify as a womon." Staff members told campers that if they honored the festival's womyn-born-womyn guidelines, they would be admitted. Furthermore, the rules stressed that "no one's gender would be questioned on the land." However, "[we may deny] admission to individuals who self-declare as male-to-female transsexuals or female-to-male transsexuals now living as men (or [ask] them to leave if they enter)." So, it appeared that the festival had borrowed the unsuccessful, wishy-washy "Don't Ask, Don't Tell" policy from the military. As long as you did not declare your gender at the gate, and kept your identity secret on the land, you could freely roam in womenspace.

When Camp Trans began, it was a group of predominantly male-to-female transsexuals fighting for their rightful place among other women. But this year, organized by both Boston and Chicago Lesbian Avengers, it was a gang of young gender queers—identified as tranny boys, dyke boys, transwomyn, female-to-male transsexuals (FTMs), boyz, andros, and simple tranz—who shook everything up. Many of them fit the "woman-born" criteria; it was the "woman-identified woman" label where things got a little sticky. You see, these Gen Xers don't identify as women, but they don't necessarily identify as men either. Riki Wilchins believes that these young, cutting-edge boychicks have every right to demand to be part of womenspace: "When lesbian feminism starts constraining women instead of liberating them, we have lost our way. This is what the success of years of lesbian visibility activism looks like: new kinds of dykes we haven't seen before and can't name yet."

Some of these genderfuckers came into the festival, and let me assure you that they blended into womenspace just fine, since there were plenty of butches, girlfags, drag kings, bois, diesel dykes, masculine women, and other gender outlaws around. The only difference was that Camp Trans-ers refused to keep their mouths shut.

The Michigan festival has strongly utopian ideals about creating a safe space for all women. "We want to encourage each of us to take this opportunity to be open to things that are new and to approach our differences with respect," proclaims the festival program. What I found there was that it is a safe space, but only for certain kinds of women. As a femme S/M dyke, I didn't always feel safe. I got harassed and shamed for washing sex toys—toys used for demonstration in workshops listed in the program—at a secluded water faucet. Staff members refused to support me and my girlfriend's First Annual Ejaculation Contest by including it among other public announcements, "due to the graphic nature of the concept." For utopia to work, it's gotta work for all of us.

Over the years, lesbian feminism has seen some radical changes, and the festival has changed along with it. Once known as adamantly anti-S/M, the festival now offers a kink-positive camping area called the Twilight Zone and more pro-S/M workshops than ever. In order to maintain the "purity of womenspace," campers are asked not to play music that includes men's voices on the land. For the first time, however, we heard the voice of Glen Campbell belt out "Rhinestone Cowboy" onstage at a worker talent show during a drag king act. The campy, sparkled send-up was an acknowledgment that drag kings stake out a crucial area of lesbian culture where we can express, interrogate, and perform the wonderful world of gender.

To quote again from the program: "Of course we don't always understand one another, but with a little effort we will come to realize that living our diversity includes bumping up against [our] differences, and constantly expanding what we consider 'our' culture and our community." It is time for festival owner Lisa Vogel and producers to read and stand by their own feel-good propaganda. In other words, welcome the Michigan Womyn's Music Festival into the 21st century, where there are people who identify as neither men nor women, but instead call themselves by names that are still evolving. Can we make room for them? The festival staff constantly encourages feedback from the community. It is a for-profit event produced by a private organization, which technically has the right—as the sign in a greasy spoon warns—to refuse service to anyone. But it has always imagined itself a grassroots, feminist affair created by and for women. In that vein, I challenge producers to poll each festival-goer on the gender admission policy, make the results public, and listen to the voices of the women.

Do you know those slightly annoying credit card ads on television about the cost of things? Well, I am tired of the price of Michigan sisterhood being so fucking expensive and available to only certain members of the tribe. Let's try this instead: Airline ticket to Grand Rapids: $280. Camping equipment: $400. Festival ticket: $340. Room for all kinds of womyn: priceless.

Porn Queens and Prom Kings

The feminist pornographer in me is still giddy from my recent trip to Los Angeles. I didn't go there just to make the rounds of all the strip clubs; I was actually working. And, boy, do I love what I do. I was there to shoot the sequel to my video, *The Ultimate Guide to Anal Sex for Women*, which I'm calling *The Ultimate Guide to Anal Sex for Women 2*. I know, it doesn't make sense grammatically, but hey, it's porno, not the video version of *The Chicago Manual of Style*.

I got to do Nina Hartley in the ass in the last video, but for this project, the porn queen served as a behind-the-scenes creative consultant. She was the ultimate sorority dance chaperone on the set, a hottie who will give you punch and cookies and flash you her tits! One morning, she made breakfast for the cast and crew. Do you know how surreal it is to walk onto the set of a porn movie you are directing and have Nina Hartley—arguably the most well-known adult film star of all time—bat her eyelashes and ask, "Do you want your egg sandwich on white or wheat?" I almost expected Eminem to come around the corner, wearing a collar, ready to drop to his knees and service me. But that would be too weird—I mean, both things happening at the same time.

Nina's presence wasn't the only thing that made the work so fun. When the performers finished their scenes, they thanked me, made off with a favorite sex toy, and generally gushed about what a good time they had. It made me feel great—creating a sexual workplace where people enjoy what they do and don't feel coerced, exploited, or generally shit on.

I returned home ready to celebrate the video production as well as my thirtieth birthday. On the actual day of my birthday, another fete, ironically related to mine, was happening in Washington, D.C. On May 9, Attorney General John Ashcroft met with Republican congressmembers and people from an organization called Victims of Pornography who are lobbying for new prosecutions and harsher penalties for purveyors of smut. The meeting was VOP's idea of a kickoff to launch its month-long antiporn campaign; that's right, you probably weren't aware that May is Victims of Pornography Month. According to many of these right-wing organizations, we are all victims of pornography, whether we make it, distribute it, consume it, or not. And, as usual, they love to talk about child pornography and abuse in order to sicken everyone into joining their censorship crusade.

If you want to see the bizarre exploitation of children, well, look no further than the absolutely brilliant HBO documentary *Living Dolls: The Making of a Child Beauty Queen*, in which filmmakers followed several players in the child pageant circuit. The fact that Swan, the little girl who is the focus of the film, is a dead ringer for JonBenet Ramsey is the least disturbing aspect of the story. Her drill-sergeant mother calls her *stupid* for forgetting the words to a song—the girl's five years old—and every other mother around her behaves in exactly the same way. Plus, we meet two gay men named Shane and Michael, the "pageant coaches" who doll up the little girls. They do image makeovers, coordinate glamorous photo shoots, choreograph dance and pageant numbers, consult on which hideously poofy taffeta mini-prom dress is best (a used one is only $1,200!), and hair-tease and mascara girls until they look like Tammy Faye Bakker. By the time these girls get to their own proms, they're going to look forty.

Speaking of proms, when I was in high school, I didn't want to be prom queen as much as I wanted to *do* the prom queen. Which, at that point, was absolutely out of the question. Maybe it's not anymore. Upon my return from pornoland, my mom told me that there was going to be a gay prom this year in my Long Island hometown, Sayville. You might think that back when I went to school, Sayville was a tiny bit hip or liberal, since it is not only a suburb of New York City but also the famed place where queers have been boarding the ferries to Fire Island since before I was born. Trust me, it was like living in the middle of Iowa, tediously suburban, but with more malls and different accents. There were no "out" gay students. There were speculations about a few teachers but no dialogue about gays and lesbians except the usual homophobic high school banter.

Maybe the organizers of the gay prom picked Sayville because it's smack dab in the middle of Long Island, easy to get to from all directions, or maybe the Island Hills Golf and Country Club gave them the best deal. Whatever the reason, it makes me proud to know that kids have options I couldn't even imagine when I was in high school. The timing was uncanny, by the way, that weeks later, R.E.M. frontman (or should I say backman?) Michael Stipe finally came out of the closet. Coincidence? I think not—he's obviously got his eye on the coveted prom chaperone job. Proms have changed a lot since the year I wore a hunter-green velvet and taffeta dress, went with a guy friend whom I ditched to go camping with my buddies later that night (sorry, Chris!), and danced to our theme song, some cheesy ballad by Bon Jovi. This year, in Ferndale, Washington, students elected a woman prom king. And not just any woman, but a big, butch, out dyke who brought her girlfriend to the prom. The openly gay senior, Krystal Bennett, saw it as a great political statement. Parents got on the phone and complained, and now the principal says there will be clearer guidelines about who can and cannot be nominated; I am sure it will be based on gender (like only boys can be kings—well, tell that to Murray Hill). This system will work for a while to squelch the gay kids from reigning as queens, and the butch dykes from flagrantly waving their scepters; however, the administrative bigots will get tripped up again when the first openly transgendered student wants to be nominated. It'll happen, and I can't wait to chaperone that prom.

Tranny Chaser

Remember the days of "We're Here, We're Queer, Get Used to It"? As the co-chairs of propaganda for Queer Nation in Los Angeles a decade ago, my girlfriend and I were in charge of disseminating fluorescent crack 'n' peel stickers with in-your-face messages like that one. Or the popular "Stop Heterosexism," "Safe Sex Slut," and "Assimilate My Fist." One sticky motto was always my favorite: "Fuck Your Gender." On the surface a bold celebration of same-sex eroticism, but with another meaning, too: a call to mess with the M or the F you're supposed to check off on the questionnaire of life.

Hearing the sayings out loud, they sound so '90s. The spirit of those stickers may still have significance today, but what they represent—radical, direct-action politics—is about as fashionable today as a faded ACT UP T-shirt. Once rooted in loud, unapologetic marches and chants, the gay, lesbian, and bisexual movement has mainstreamed itself into polite task forces and lobby groups like the Human Rights Campaign Fund (with a name so closeted you can't even tell it's gay!). And some of our transgendered friends are following suit.

When trans people began to have a voice in the political arena (first as part of the gay, lesbian, and bisexual movement, then breaking out on their own), the first wave of activists wanted to raise awareness of what lay beyond M and F; specifically, to educate people about male-to-female (MTF) and female-to-male (FTM) transsexuals. From there, "transgender" was born to include people who crossed gender boundaries without necessarily having surgery or legally changing genders. Some members of the movement want to transcend "trans" altogether, and focus on just gender (just gender—how loaded is that?).

So it comes as no surprise that a blinding pink square with the thick and blatant "Fuck Your Gender" has been replaced by an understated white sticker that reads "Gender Rights Are Human Rights." This radi-cal-yet-digestible phrase (I mean, who's against human rights?) is the mantra of Gender PAC, a national advocacy organization at the forefront of the newly made-over "gender rights movement." Gender PAC presented its First Annual National Conference on Gender and Sixth Annual Gender Lobby Day in Washington in May 2000. More than four hundred people attended the three-day conference that came complete with a con-gressional gala and corporate sponsors. That's right, American Airlines is the official carrier of gender rights. And in this kinder, gentler gender movement, as a fucker of genderfuckers, I learned that I am no longer a tranny chaser, I am a "trans ally." So much more civilized, don't you think? (So, what does that make the transsexual woman who hit on both my genderfucking dates at the gala? Trans ally, my ass.)

Like any other minority movement gathering, the conference brought forth numerous tensions. The absence of significant transgender activists (and their recent defection from Gender PAC's board of direc-tors), who openly boycotted the conference, symbolized a growing schism in trans politics. Some believe that the rights of transgendered people are being diluted or erased by Gender PAC in favor of an amorphous, more mainstream and marketable "gender agenda." Certainly, having a broader scope beyond "transgender" can incorporate all forms of gender identity and expression into the mission. And money from corporate America can buy us a seat at the big boys' table. But how did genderfucking go from radical to just rad?

The media representation of gender crossing has come a long way in its diversity and acceptance. Jack of TV's *Will and Grace* can swish about like a fag at Banana Republic. Mayor Giuliani can dress in drag for laughs. RuPaul can have a new series next season (on the WB network) about taking care of a rich guy's children, called *The Tranny* (proving that the network isn't just after black viewers, it's after black tranny-chaser viewers, too). Crossing over from blue to pink is now acceptably cute in the media. (From pink to blue is a little more unsettling, and forget about being in the middle.) But look away from your television screen for a real-ity check: Genderfucking constitutes a serious offense in our society.

Dana Rivers was a beloved and award-winning teacher in California before she lost her job for transitioning from male to female. In a New Orleans suburb, Peter Oiler was teased by coworkers who labeled him gay. Pressured by his supervisor, he revealed that he wasn't gay, though he was a cross-dresser in his personal life. He was fired. After working at Harrah's Reno Casino for her entire adult life, Darlene Jesperson was told she had to wear makeup to work every day; when she refused to comply, she was let go. What do the three have in common, besides being unemployed and pissed off? These accidental activists are among the thousands of people who face harassment, discrimination, and violence every day because of their gender identity or gender expression. They are why we need to organize, to educate people about gender identity, and to fight to change the institutions that breed the bigotry that leads to bad attitudes and even worse behavior. They are why Gender PAC's work is undeniably important, even though their stickers are still too quiet for me.

Not quiet at all is a new breed of young people who prove that genderfucking can still be in-your-face. This second wave is hell-bent on creating their own labels: baby butches, tranny boys, girlfags, genderqueers, pansexual girls and bois. They eat Judith Butler's cultural theories for breakfast. Some of these exceptional specimens of the future of gender were at the conference, and they give me hope. Many of them say "Fuck Your Gender" and mean fuck gender altogether. The I-don't-identify-as-anything-but-me generation wants to toss out the baby, the bathwater, and especially that silly blue bonnet. Can't wait to see the stickers and the riots they create.

Drag Kings Make Me Wet

There's nothing like a stuffed jockstrap to get this girl going. And I like it even better when I am not exactly sure what's making the cotton fabric stretch and strain against a pair of tight 501s or well-tailored suit pants. I love illusion, mystery, and desire that waves itself in your face. That's why drag kings make me wet.

While female impersonators have dozens of clubs, books, and documentaries, and even an unofficial national spokesqueen in RuPaul, their drag brothers are still finding their own way in the world. With *The Drag King Book* by Judith "Jack" Halberstam and Del LaGrace Volcano, several independent films and documentaries, and appearances on *Sex and the City, Queer as Folk,* and *The Maury Povich Show,* the performance of masculinity has dramatically increased its visibility in the last few years. Several weeks ago, more than two hundred drag kings, performers, artists, and their admirers from nineteen states gathered in Columbus, Ohio, for the third annual International Drag King Extravaganza (IDKE), a weekend of gender-bending workshops, panels, and schmoozing.

Like their laméd and lipsticked sisters, these cross-dressing impersonators embody campy cuteness, with catchy names like Izzie Big, Rusty Nails, Duncan B. Deepe, Mario Testosteroni, Arty Fischal, and L. Camino. Their names aren't the only clever thing about them: Lots of kings choose stars, songs, or styles to poke fun at gender, criticize misogyny, and fuck with their audience's heads and libidos. As the designated Barbra Streisands and Chers of the king world, the Backstreet Boys and 'N Sync get more than their fair share of mockery from girls who play boys. (After all, their brand of prepackaged masculinity makes them ripe for caricature.) But there are also dead-on ringers for such diverse artists as Little Richard, Axl Rose, Fred Durst, Andy Gibb, and even Eminem. As princes of parody, drag kings know one thing for sure: Size does matter, and the breadth and width of masculinities these guys take on is extremely impressive. In two nights of performance at IDKE, I saw a mac daddy pimp, '40s swinger, cowboy crooner, Vegas lounge singer, budding Boy Scout, gangsta rapper, swishy sailor, investment banker, disco dude, kinky leatherdaddy, '50s greaser, angry punk rocker, flamboyant diva, strung-out metalhead, and plenty more models of manufactured manhood.

Among the acts, there were many standouts: the hot hip-hop/rap duo from Kentucky, the Underground Kingz; the campy country-western stylings of Troy Andrews from Michigan; the glitz of Canada's sequin-drenched glam cowboy Carlos Las Vegas; and two brilliantly choreo-graphed pieces by Santa Barbara's Disposable Boy Toys, including a Broadway musical tap and swing dance number with ten boys and girls who look straight out of *42nd Street*.

Polished routines, clever costumes, and well-rehearsed acts are not all that is on the agenda for drag kings. Many of these gender illusionists convey a political and social message in their performances, something that seems more popular among them than their queen counterparts. A perfect example was the dark but hilarious look at the inhumane slaughtering of cattle by Andy and Elroi from New York. (Bet you didn't know there was such a thing as a pair of antiburger kings with a provegan manifesto.) Jake Danger and Rian of Santa Barbara conveyed an intense, complex Master-slave relationship better than some S/M films I've seen. Tackling hate crimes and repressed homoerotic desire, Chicago kings Billy T. Holly and Jeff Stroker portrayed a fag-bashing frat boy who falls in lust with the gay leatherman he attacks. They may be lip-synching the words to their songs, but that doesn't mean that drag kings don't have plenty to say.

Four performers—Pat Riarch, Ray Cruiter, Brandon Iron, and Leo, all from New York—dedicated their performances to the tragic events of September 11, and two used actual video footage of the devastation of the World Trade Center. Showstopper Iron staggered onstage in a gas mask and a soot-covered suit clutching the flyer of a missing woman. When he ripped off his pinstriped corporate uniform, the back of his T-shirt read MY TEARS ARE NOT A CRY FOR WAR. Drag kings know their audience, too: people who appreciate—maybe even expect—social satire with their glued-on facial hair, political statements with their bound breasts, and cultural commentary with their cunts-turned-cocks. It's entertainment laced with gender activism, feminist ideals, and plenty of sexual innuendo. IDKE is the thinking man's Wigstock, a Midwestern Cockstock.

There was talk that the conference may not be in Columbus next year, yet the community has grown so much that if Ohio cannot take on hosting responsibility, there are clearly other groups out there willing to grab the torch and set their own town on fire. Because there are so many kings from places like Missouri and Indiana, the next gathering seems destined for somewhere in the heartland. Plus, it feels so much more sub-versive to take gender performance out of the major cities (where it really can be a way of life) and put it on the road.

Taking her own show on the road, San Francisco–based photographer Erin O'Neill has traveled around North America to document drag kings for a series called "Kings of the Road," which she presented this year at IDKE. Each king is shot with a mode of transportation, from a cool con-vertible Cadillac or sexy Harley to a set of sandy surfboards or scratched-up Rollerblades. Simultaneously gritty and slick, seductive and unnerving, the black-and-white images capture multiple masculinities, and O'Neill says her intent was "to look at our bipolar gender culture with kaleidoscope eyes." Well, the rose-colored bifocals that see only M and F are off for sure, and O'Neill's pictures left me feeling pleasantly confused, helplessly turned on, and questioning the gender of nearly everyone around me.

Every seemingly male person I saw for the next few days immedi-ately had me asking, Can I see evidence of the Ace bandage that binds his tits through that shirt? Are those sharply defined sideburns attached to his face with spirit gum? When he goes into the men's room, do you think he'll get some funny looks? A gay friend of mine who attended the conference went to a men's sex club after the show and reported, "All the guys had these well-trimmed goatees, extreme facial hair, bulging pack-ages…. They all looked like drag kings to me. In fact, some of the drag kings were better-looking guys than the ones at the club. Some of them gave me a total boner."

Building a Better Cock

As soon as I reveal to someone that I'm involved with a female-to-male transgendered (FTM) person, I inevitably get the same questions: Has he had the surgery? Has he gone all the way—the dick and everything? It's not enough to simply say my lover was born female and now lives his life as a male: He prefers male pronouns, uses the men's room, and looks like a guy. No, this explanation doesn't seem to satisfy most people. They need to know what his body looks like, how it works, what *physically* makes him a dude.

This response is linked to our society's deeply entrenched beliefs about biological sex and gender: In other words, genitals determine gender. I suspect that it's also based on some people's awareness of male-to-female (MTF) people, for whom sex reassignment surgery (SRS) is common. When folks ask about "the surgery" of FTMs, most don't know that there isn't one option, but many. In fact, the most popular method of body modification is nonsurgical—testosterone hormone therapy can broaden shoulders, narrow hips, enlarge the clitoris, and cause facial and body hair growth. When it comes to what's often referred to as "top surgery," some transmen opt for a double mastectomy followed by chest reconstruction. FTMs with small breasts may opt for the "keyhole" procedure, in which a small incision is made just below the areola, and breast tissue is removed through liposuction with little scarring and a better chance of retaining nipple sensitivity.

"Bottom surgery" options are more complicated. The most common are hysterectomies and metoidioplasties, in which skin around the clitoris is removed, freeing the clit from the pubis. Some trannies get silicone implants for balls and a scrotal sac crafted from the labia. Phalloplasty is the most complex, least successful, and least common option. Surgeons can create a cock out of skin taken from the forearm, the abdomen, or the upper thigh, but a urethral extension is needed for peeing out of it and the sexual sensitivity varies (many leave the clitoris at the base of the new dick). Erections are also tricky: Surgeons can leave a hole to insert a rod or a built-in inflatable pump. These phallic devices may resemble high-tech Sharper Image toys on paper, but most of them don't seem to look (or work) as good as they sound.

And how do I know what they look like? Photographer and trans-man Loren Cameron has documented the bodies and narratives of twelve FTMs in his new e-book *Man Tool: The Nuts and Bolts of Female-to-Male Surgery*. Building on his first book of transsexual portraits, *Body Alchemy*, this interactive collection closely captures transmale bodies, making the hidden visible. While the owners of these new man tools are content and upbeat about the results, you can't help but see big differences between SRS for transmen and transwomen.

For MTFs, surgical options are more advanced, performed by more physicians, and potentially a lot less expensive than their FTM counterparts ($5,000 to $25,000 for vaginoplasty and $15,000 to $150,000 for phalloplasty). I saw an extremely explicit slide presentation by Beverly Hills physician Gary Alter (one of only three doctors in the world who is board certified in both plastic surgery and urology), who proclaimed that every one of his MTF patients were orgasmic post-op. I don't know how he gauged that, but I do know that they had pretty good-looking coochies. And I wouldn't be able to tell the XX from the XY in a pussy lineup. But while Alter has been trained to perform FTM sex reassignment surgery, and has even done a few, he won't do it any-more. He's a perfectionist—a great quality for someone modifying bodies for a living—who says he can't achieve anything close to perfection with the available operations.

In her comprehensive research study, Dr. Anne Lawrence, a Seattle physician specializing in transgender medicine, found that the happiness, satisfaction, and quality of life of one group of MTFs depended greatly on the physical success of their sex reassignment surgery. "Buying a vagina these days is like buying a Toyota Camry. The technology has largely been worked out, and consumer satisfaction is very high. You can even shop around for the particular model you want," says Lawrence. "On the other hand, buying a penis is more like buying a Wright brothers airplane. Can it fly? Yes, sometimes. But how high, and for how long? Is it something you'd really want to fly in? In female-to-male surgery the engineering challenges are far greater, and the technology is still being worked out."

When you dig into the medical issues of building a cunt versus a cock, you see why it's much easier to make an aesthetically pleasing, sexually sensitive, and functional vagina than a comparable dick. But politically, the imbalance is still glaring. There are far fewer well-reputed, experienced physicians performing FTM surgeries. There is less research on FTM body modification and the relationship between transmen and their bodies. One can't help but hear the male-centered medical industry whispering, "We'll move you down the patriarchal hierarchy, but we won't move you up."

To look at trans bodies is to see the ways in which our sex organs are more alike than different. Big clits look a lot like small dicks, for example. One person may have a flat chest and a testosterone-enlarged clitoris, and another breasts and a member from metoidioplasty. To many FTMs, their working parts are not in limbo between male and female; they simply live in a different kind of body that transcends clits and dicks, and moves beyond male and female into exciting gender territory. For some, the tool doesn't necessarily make the man.

Paying for It

My Virgin Lap

"I want to get a lap dance, and I want to know a good place to go."

That's not an easy task these days since Mayor Giuliani has declared war against the sex industry in New York City, and Times Square has turned into an urban Disney World. The world of porno theaters, strip joints, and peep shows isn't what it used to be.

"Well, it depends on what you're looking for," says my friend Mario, the girlie-magazine editor I'm consulting about where to have my fantasy fulfilled. "Do you want an overpriced, strictly hands-off dance from one of those high-glam, busty blondes who looks like a porn star? You know, a place like Demi Moore went to to research her stripper role? Or you could have it down and dirty, do whatever you want for whatever you want to pay, but some of the girls are definitely junkies."

"What about somewhere in between—not too classy, not too sleazy?"

He ends up sending me to New York Dolls. All my dyke friends are either busy or not interested, so I recruit my friend Ron, a nice Jewish straight guy who's never had a lap dance either.

Seven thick, mean, cartoonish bouncers are on guard at the door. The mood is chaotic as we make our way to the only empty table in the main room. A T-shaped stage sits in front of a mirrored wall: a short-haired red-head in a white lace G-string to the left, a bronze-skinned woman with a fuchsia orchid in her hair to the right, and a tall brunette with Betty Page bangs in a patent leather thong on the catwalk. Above the mirrors, the Dow Jones index dances in red dots across a long black screen. It doesn't feel scary like my nightmare of a strip club: creepy men groping wasted runaway girls in some dark, dirty place. We're surrounded by well-dressed men in gray flannel and pinstripes, and about twenty topless women gyrating in G-strings. It's strange to be the only fully clothed woman, but I'm not intimidated, just curious. No matter how bold I feel, some patrons stare suspiciously. There is a certain alienated camaraderie among all the men here that I have disturbed. They weren't expecting me, and they don't know how I fit into the scene. *I* don't exactly know how I fit in.

I watch intently as each dancer takes her turn on stage, then moves through the audience seeking takers for a $10 dance. There is a wide variety of women, from blonde bombshells with silicone breasts and tanning salon skin to ordinary-looking girls with bright eyes who look like my college classmates. The good ones have a way of connecting with a customer, establishing some immediate sense of intimacy. Making him think she really likes him, that he actually has a chance with her. That the seduction is real.

At first, when the petite blonde gets on stage, she looks really young to me, and I usually don't go for that little-girl look. When her dress comes off, she has an arched back and tiny breasts. Then she starts to dance, first in front of the mirror, looking at herself, running her hands over her curves. As she wraps herself around the pole, her moves are sensual, sure. When she struts down the catwalk, she immediately locks gazes with me. She's checking me out and all the men in the place know it. Brazen. When the music changes, she makes a beeline for my table. She doesn't even ask me if I want a dance. She simply takes my hand in hers and leads me over to the leather banquette. I ask her what her name is.

"Sinderella—with an 's,'" she coos, "What's yours?"

"Tristan with a 't.'"

She sits me down on the leather seat and tells me to spread my legs; as she says it, her hands slide up my satin pants, and she spreads them for me. Slowly, she begins moving her body in front of mine. Even though I know I'm not supposed to, I want to touch her long blonde ponytail.

"Sinderella, this isn't your hair, is it?"

"No, but don't tell *them* that. The ponytail is part of my look; besides I don't want to show my real hair, not here." I picture her then without the hairpiece...her blue eyes framed by short, spikey bleach blonde locks. Still cute and naughty, but tougher, definitely more like a dyke.

I suddenly feel overwhelmed by all of it, and I want to ask her so many questions. Some dancers stop by our table and chat. I want to ask them all sorts of questions. How much do you make on a good night? How long have you been dancing? How many hand jobs have you given upstairs in the VIP Champagne Lounge? Why do some dancers ask me if I want a dance but others avoid me—isn't it all the same to you? But all that comes out of my mouth is: "You look awfully young. How old are you?"

"I know. I'm twenty-four." She flashes me a space-between-two-front-teeth smile, and I glimpse a twinkle in her mouth.

"Hey, open up again."

She obeys and I get a look at the round solitaire diamond piercing her pink tongue. Mmmm—that turns me on.

Then she starts to grind against me, not keeping the distance between her body and mine like I watched the other dancers do with other customers, but brushing right up against me, rubbing her face against my cheek, kissing my neck and nibbling on my ear. I like the idea that we're breaking the rules.

"I thought you weren't supposed to touch me," I say playfully, letting her know I am absolutely enjoying it.

"Oh, I don't give guys a dance like this," she whispers as her hand finds its way up my thigh and between my legs. I feel a wave of warmth surge to my pussy.

"I like girls, and I like to dance for them." She's playing right into my fantasy that because I'm a woman, she enjoys this more. Or hates it less. After all, we're sisters, I'm not The Man. In real life, maybe it's all the same to her. She turns around and bends over, pushing her firm, round ass to just inches away from my face.

The music changes then, signaling the end of the dance. Time to pay up.

"You have a great ass," I say, and I mean it. But after I say it, I think I sound piggy, like all the others. And I think she's playing me just like I've seen dancers play the men all night. She's close to me, but out interaction still doesn't feel real. If I am using her, she is also using me—it's a typical capitalist transaction in that way. But does the absence of cash make for a more intimate sexual exchanges with a stranger in a club? The money clarifies everyone's expectations. We don't have to wonder what the other person wants. No games, no dyke drama. It does feel a little lurid, a little sleazy, a little strange. I slip $25 under Sinderella's garter. I don't know how much of the money will go to the house, to the bouncers, to the bartenders, to the DJ. I want her to keep all of it, but I know that's a fairy tale. She looks surprised for a minute, then she kisses me on the cheek, trots off, and vanishes into the crowd—not even an open-toed Lucite spiked heel left behind.

Tips for Tricks

"Hey, this is Tyler," he says. His voice is flat, devoid of all the bubbly queeniness that marks it when he talks to me. "Where'd you see my ad?" he asks, and I know it's a prospective client on the other end of his cell phone. He continues, "I'm six feet tall, slim, tight, muscular build, very defined, naturally smooth. I've got six-pack abs. I'm eight inches cut. Short blond hair, blue eyes, clean-shaven, clean-cut."

I can hear the voice talk, but can't make out what he says. "One-eighty." More talking from the cell phone. "What do you want?" Pause.

"Ohhh-kay," he says. His voice has changed and now it's clear he's talking to me again. I have witnessed the conversation between Tyler and trick because it interrupted our phone interview. "He hung up."

"Do you get that a lot?" I ask.

"Well, he's probably from my ad in the *Observer*. They're usually straight-identified Upper East Side guys. They have a lot of hang-ups—you know, they're nervous, they don't know what they want."

Tyler's real name is Matt Bernstein Sycamore. He's a twenty-six-year-old who has been a sex worker for seven years. He actually describes himself as a *whore*—a term that he and some of the more educated, politically conscious prostitutes have reclaimed (much as gays and lesbians embrace *fag* and *dyke*). Matt earns about $200 per client per session, and he can make up to $2,000 a week. Also an accomplished writer and activist, he is editor of the titillating new book *Tricks and Treats: Sex Workers Write About Their Clients*. Written entirely from the point of view of a class of workers who seldom get to speak for themselves, the collection illuminates the unique perspective they have on our culture.

In reading *Tricks and Treats*, I was struck by just how intimate some hookers and hustlers get with their clients. They hear secrets, know intensely personal information, and see a side of their clients no one else does. Matt says this was one of the driving forces behind the anthology:

"Everyone I know who does sex work can tell you amazing stories. The trouble is that these aren't the stories you hear in the mainstream media." Think of the tabloid-style coverage of infamous Hollywood madam Heidi Fleiss, the Hugh Grant hooker bust, and LAPD civilian traffic-officer-turned-call-girl Norma Jean Almodovar. "Instead of letting sex workers speak for themselves, talk-show hosts, televangelists, law enforcement, social workers, and politicians prefer to present pathologized, glamorized, or sensationalized images of sex workers. We are either sex-crazed maniacs or trapped victims. I wanted to let sex workers take control of the spotlight and shine it on their clients. This is their turn to put everyone else under the microscope," emphasizes Sycamore.

Contributor Carol Queen, a former sex worker who has a doctorate in human sexuality, describes one of the roles working girls (and boys) play for johns: "We make them feel safe enough to drop their pants and talk about what they want. To hear a lot of them tell it, they can't do that anywhere else." Her piece is about "What Johns Want," and it led me to ponder what *whores* want. What makes a client a good one? Sex workers don't have the luxury of a union, industry standards, legal protection, or a reference guide for johns on proper procedure and behavior. So, before you move on to the back section of your favorite publication, here are six tips for tricks:

Time is money. My shrink has a new cancellation policy. In addition to the requisite twenty-four hours' notice, if she can't fill my time slot, I still have to pay for it. Imagine if sex workers could demand the same. Matt's biggest complaint about johns is their unreliability. If you aren't planning to keep an appointment, call and cancel, just as you would do with your favorite restaurant. This is basic consideration for other people's time. If you can afford a whore, you can afford a one-minute phone call to cancel or reschedule.

Don't be cheap. If someone names a price, consider it printed on a Tiffany's price tag. Eva, a contributor to *Tricks and Treats* and a retired sex worker, says, "I hate clients who try to talk down the price. It's really rude. It makes me not like them and not do as good a job. This is not a swap meet."

Tipping is customary. And speaking of money, here's a general rule to live by: Real men tip. As with an excellent waiter or a superb hairdresser, it's appropriate to tip for a job well done. You can apply the 20 percent rule here, but Matt reminds me, "Any tip is a good tip."

Communicate. You have plenty of time to be the strong, silent type or shy and reserved with your wife, girlfriend, or boyfriend. When you are with a sex worker, step up to the plate. Be verbal and vocal about your desires, wants, needs. You are paying, so you might as well get what you want. Not everyone just wants a blow job. They're whores, not mind readers, so you need to tell them your secret wishes before they can make them come true.

Respect boundaries. Sex workers have their own rules and limits, and most will tell you up front what the deal is. Don't try to push those limits or test them. Don't agree to one thing and think in the back of your mind you're gonna get something else. That's not the way it works. (Matt's other complaint about badly behaved clients: "When a john tries to shove his dick in your ass without asking first and without a condom—that's a pet peeve of mine.")

Business versus romance. "Understand it is a business transaction that can be mutually pleasurable, but it isn't a date or a romantic encounter," says Matt. Eva agrees: "Don't ask me too many personal questions or if I have a boyfriend. And don't tell me 'I love you.' I don't want to hear that." I asked Eva what she wished every parent would teach their sons about hookers: "Just because you're paying, you don't have to treat someone any differently. Show her respect the way you'd show any woman respect."

There you have it—consider it a buyer's etiquette guide. Next time you take out your dick and a wad of bills, make Miss Manners and me proud.

Organizing Jizz Joints

Imagine if you had a job where your work schedule and location depended on your race. You couldn't call in sick, and you could be fired without reason or notice. You could be put in unsafe situations, and management would look the other way. All this sounds illegal and unfair, right? While you might assume that Kathie Lee Gifford or Nike has another third-world sweatshop up and running, think again: These are the conditions that a certain class of workers face every day in this country. Would you support their efforts to organize a union in order to secure a better work environment? If I told you that these workers bend over, shake their asses, spread their legs, and play with their pussies in front of strangers for a living, would it make a difference?

After eight months of stripping, student and stand-up comedian Julia Query and her fellow dancers were sick of the draconian rules and unfair practices at the club where they worked, the Lusty Lady in San Francisco. They decided to organize and attempt to form a union. Media-savvy and aware that their activism was historically important, Query also picked up a camera to capture their efforts on film. She later joined forces with filmmaker Vicki Funari, and the result of their collaboration is a documentary called *Live Nude Girls Unite!*, which follows the dancers' struggle to unionize.

The Lusty Lady was a unique place even before all the union hoopla. It's the only sex shop in the city that promotes itself as the hip, feminist peep show; its recruiting ads emphasize that it is owned by women (actually, some, but not all, of the shareholders are women), managed by women, and therefore a great place for women to work. Yet, this same supposedly cool company had a policy that if a dancer could not work her designated shift, she was required to find a replacement dancer whose skin was as light as hers or lighter and whose breasts were as big as hers or bigger. Not even a wacko "neo"-feminist like Camille Paglia would go for that. By setting itself up as a fun, slightly slutty, grrrl-powered slumber party, the Lusty Lady was a perfect target for union organizing. Of all the clubs in San Francisco, this one had an image to protect and couldn't afford the bad publicity.

Because of the way it positions itself, this particular jizz joint is not a haven for working-class girls in a dead-end town or junkies supporting a habit. Peering into the mirrored box from a booth, one sees a carpeted room full of brainy strippers—grad students, lefty activists, and starving artists. They are bright-eyed, intelligent girl-next-door types. The politically and socially conscious stripper has been around since the '70s (thanks to the women's movement), but there are a lot more of them now, and plenty of these liberated chicks are at the Lusty Lady. To me, the Lusty is so San Francisco—a city overrun with idealistic, sex-radical women who need real jobs and plenty of dot-commers titillated by the idea that the girl behind the glass might have been his sister's college roommate at Vassar. What's next, a worker-owned cooperative strip club? Hey, if it can happen anywhere, it's San Francisco, where lefty collectives are an institution.

So the peep-show girl who's working on her Ph.D. may appeal to consumers, but this brand of stripper is a club owner's worst nightmare. Management should have seen the union effort coming: When you hire strippers with college degrees in women's studies, they aren't gonna take any crap. Like all other clubs in the industry, the Lusty Lady counted on the marginalization of sex work to thwart any attempts to unionize. What credible union would actually take on the fight to get strippers a fair contract? Fortunately for the women of the Lusty Lady, the Service Employees International Union (SEIU) did take on the Lusty owners— and they won, forming the first and only Exotic Dancers Union in 1996.

The Lusty Lady is the only peep show or strip club in the country where workers belong to a union. While membership in the union is not mandatory (management would not agree to become a union shop), Query says that of all the workers who've been on staff for more than four weeks, 100 percent are union. The film is tedious and self-indulgent when it veers away from the unionizing effort and toward Query's own stripper experiences and her relationship with her mother, prostitute-rights advocate Dr. Joyce Wallace. I overlook that flaw and give credit to Query for documenting such an important moment in the women's movement, the sex-worker movement, and the union movement. Says Query, "It was a powerful experience for everyone on the bargaining committee, and our working conditions have improved dramatically. We fought against the odds. It took the miners a hundred years to have enough work sites unionized so that they could get better working conditions. We did it in less than a year. Stripping is such a stigmatized profession, and there is so much internal shame, that the fact that we accomplished what we did made us feel like superheroes!"

Query and Funari have made an incredible piece of propaganda— a smart, engaging, and useful organizing tool that I hope inspires dancers everywhere. The union movement among strippers is not exactly catching on as fast as you can pump quarters into a machine to keep the window shade in your booth from sliding down, but I for one hope it will. Since they began to organize and especially since the film has hit select cities, the Exotic Dancers Union has gotten calls from dancers in every single state.

Women become live nude girls for many different reasons, including the high pay and the flexible schedule. We are still taught that if we dress a certain way, we can expect—and maybe we even invite—harassment and violence. Thus, if we dare to parade around in our birthday suits, well, then we're definitely asking for it and deserve even less respect and safety. Sex workers are bombarded with the mixed message that consumers will gladly buy what they're selling, but because they're selling it they shouldn't expect safe or fair working conditions. The fact of the matter is that sex is work and as such should be treated like any other job. Contrary to popular opinion, when a woman takes off all her clothes for money, she is not stripped of her dignity as well. Or her human rights. If you have any doubt that strippers are people too (and deserve to be treated fairly by their employers), this film will change your mind.

Lap Dancing in Queens

When the stripper's-worst-nightmare-for-a-mayor first began his bogus, antisex "rezoning plan," I heard that adult playgrounds would be relegated to industrial areas in the 718 area code. Is the sex industry thriving in the outer boroughs? Where can a girl go these days to get a lap dance in, say, Queens? I recruited my friend, Susan, and her friend Patricia—both lap-dance virgins—to accompany me on my quest.

Our first stop: Phenomenon, a strip club/sports bar combo. Before we passed through the metal detector, our doorman asked us for ID. Fifty feet away, another thick-necked bouncer shook his head at us, then at Mr. Doorman, who explained: "You're gonna think it's discrimination, but it's not. It's the owner's policy: no unaccompanied women." To give him a second chance, I then identified myself as a *Voice* columnist and told him that I would report his refusal.

"Yeah, you can print that. And say that Raul didn't let you in. That way my boss knows I was doin' my job."

One bouncer told me that single women don't get into strip clubs because the management assumes they are sex workers looking for clients, and the club could get busted for prostitution. Another manager told me that women aren't allowed in because they may be hunting for their husbands. I think the policy is clearly intended for the comfort of the male clientele. In a strip club, to be a woman who is not for sale upsets the balance of men-as-buyers and women-for-purchase.

We headed toward the 59th Street Bridge, where there are three clubs close to one another. Outside Goldfingers, we recruited two guys to "accompany" us—$40 for the male escorts, $10 each at the door, and we were in.

In its heyday, Goldfingers—then located on Queens Boulevard in Forest Hills—was one of the most popular strip clubs. The mayor held a press conference on its steps to announce its closing as a victory over sin and sleaze. The fact that Goldfingers reopened in a different location a month ago is a testament to the enduring spirit of the sex industry: Underneath the steel girders of the elevated N train in Long Island City, a puffed-up phoenix rises from the ashes to spread its wings and dance again.

The parking lot was crowded, but the place appeared to be empty. Then we saw a thick velvet curtain with two signs over it: THE ENTER-TAINERS WHO PERFORM IN THIS PORTION OF THE CLUB ARE NOT EMPLOYEES OF THE CLUB and ENTERTAINERS ARE ONLY PERMITTED IN THE SPORTS BAR OR CIGAR CAFE TO EAT OR BY CUSTOMER REQUEST ONLY. NO EXCEPTIONS. Symbols of the impact of Mayor Giuliani's sex war. Because Goldfingers is near a church, it has to abide by the 60/40 rule. The 60/40 rule is a way for a strip club to legally remain in an area where it is less than five hundred feet from a "sensitive receptor" (i.e., a school or place of worship). Sixty percent of the space must be dedicated to nonadult activities; that explains the full dinner menu, cigar bar, pool table, big-screen TV, and espresso bar. The 40 percent that everyone comes for is behind the curtain.

For a Wednesday night, there were enough customers, and the dancers worked them all. The girls were pretty, engaging, half of them natural, the rest silicone-enhanced. No one looked too drugged out or desperate, which always depresses me. We felt comfortable there; no one was leering or overly concerned about our presence. Some of the women seemed genuinely glad we were there, and they sat and talked with us. We met Coco, who did a table dance for Patricia and told us about her girlfriend, who's also a stripper; Angel, a Russian beauty with a pierced septum, who was wearing a blue wig and silver dress; Kitty, the mother of a three-month-old, who was nervous about dancing again because of her slightly bulging tummy and stretch marks.

After only twenty minutes, a manager came over: "So I heard you're the girls from *The Village Voice*." When I asked him how he knew, he said, "I just know everything."

He launched into a tirade about Giuliani—he clearly had a lot to get off his chest—and I felt for the guy because he's angry, frustrated, just wants to run a strip club in New York City. He talked about undercover cops coming in every week, all the paperwork and rules. Meanwhile, I missed Angel doing her three songs onstage. He rambled on about statewide zoning policies, but I was there to see a girl shake her butt.

I wanted my friend to have the full strip-club experience, complete with a private dance. She liked a woman we had seen when we first walked in—red dress and lipstick, long dark hair, nice round ass, black spiked heels with straps that wrapped all the way up her legs. We described her to one of the VIP guys, but he brought out another woman. This one was dressed in pink, had light brown curly hair, big fake boobs, and the culprit—the same strappy shoes—which explained the confusion. Susan said she felt bad when the guy asked her, "Is this the one?" She didn't want to reject the girl, so she said, "She's fine." The dancer took her dress and bra off, danced in front of my girlfriend, but didn't get near her or her lap. You can't really get a lap dance anymore, according to the management, only a table dance. Susan didn't think it was too big a deal, but she doesn't know what a lap dance was like in the old days, where a girl might actually rub up against you. (FYI: Even if one of her sensitive receptors *had* gotten rubbed, if I say so, Goldfingers would get busted.)

The next morning, I woke up and realized that my only complaint about the club was that it was too well lit. Bright lights don't help anyone, not the girls, not the customers. So, Goldfingers is a clean, well-lighted place to get a clean lap dance. I wonder if that's what Giuliani had in mind.

Hollywood and Sunset Strippers

The Spearmint Rhino in downtown L.A. is an "upscale gentlemen's club," meaning it's $20 at the door for men (which I was happy to shell out for my companion, a tranny boy, because if you can pass to a strip club bouncer, you're in business) and ten bucks for chicks. (I like to think of this as the club's nod to the continuing inequality in wages.) The cover charge supposedly weeds out the riffraff, and the crowd seemed quite well behaved as we found seats with a good view. This wasn't difficult, since the stage was round and every spot was the best seat in the house. People who design strip clubs are like casino planners—when they get you in, they want you to stay as long as your wallet will let you. We also had a peripheral view of the alcoves with big leather banquettes behind us, where women were grinding their hips on men's laps.

We watched as one dancer after another took the stage, wriggled out of her costume, crawled around with her ass in the air, touched her pussy, collected her tips, and departed. Classy strip joints like the Rhino offer mostly all-American girls, too clean and WASPy for my taste, with bodies modified in all the wrong ways. I'll take ink and metal over silicone and saline any day. But I would suffer through the implants and the fashion faux pas in order to see the featured dancer that night—my favorite porn star, Chloe.

Besides being smart, super sexy, and the queen of anal sex on the small screen (must be all three to be my favorite), Chloe is the Antichrist of strippers—no fluorescent pink spandex peekaboo dress, fake tits, and over-dyed blonde tresses for her. Her body is 100 percent Chloe, and so is her style. She floated to the stage in an amazing white kimono trimmed with red sequin accents; it covered her entire tiny frame. With a flick of the wrist, a crimson fan appeared, and like a consummate drag queen, she executed her clever, raunchy choreography as that fabulously cheesy '80s tune "Turning Japanese" blared from the sound system. I am afraid her sense of camp and stripper irony was lost on most of the room.

When the silky robe was finally tossed aside, she revealed a red sequined bra and G-string that Judy Garland (or any Judy Garland imitator) would have died for. Spearmint Rhino is an all-nude club, so the sparkled set eventually came off too. For her finale, she dripped red candle wax on her pale, naked skin and encouraged audience members to drip it on her pussy and ass. (Don't try this at home, wannabe strippers; Chloe is a seasoned S/M-er and knows her way around hot wax.) Chloe has such a queer sensibility for a straight girl in the sex industry (another reason I adore her). The ultimate female impersonator, she can shake her tits and ass with the best of them, yet there is always some sense that a kickass being with big cojónes lurks underneath the glitter. Someone who can put on a girl look and take it off like nail polish.

In a different part of town, on Hollywood Boulevard, there wasn't any admission price at Cheetah's. People crowded the bar or played pool in the corner, and it felt more like a local dive where women just happened to be stripping. A big-boned punk girl with purple hair extensions and tattoos took the stage. She had a giant red ribbon etched on the back of each thigh. On the left, below the bow, in girlie black script, the word WHITE covered the entire creamy space above her knee. On the right, TRASH completed the picture. A different kind of stripper irony. My friend Thomas went into full-drool mode for her, ready to support a semester of college or ten more tattoos. (Note to dancers: Play to the sex activists in the crowd. We are simple targets. We will easily part with hundreds of dollars because we want to support sex workers!)

I can always spot the best dancer in a place within thirty seconds. She arrives onstage and she captivates. Her presence and charisma stop conversation, traffic, and anything else in her way. Cheetah's top girl was a leggy brunette with an all-natural body dressed in a leopard-print ensemble. She was definitely pretty, but otherwise seemingly unremarkable as she made her way through the crowd. But when her heels touched the shiny neon stage, she transformed. She was raw sexual energy, electric eyes, melting smile. As she wiggled around collecting dollar bills at the end of her routine, my friend Rachel complimented her on her animal-print outfit, and the two of them giggled to each other. Everyone decided she was the one. The one who'd give Rachel her very first lap dance.

As Rachel sat down across the room for the leopard girl to strut her stuff, a mature woman (read: not twenty-two) appeared onstage. She had short, perky blonde hair, a red sheer robe trimmed with feathers, and black patent-leather thigh-high boots. The dramatic opening of a jazzy rendition of "Summertime" caught me off guard, like Tupac playing in the supermarket. The blonde's moves were polished, fluid, crisp, sensual, as if she was auditioning for the chorus of *Chicago* or *Fosse*. (And by the way, she would get called back.) Was that a double-woman symbol tattooed on her right shoulder? Later, as she collected her tips, I smiled at her. She noticed that we had emptied all our ones onto the stage for her.

"If you're gonna do something, do it well," she said to me, and I detected a slight English accent.

"I could not agree more," I returned, convinced that she was a veteran stripper, possibly a dyke, and a real dancer in another life.

"I've only been doing this for nine months. I used to be a customer here, you know; I'd come in and hang out. One day, I thought, 'Hey, I could do that.' It's the best thing I've ever done for myself." I bet the guys in the place wouldn't have a clue what she meant, but I did. I am a sucker for smart strippers.

Hot Potato Sex!

One potato, two potato, three potato (*gettin' excited?*), four; five potato, six potato (*yes!*), seven potato, more. I love potatoes in all their forms: salt-and-vinegar chips; garlic mashed; baked with melted butter; fresh herb-dusted baby potatoes; Cajun-spiced curly fries; well-done hash browns with peppers. When Oprah became obsessed with "carbohydrate addicts," she may have characterized my constant craving as biological rather than simply obsessive. She often raves on her show about how she adores potatoes. Why not? There's a lot to love.

I met a woman who's got me and Oprah beat—I mean, she *really* digs potatoes. For Pommela de Terre, potatoes are her passion—for nearly a decade, she has been carving them into dildos for masturbation. When I first visited her website, I must say I was impressed. I've seen a lot of turn-ons and bizarre sexual practices, boys and girls, and this one is wholly unique.

When the petite, curvaceous dental hygienist–turned–stripper walked into the lobby bar of Manhattan's midtown Hilton, everyone's head turned. Maybe it was the cream-colored sweater that barely covered her breasts, the dark movie-star glasses, and the black Cleopatra wig. Little did the onlookers (who, incidentally, were there for a Society of Cosmetic Chemists convention) know that she was gonna take me to her room and show me why the apple of the earth is the apple of her eye.

In her quest for the perfect dildo material, Pommela has tried everything: sculpted phalluses of clay and Play-Doh; carrots, cucumbers ("They break"), bananas, candles; store-bought dildos ("They don't feel real and sometimes they chafe"); even Coke bottles ("I like old-fashioned glass ones over plastic"). For her, potatoes are the penultimate: natural, easy to carve, firm yet pliable, and they conduct heat and vibration. She claims their texture and shape are the closest you can come to a real cock, and she has never had a potato break: "Never, and I know how to push it."

On a tray in her hotel room sat three potatoes, an ordinary steak knife, a spray bottle of olive oil, a plastic lemon full of lemon juice, and a bottle of lube. She laid a towel down on the bed, brought the tray over, and went to work. She selected two potatoes, one six inches long and three-and-one-half inches around, the other five inches by three inches. She started peeling with the steak knife, and pretty soon she was whittling dick, see.

As she carved, she squeezed lemon juice on the potatoes ("a natural preservative that prevents the spud from turning brown"). Here's the thing: They were amazingly realistic—circumcised bulbous heads, impeccably detailed frenula, even veins in the shafts, which she scratched in with her manicured nails. And when she carved them, she seemed to be in her own world, potato chunks flying everywhere; peels stuck to her inner thighs and the bottom of her spiked heels. As the starch stiffies took shape, she doused them in olive oil, which helps make them more pliable.

She rubbed her creations on her breasts, sucked them, glided them along her clit. When she was satisfied with her sculptures, she invited me to put one in her pussy. I obliged with the larger spud and slid it inside her. She wriggled around, then turned over so that she was on her hands and knees. She rubbed more olive oil onto the smaller potato and worked it into her ass. She had one carbo cock in her pussy, one in her ass, and she was in potato heaven. "It's like they come to life inside me," she moaned, and sure enough both were warm and more flexible once they'd been in her for a while.

Usually when she's giving a private show (the majority of her clients are men, some couples), she's talking sexy to her watchers or they are talking to her. I wondered if my direct questions, like, "Does the lemon juice sting your pussy?" were distracting. But I did want some answers about the health and safety of hot potato sex. Because, if I know my readers, some of you are going to try this at home.

In all the time Pommela has been whacking off with her delicious dildos, she's never gotten an infection. I asked masturbation guru Dr. Betty Dodson for her expert opinion on the matter, and she said, "For some people, the starch in the potato could lead to an overgrowth of yeast.

I think the lemon juice may neutralize the sugar in the potato, but everyone's body is different." Pommela also has never lost a potato up her ass, though because her carvings don't have a flared base, as Buttgirl I must warn you that it's a risk you should consider.

Although Pommela doesn't politicize her fetish, making her own masturbation tools seems liberating to me (at least worthy of a grrrl zine); before manufactured dildos, many women (especially dykes) made their own out of household items and vegetables. Pommela may be the mother of potatophilia, but there are others who've plowed the field for her. Pommela de Terre is a revolutionary. She creates the object that fucks her, she hand-makes what she fucks, and she brings to life what gives her pleasure.

Pommela's artistic mission doesn't preclude economic reality: Let's face it, she needs spud money. She's found a way to make her art pay off. She sells memberships to her website for $9.95 for two months. She currently has 123 members, and is proud that she just signed up her first female. For $95, less than the cost of a night at a strip club, a man can send Pommela a photo of his dick, from which she will carve a realistic potato representation. Then she'll jerk off with the pet potato cock, send him the cum-soaked spud penis, a photo of her doing herself with it, and her cum-soaked panties. Since the website launched in June, she's received eight orders for custom cocks. She also performs private hot-potato sex shows; that'll run you $500, plus travel and hotel expenses.

Pommela gave me the pet potatoes as souvenirs of our meeting, and they sit side by side in a plastic Hilton shower cap in my refrigerator. (They last for about eleven hours without refrigeration; you can also freeze them.) I take them out and show them to friends when they come to my apartment—everyone is in awe of the detail and realism. I'll never look at a potato the same way again.

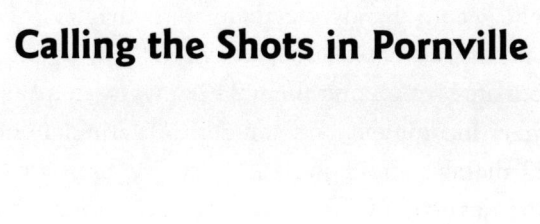

Calling the Shots in Pornville

On Being Buttgirl

When I began writing a book on anal sex for women in 1997, there was only one other guide devoted to the subject; *Anal Pleasure and Health* by Jack Morin was a wonderful resource, but it was over ten years old (later, in 1998, a third revised edition was released). Other than Morin's book, anal sex information was pretty hard to come by. I searched every sex manual I could get my hands on; there were chapters or entire tomes devoted to many aspects of sexuality, yet I found only a paragraph or a few sentences about anal sex among them. What was written was often mis-informed, always incomplete, and sometimes alarmingly negative about anal eroticism. Rather than illuminating a subject unnecessarily shrouded in mystery, the details I did find reinforced the misguided myths and fear-based warnings that many of us hear and take to heart. No other body part carries with it so much cultural baggage, and it's that stigma which causes people anxiety about anal sex or makes them avoid it altogether. I knew that I couldn't possibly be the only woman who was curious about the erotic potential of the ass, experimented with the back door, adored anal sex, or had earth-shattering orgasms from it. Since *The Ultimate Guide to Anal Sex for Women* was a book I wanted on my own bookshelf, I decided to write it myself.

To create a manual that would help people achieve safe and pleasur-able anal erotic experiences, I wanted it to be accessible to a wide variety of women *and* men—lesbian, bi, gay, straight, tranny, young, old, sex-positive, sex-neutral, sex-curious. I think accessibility is critical in sexual how-to books, and especially crucial when the topic is one like anal sex—an act still laced with embarrassment, taboo, and shame for many. I decided that rather than take an approach of distant, coolly aloof, and knowledgeable expert, I would strike a different tone altogether and infuse my writing with my adoration, enthusiasm, and curiosity about anal sexuality. I wanted readers to know that I have undeniable respect and ardor for my subject. I wanted to communicate how much I love—really love—it in the hopes of giving them permission to love it too.

The response to my book was totally overwhelming. I thought that it would strike a chord with people, but I never imagined the scope of the reaction: It was a bestseller on Amazon.com, it won a Firecracker Alternative Book Award, and it garnered national media attention. Since traditional readings and book signings didn't lend themselves to my subject matter, one of the ways that I began to promote the book was to teach workshops on anal sex, and I still teach them today. The crowds I get at the workshops are never predictable—women, men, gay, straight, bi, trans, single, coupled, old, and young.

One of my first classes was at Toys in Babeland, where I worked at the time, and as soon as an ad hit the local papers, the store's phone was ringing.

"Hi, I'm calling about this anal sex month, so is there a party or something?"

"At this workshop, will there be demonstrations?"

"Are you selling tickets for the anal performance?"

"Do the students get to try out the anal sex?"

"If I wanted a private lesson, uh, for me and my, uh, wife, with this woman, how much does that go for?" Just a few examples of people's eagerness about the topic.

The people who attended the workshop were mostly straight, mostly well-behaved. They were attentive and asked thoughtful questions:

"Any suggestions about how to sweeten the anal area?"

Well, some people like the taste of butthole. You could try a flavored lubricant like ID Juicy Fruit. The Vanilla Creme is delish.

"How does one go about removing the hair from the anal area?"

Use the same methods you would to remove hair from the bikini line—shaving with razors or clippers, waxing, electrolysis. Skip Nair, which shouldn't be used in the genital area. This question tapped into one of my secret pleasures—I love to shave my ass. I am so familiar with every millimeter of my ass—all the puckered flesh and tiny, sensitive folds—that I can shave it with a brand-new razor, without a mirror. I love the way my ass (and my pussy, for that matter) feels when it's been freshly shaved—smooth and soft and new. I love the danger of doing it and the results of a job well done. I love the thought of someone pulling down my panties, bending me over, and thinking, "What a nicely shaved asshole she has." And since my lover is such a fag when it comes to grooming, I know she notices and appreciates it.

My favorite question of the evening articulated a new battle of the sexes: "When I ask a woman to have anal sex, she says, 'Let me fuck you in the ass, then you can do it to me.' What should I do?"

Well, after the disclaimer that no one should force anyone else to do something they do not want to do, I gave it to this guy straight. Let her fuck you in the ass. You might be surprised to see how good it feels. Men do have a prostate gland, and when stimulated, it can rock your world. So let her explore your back door, then you can do hers.

That's another thing I love about my area of expertise: The butthole can be the great equalizer—everyone has one. It is the most democratic of our orifices. We can all experience what it feels like to be pitcher or catcher on the butthole diamond. And no one can accuse you of anus envy.

There was a guy who brought an attaché case of sex toys, which he wanted to show me. (I looked them over and told him my favorite was the dildo he can strap to his face.) Another fellow asked me incessantly about swingers parties and sex clubs. And then there was the shy, nerdy one who sat in the front row, took notes, and lingered long after it was over, asking question after question, desperate to be teacher's pet. In another time, this lanky, Jewish, bespectacled boy would have been just my type of guy—submissive and dying to get fucked in the ass—but I'm not there anymore.

There was one question that I was asked at nearly every one of my early workshops: When are you going to make a video? Apparently, people wanted to see my teaching in action. I'd watched my share of sex ed videos, and I had always been a fan of porn, so a video based on my book seemed like the perfect next project for me. But I didn't want to make a traditional how-to flick. I think the problem with most sex instruction

videos is that they teach you how to do something, but they don't inspire
you to run out and do it. I wanted to make a video that would be educational as well as sexy and hot.

The way I saw it, I had two options to produce the video. Number
one: Beg (including making all my friends and friends' friends work for
free), borrow, steal, make it on a shoestring budget with amateur actors,
and attempt to self-distribute it. That's the traditional lesbian feminist
approach. Or two: Sell out to The Man. I chose the latter for several reasons. My first time calling the shots, I decided that adding first-time performers to the mix was too many unknown variables; I wanted seasoned
adult performers who knew what they were doing and were excited to do
it. I also wanted to reach as many people with my video as I could, so
mainstream distribution was a must.

I pitched the idea to several top producers in the adult industry, who
all turned me down. When I described the video as both "educational"
and "for women," the way porn people responded I might as well have
been speaking a foreign language.

One of the people who turned me down was legendary porn mogul
John "Buttman" Stagliano. John is the head of Evil Angel Video and
creator of the wildly successful *Buttman* video series. I first discovered
John as a fan when I saw a *Buttman* video. John created the character of
Buttman, a man obsessed with women's asses. One of the arguments
made against porn is that it is produced by and for straight men, and
therefore couldn't appeal to women. My identification with Buttman's
point of view—one that worshipped and adored women's asses—directly
contradicted this assertion. I could totally relate to Buttman! But after our
first meeting, John seemed less than interested. Several months later,
seemingly out of the blue, he called me at home. I remember that I was
sitting on my couch, laptop glowing in front of me, typing up a freelance
article when I answered the phone. He identified himself, and I wanted
to scream, "Oh my God! Buttman is calling me!" but instead I listened to
what he had to say, and we set up a meeting.

Besides our common lust for derrieres, another reason that John
appealed to me was that he is credited as the father of "gonzo" video.

Gonzo is a genre of adult video where the camera is acknowledged as part of the storytelling; call it documentary-style porn or *Real World* porn. Spontaneity, realness, and hot, raw sex are emphasized over stylized plots, sets, and other elements of big-budget productions. I identify heavily with the gonzo genre, perhaps because I am a Gen Xer raised on MTV. I think that if porn stars are good at something, then we should just highlight that thing—giving them elaborate dialogue, sets, props, and costumes only distracts from their talent: delivering a scorching sexual performance. Show me the sex!

I met John for the second time at the Consumer Electronics Show in Las Vegas, which coincided with the Adult Video News Awards (think Oscars for porn). He agreed to fund the project, but his one concern was that I had never made a movie before, and I needed someone to show me the ropes. I didn't blame him: I'd never taken a film class, read a book, or picked up a video camera. We added fetish master Ernest Greene to the mix, and John was satisfied that it might just work. I was photographed the night of the awards with John and porn legend Nina Hartley, and the picture is an important representation of the beginning of my porn career: Flanked by two mentors, I grinned ear to ear.

Casting was a crucial part of the process. Lots of actors can give what porno people call a "strong anal performance," but I wanted to cast people who actually loved anal sex and who were really into the project. I only knew one of the actors that I cast—Chloe, known throughout the industry as "The Anal Queen." For the other actors, I had to rely on past performances and reputation. Naively, I wanted everyone to come to the set enthusiastic and psyched to be part of something altogether different. Perhaps that didn't work out in every case, but the entire cast was very open, honest, and articulate on camera about their experiences with anal sex, and that became an important component of the video.

Porn stars are a tricky bunch; like the industry, as a group and as individuals, they are full of contradictions. There are women who love sex and women who hate sex; women with low self-esteem and women with strong self images; women addicted to plastic surgery and women with less than perfect bodies who like them just the way they are; women with drug habits and women who are clean and sober. I have met women who are sexually feisty, in control of their bodies, lives, and careers; I also know women who feel exploited by the industry, don't feel they have a lot of work options, feel compelled to look a certain way to "make it." Somehow, my cast of eight women and three men was like a microcosm of the industry; I had to take the good with the bad, and make it all work somehow.

I went into the experience as a cheerleader for porn. I thought porn was great, and I couldn't wait to be a part of producing it. The first day on the set, there I was—I'd never made a movie, never even read a book on how to make a film—and I got to watch people have sex all day. It was incredible! I was simultaneously stunned, inspired, aroused, and dumbfounded at what porn stars do every day. We ask them to perform pretty incredible feats and they do, practically on command.

What I learned that first day, and would relearn each day of shooting, was that sex in front of the camera may look like sex (as I knew it, in private), it may feel like sex, but in actuality it is something altogether different. It's a copy of sex, a performance of sex, sometimes even a parody of sex. Positions that feel good don't always look good, so pleasure is often compromised in the name of seeing more pussy, more ass, even more face. The timing is not as it is in private. Sometimes, we would capture an awesome, real orgasm on film, then Buttman would say, "Okay, that was great. Now, I need about ten more minutes of footage in that position." Later, we would switch it around in the editing room, so the scene still culminates in the kick-ass orgasm, but we just have some more footage before the climax. Now, I don't know about you, but after I've had an orgasm, I don't feel much like doing the same thing for ten more minutes.

I've heard horror stories about women who've had to work with (remember, *work with* here equals *fuck*) men they didn't much like. Even in the best-case scenario when you get to work with people you genuinely like, the most you can hope for is some authentic chemistry and a good time, but there isn't a lot of intimacy on the set of a porn movie. There are exceptions: Some real-life couples who work together can explore their exhibitionism, get off on people watching, and add a different component to their sex life at home. As an actor, you are always aware of the cameras, and actually that's not a bad thing since you are performing and that's what you are being paid to do. Simply having sex with a camera rolling isn't necessarily sexy at all. You have to make it look good. That's why porn stars are porn stars. They make it look easy, sexy, fun.

Not only did Buttman serve as executive producer, he shot the movie himself in his own house in Malibu, which meant I got to work very closely with, and learn from, one of the best. Buttman footed the bill for my virgin voyage, but the process was still a collaboration, and amazingly he let me call many of the shots. John's loyal audience is primarily straight men who like a hot anal sex vid; I knew going into it that I would tailor the video accordingly. I wanted to make a video that not only taught people (especially women) about anal sex but actually inspired them to do it, and I think I achieved that, without losing sight of what sells tapes— the jerk-off factor. Before he agreed to do the movie, other adult industry folks discouraged me from even approaching him. One insider warned, "John doesn't do movies with condoms. He'll never, ever make a picture with a single condom." In fact, there were condoms used in all the scenes but one, and that one was between a real-life couple, which was established on camera.

The rubbers were just one of many compromises I made to create the film with John. As a sex educator, I encourage people to protect themselves and practice safer sex, but the adult industry is notoriously latex-free. After all, it took several cases of HIV to kick adult producers and performers into making condom-only films; others are condom-optional, but others still continue to have unprotected sex. In addition to condoms, I managed to get about half of the performers to use latex gloves for digital penetration, including a few who had never used one before and said it actually improved the experience. One of the reasons that you don't see more vibrators in video, especially with male–female couples during intercourse, is that the vibrator often covers what the cameras can't take their eyes off: the pussy. And some of them can be so loud that it sounds like there's a blender in the background. Visual and sound challenges be damned: I wanted performers to use vibrators if vibrators were going to turn them on and enhance their experience and thus their performance. I decided before the shoot that I wasn't going to have any facial cum shots. I felt that it had become a cliché in porno, to say nothing of being a stereotype of the male-centered world of adult film. It's the one moment onscreen when most women look bored, turned off, or downright miserable. Having a guy come on your face can be spontaneous, fun, and a total turn-on for plenty of women, but at least in videos I've never been impressed with this typical "pop shot." When I directed my performers that there were to be "no facials," they expressed surprise, even shock, but they went along with it reluctantly, as did John.

Lots of people ask me why I decided to be in the movie. After spending six scenes dishing out tips and techniques, I surrender to my entire cast, who show me what they've learned in an anal orgy where they each get to have their way with my butt. It was important for me to be in the video to show not only that porn stars can enjoy anal sex, but that any woman can. Besides, I can't be the poster girl for anal sex without putting my own ass on the line. I think lots of women are intimidated by porn stars, and believe either that their performances are fake or that they can do things ordinary people can't do merely because they are "professionals." I needed to show those women and others that the girl next door, which I am myself for all intents and purposes, can have just as fabulous a time getting nailed from behind. Plus, as a director/ producer, I knew I had a unique hook in my film. Not an original story line per se, but the idea that a respected writer who's never performed on film would make her debut in a ten-person anal orgy...well, *that* should get the movie some attention.

It was important to me that I got to call the shots (so to speak) in my debut. Since I also directed it, I created a safe way to be fucked by a group of ten people I'd never had sex with—I told them what to do to me and how to do it, then I momentarily surrendered and just let them all do what they do best. They teased me when I ran down the list ("Nina, talk dirty to me"; "Kyle is the first guy in the line-up"; "Sydnee, do my ass with the big red dildo") and they also taunted me—"Sure, we'll do exactly what you say..." (wink, wink). In the end, if you listen to my direction (which I included as part of the behind-the-scenes footage at the end of the video), then watch how the scene goes, they do, in fact, follow my instructions almost to the letter. And, for me, that was an important element in creating the ultimate feminist gang bang.

When I sat down to watch myself for the first time on video, I was with my codirector and editor and we were reviewing the raw footage (all twenty hours of tape). They were thrilled, said I looked great, said it was a hot scene. I wasn't so sure. For one, though I am very expressive, I didn't always seem to be able to communicate my arousal and zest. I knew I was having a great time, but I couldn't always bring those feelings to the surface. Some of my pleasure was subtle, very internal, not good porn star material. I saw all the flaws, the funny faces, the awkward body positions. We are our own worst critics, after all.

So, the most popular question: Would I do it again? I'm not sure. I definitely enjoyed being a producer and director, and I will make more porn, but as for stepping in front of the camera, I am ambivalent. Two of my mentors in the industry, both men, both of whom work primarily behind the scenes, warned me the minute I stepped foot into the Valley (the hub of the porn world): "Tristan, do not become a porn star. It will swallow you up. You actually like—hell, you *love*—sex. Sex is a big part of your life and it's important to you. After being in this industry, you won't like it anymore, you'll probably hate it. Please do not become a porn star." I trust both these people—they are smart and insightful and know their shit, and I have taken what they've said seriously. It's true that working in any segment of the sex industry as your life all day every day can numb you to the pleasures of fucking, can dilute all the high-velocity possibilities of great, mind-blowing, awe-inspiring sex.

I didn't like having sex on camera as much as I thought I would. I mean, I love public sex, exhibitionism, and sex parties, plus I love having an audience. I have go-go danced and stripped for men and women and really, truly enjoyed it. I also liked being in front of the camera, but once I was the one getting fucked, I felt too exposed, too vulnerable—I like to feel those feelings with a lover in private, but I am still not sure how I feel about them being captured on film. And my feelings about all of it are still changing, still being formed. I am still learning.

Writing the book, teaching workshops, and creating the video—a multimedia coming out to the world about my love of anal sex—have produced a variety of pleasures and pitfalls. The pleasures come in the form of brief encounters with both women and men around the country who have benefited from my book and video, who really enjoy anal sex, and who are finally talking about it. In my travels, complete strangers have approached me and told me about their secret love of anal sex, their anal experiences, desires, fears, anxieties, and fantasies. People have confided in me why they love to do it, how they love to do it, when they love do it, and with whom (or what) they love to do it. Plus, people will ask me questions they wouldn't ask anyone—not a lover, friend, parent, doctor. I'm happy to hear them because it means people are finally talking out loud about butt love.

But people also make a lot of assumptions about me. First, they think that I love anal sex so much that I will have it—indeed, I want to have it—anytime, anywhere, with anyone. I think people often mistake sexual openness for "I'm game!" I am sexually honest, and I'm pretty adventurous and slutty, but I'm also careful, cautious, and choosy about whom I have sex with—and especially whom I have *anal* sex with. Sometimes I have to spell that out to people clearly who think "anal sex" equals "no boundaries."

So, despite all the people who have benefited from the ways in which I have talked and written about sex, there are a few who just don't get it. I think it's still daring and dangerous for a woman to talk so openly about sex, and my public pronouncements of sex-positivity always put me in danger of being branded a slut, whore, nymphomaniac, sexual deviant. Okay...I am, I am, but you know what I mean.

I'm a Porn Star

I was nervous on the drive to the East Coast Video Show (ECVS) in Atlantic City. I've been to adult industry trade shows before as a fan, consumer, and reporter, but this year was different. I was there to promote *The Ultimate Guide to Anal Sex for Women*, the video based on my book. It's true—I'm a porn star now.

A trade show is a trade show no matter what the product—crowded, overstimulating booth displays; salespeople, distributors, and retailers making deals; free candy. ECVS is as mainstream as any industry showcase, except that a portion of it happens to be devoted to pornography. In one corner of the Convention Center there were displays (how many blow-up dolls can you fit in a ten-by-ten-foot booth?) and deal making (overheard: "What's the wholesale price on *Gag That Bitch?*"). But the candy here was blonde and busty eye candy. By taking part in the mainstream video biz, the adult-film industry cleverly allows businesspeople to attend on the company's dime and see their favorite porn stars five aisles away.

So, there I was on the convention floor, where producers, distributors, and other adult-related businesses had adult-film stars on hand to sign autographs. I had the pleasure of strolling by the gorgeous, perfectly coiffed likes of Shayla LeVeaux, Anna Malle, Stephanie Swift, and Jenna Jameson to get to the Evil Angel booth. It was intimidating, electrifying, and funny. After all, here was a world of stars named Allysin Chaynes, Jewel De'Nyle, Candy Apples, Cinna Bunz, and Stryc-9, and video titles like *Cornhole Armageddon, Anal Addiction, Missionary Position Impossible, Inner City Black Cheerleader Search #28, Tushy Con Carne,* and *Biker Pigs from Hell.*

This is beyond parody, which is also to say it's damn complicated to be a woman in porn. It's a place where women are objectified, are hypersexualized, and work their asses off. But women also have power: They get paid more than male actors, they call the shots on whom they work with, they demand respect. There are women like Nina Hartley, Candida Royalle, and Veronica Hart who've successfully transitioned from porn starlets to directors. Younger actresses like Jill Kelly and Juli Ashton appear to be following in their footsteps.

Irony and contradiction abound in porn: Women perform intimate acts for our viewing pleasure, then are often vilified for doing their jobs. Within the industry, there are women who adore sex and women who abhor sex; women in love with plastic surgery and women in love with their 100 percent natural bodies; women on drugs and women in AA.

I confess I am a reluctant porn star.

Making my movie was an intense, complex experience in which I worked with a diverse bunch of anal sex–loving women and men. Since I also directed it, I created a safe way to be gang-banged by ten people I'd never had sex with—I fulfilled a fantasy and told a great story.

When I make my next movie, I will only change one thing: I hope to independently fund it so that the money shot is mine, all mine. Sex is a powerful, seductive force, and so is money. Both draw women into porn. I want to harness that power to make sexy, quality porn that does justice to the women who make it and the women who buy it.

At the convention in Atlantic City I watched the legendary Nina Hartley, an ultimate pro, interact with her fans and make it look effortless. Wearing false eyelashes, an itty-bitty dress, and mile-high heels, she can stand for eight hours greeting fans, signing autographs, posing for photos. From the first fan to the end of the line, she was gracious, warm, and sweet. In return, fans adore and respect her. She helped teach me to treat the whole experience as a performance: I was playing a porn star who happened to be named Tristan.

When fans approached me to sign a slick photo from my video, I made eye contact with them, chatted, and smiled. When they asked to have their picture taken with me, I positioned them sitting in a chair, climbed on top, ass stuck out, and looked back over my shoulder and smiled. A few men (out of hundreds) asked if they could touch my ass or breasts, but most were content to enjoy our cheesy porno pose. (A Nina tip! Take his hands and place them on your body where you feel comfortable being touched. She's right, then it doesn't become a free-for-all.) I found that if I just took charge of the situation, the guys were more than happy to do what I said. I appreciated their mild ardor, and I wanted their respect. Yet I couldn't pretend that most of them were there to have a conversation with me.

Some did want to engage me and were surprised to find an articulate sex educator underneath all the shimmering body glitter. I'm not blonde and I don't have huge breasts, but I can work the smart girl routine. After all, an intelligent girl in glasses who can suck cock and do calculus is erotic because she's enigmatic. Rather than transform myself into someone I am not, I've got to work with what I've got. It's who I am and it happens to sell—I know it and the porn makers know it too. And there are plenty of women like me getting into the industry at a time when producers strive for the authentic, who want to catch the "real thing" on tape. That's why amateur videos have been so successful. Contrary to what critics say, not all porn stars are Barbie dolls with boob jobs. Some of us have brains, and some of us will make great porn. All I need is the cash.

Who Does Your Pubic Hair?

When I see a naked woman spread out in the centerfold of *Playboy* or a porn queen sitting atop some stud in reverse-cowgirl position or a sassy stripper showing her pink in a gentlemen's all-nude club, one burning question always comes to mind: Who does her pubic hair? Sure, I appreciate a tasteful pose, an artful fuck, and an athletic pole dance as much as the next woman—I just can't help but notice a well-groomed cunt when it's staring me in the face. Inevitably, my inquiring mind wants to know how it got to look so inviting (and how I can get mine to look just as fetching). In his commercials, mousse and manageability guru Paul Mitchell says, "Got a question? Ask your hairdresser." But something tells me that the folks at Vidal Sassoon aren't gonna return my call on this one.

A tastefully trimmed twat doesn't happen by accident; it takes time, technique, and talent. For girls in the sex biz, whose pussies are their paychecks, a stylish snatch is just as important as false eyelashes and smudge-proof lipstick. I suspect they learn and develop their own techniques for keeping up the appearance of their private parts. But when it comes to a coed freshly plucked from a Midwest farm to be *Penthouse* Pet of the Month or a celebrity showing it all off for Hugh Hefner's audience—do they call in a professional? I mean, did the *Playboy* editors recommend someone to style wrestler Chyna's vagina? Did the WWF diva do it herself with Lady Gillette? Or is her carefully coiffed cunt a product of modern technology—you know, like Shoes by Prada, Pussy by Photoshop?

Shearing our slits is not just for porn stars anymore. Some of us haven't yet received an invitation to pose from Mr. Hefner (hint, hint), but we still prefer to preen our pusses for our own enjoyment, for aesthetics, or both. How does the everyday girl get helpful hints on selecting an appropriate shape, preventing razor bumps, using clippers versus hot wax?

How come no one has lectured at the Learning Annex or written a witty how-to book on the subject? (Note to self: Fax proposal to Judith Regan at once!) *Cosmo* may mention where to get a good bikini wax for that trip to the Bahamas, but what about the girl who wants to go beyond the bathing-suit line? Where is Martha Stewart when my pussy needs her magic?

When it comes to mowing our lickable lawns, the hairstyle you choose for your kitty can be an expression of your personal taste. You may want to neatly trim the edges, leaving the fullness of your bush mostly intact. Or opt for a traditional triangle and create the bottom of an arrow to point the way to pleasure. Alternatively, crop your hair into a vertical so-called "landing strip" (obviously named by a jet-setting man). Once you've decided on a general shape, think about height and fullness: Do you want a fluffy tuft or a shorter, trimmed-to-the-nape-of-the-neck look? Perhaps you're daring enough to make your beaver completely bare.

To manicure your muff's mane, you can go the way of the *Sex and the City* chicks and choose hot wax. Unless you've experienced another part of your body being waxed, I would not recommend that your first waxing experience be South of the Border. While I know some folks who wax at home, I say leave it to the professionals. Electrolysis is permanent, though it requires several treatments and is your most expensive option. Another disadvantage of both waxing and electrolysis is that they are best done by someone else, and unless your partner is a licensed beautician the experience is not exactly sexy.

Shaving is simple, is painless, and can be a two-person job. Entrusting someone else to take a very sharp object to a very tender spot can be scary, exciting, and awfully arousing—a close shave can be the perfect presex practice. Or perhaps you want the skill of a pro with an erotic twist. My friend Audrey wants her fiancé to open a shaving parlor, where, for a nominal fee, women can go and have their pussies shaved in a sensual way by a handsome stud. "Why should I go to a salon and have an old woman spread my labia and wax every inch of my pussy while she acts like she's giving me a pedicure? I'd rather have a cute guy shave me, and do it in an erotic way." (Note to self: Draft business plan for Stylish Snatch Salon tomorrow.)

Personally, I absolutely love to take a blade to my cunt. Shaving is not only a do-it-yourself (or with a lover) project, but an intensely erotic ritual for me. I have a very particular routine. First, I trim any long or bushy areas with scissors. Using a soft face brush and Aveda Body Polish, I gently exfoliate the area, rinse with cool water, then lather up with Aveeno Shave Gel. Using a sharp Gillette Mach 3 (way better than the cheap disposable single-blade kind), I begin with the pubic mound and work my way down to the more tender parts, shaving with, rather than against, the direction of hair growth and pulling the skin taut to prevent nicks.

Shaving lets me stare intently at my pussy for quite a while, fussing over every inch of it. Last year, during a one-on-one masturbation coaching session, Betty Dodson commended me on my grooming job. She told me that women who style their pubes often have a better relationship with their pussies as a result of preening them on a regular basis.

After I shave it, I feel so much more connected with my pussy. For one thing, every time I pull down my panties, there she is. Not hidden by a bush, but right out in the open for me to see. I absolutely feel sexier too; once all the hair comes off, I can see every inch and every fold. Left unprotected, I become hyperaware of what's between my legs when I walk, sit down, or make any kind of move. My sensitivity also skyrockets: A tongue, a touch, or a vibrator feels ten times more intense. I can't decide which I like better: sliding my tongue against a freshly shaved cunt or having someone's mouth on mine. Must I choose?

Desperately Seeking Dyke Porn

Full of fake boobs and clichéd images, the slipcases of porn videos rarely catch my eye. But a particular one arrived in my mailbox from San Francisco and dampened my panties even before I popped its contents into the VCR. A woman is captured by the camera from above as blond waves of hair cascade over creamy shoulders. Her head is thrown back in ecstasy, her eyes are closed. Her pouty lips, painted crimson, are slightly parted with desire. She's wearing a sequined bra that matches her lipstick, and she's got a bright red dick strapped between her legs. Perched on silver platform shoes, she suggestively holds the cock. The copy reads, "Outrageous sex-ed, serious stilettos, scorching dirty talk, and daring babedick action." The blond is Shar Rednour, and she and her partner, Jackie Strano, are the producers, directors, and stars of this new dyke porno with two movies on one tape: *Hard Love* and *How to Fuck in High Heels*.

Dyke drama at its finest, *Hard Love* is the story of two former girl-friends who can't resist a last roll in the hay. It's brimming with dys-functional breakups, girls with questionable boundaries, and a heated argument that fuels steamy sex between ex-lovers. There's a little too much dialogue for my taste, but some of the acting is good, and the sex is surprisingly real, fierce, and provocative. The plot's climax between the exes—Strano and newcomer C. C. Bell—is genuine, explosive, and one of the best lesbian sex scenes ever made.

When was the last time you found a girl who not only could sport a sizable camouflage-colored dick that perfectly matches her perky bra, but who could also put her hips where her style is and pump the daylights out of every chick in the room? In *How to Fuck in High Heels*, the scripts and characters are tossed in favor of a music-video-style "mockumentary" with lots of wall-to-wall sex. There's no real story, but there's certainly a thread and a purpose to the rapidly changing scenes: how to fuck in high heels. Part erotic education, part girlie bangfest, the movie lets us witness as box-cover diva Rednour fucks everyone in sight, pausing only to change her high heels and strap-ons. I just love an ambitious woman.

Rednour and Strano have funneled their ambition into their new company, S.I.R. Video. S.I.R. is already known for its sassy series *Bend Over Boyfriend*—the third volume is in production—where women learn how to give men anal pleasure. This twosome, recognized for breaking boys' asses in, ought to also be acknowledged for breaking new ground: They are among the few dykes out there making dyke porn. They learned from the best. S.I.R. coproduced *Bend Over Boyfriend 1* with Nan Kinney of Fatale Video, the most successful lesbian porn company to date. Kinney was a founder of *On Our Backs*, the first lesbian-produced, lesbian-aimed magazine, and Fatale began in 1985 as a natural outgrowth of the mag. However, Fatale released its last lesbian porn video, *Safe Is Desire*, in 1993, leaving a huge hole in an already struggling porn pocket. While the straight and gay male porn industries burst at the seams with growth, the world of lesbian porn withers on the vine.

A towering obstacle to producing lesbian porn is money. Women, lesbians especially, just don't have a ton of cash to throw around. "Producing our own porn has not been on the No. 1 hit parade of important endeavors by lesbians," Kinney observes. "It's not that easy to do, especially not that easy to get distributed; there's not a lot of money in it, so it's really kind of a labor of love." The dot-com boom leads Rednour to think the capital is out there: "Yeah, a lot of dykes don't have that much money, but hello, Silicon Valley. In this day and age, there are plenty of dykes who have ten thousand bucks who could spend it on making a porn if they chose to."

Investment tip for rich lesbians: smut.

Antiporn feminists protested the evils of pornography in the '70s, arguing that it exploits and objectifies women; some of that rhetoric lingers, leaving many lesbians ambivalent about visual erotica of any kind. If we make it, buy it, or—goddess forbid—enjoy it, we become The Man, degrading and abusing our own sisters. On the set of her movie,

Rednour explains, "I really believe that I am doing important work in this world. And I still feel weird when I have to ask people to come. I mean I have this moment where feelings of guilt wash over me about what I am asking another woman to do." We're still figuring out how to make grrrl-powered porn and retain our feminism.

In general, women aren't seen by the mainstream (and, in turn, we don't see ourselves) as consumers of pornography or other sexually related products and services in the same way that men are. Women rarely go to peep shows to jerk off, strip clubs for a lap dance, or prostitutes to pay for sex, and this extends to their relationship to porn. I am convinced that if a man were raised in the wild by apes, and on his twenty-first birthday you brought him to a strip club, he'd whip out a wad of bills. Men just have an easier time coupling sex and money.

Most producers are only recently (and slowly) acknowledging women as porn viewers and buyers. The lesbian porn market is even smaller and less recognized. *On Our Backs* is the only dyke porn magazine, and the by-and-for-dykes porn video is a rare treat. The question remains: If we film it, will they come?

Even if we've got the money and the balls, we still need talent. There are plenty of lesbians who strip *and* hook, but finding dyke porn stars is a whole other challenge. Strano recalls their casting difficulties: "We needed a butch bottom. We're in San Francisco where butch bottoms are like weeds, they're everywhere. But to find one who will actually take off her clothes and get fucked on camera was another story."

So you can see why I get all worked up over a new dyke porn tape like *Hard Love* and *How to Fuck in High Heels*. It's a miracle that S.I.R. Video exists, and that it shows no signs of slowing down. Says Rednour: "We've got plenty of dyke movies that we're gonna make. We have porn coming out our ears. We want to start the dyke *Boogie Nights* porn empire." I for one can't wait to meet the dyke Dirk Diggler.

Me and Juli Ashton's Ass

The first time I went to Canada, I was eight years old. My mother and I went to Montreal with a friend of hers who happened to be a priest. The only Canadian memory I have is of visiting an old church where I climbed on my knees up hundreds of steps to the place of worship, which was the tradition (those Catholics are always good for some old-fashioned S/M). When I thought I had dreamed this particular part of our vacation, my mom produced a photo of me in a green hooded sweatshirt, knees against the concrete, with a huge grin on my face.

Two decades later, I returned to Canada on a crazy dyke road trip in a camper van. This time, I was still after some submission and masochism and hoped I would find it at the 14th Annual International Ms. Leather contest. No longer a kid with a heaven shoo-in as an escort, I was more than a little nervous when we arrived at the border. Canadian customs officials can be a real pain in the ass, and the country's antiobscenity laws are worse than any in the United States. We'd briefed ourselves on the no-no's—no implements or pornography that could be classified as obscene, offensive, or violent. Yup, that's right folks, we were going to a big leatherfest and had to leave all our whips, floggers, paddles, and knives at home—that's like going to a Martha Stewart convention without a glue gun. I did bring along several copies of my anal sex book and video, which could have been confiscated if some numb nut wanted to watch it for "evaluation." Luckily, we answered a few questions, and they let us drive right through.

Once we were across the border, I had a horrible realization—I forgot my ass. Not my own behind, but the ass I use for demonstrations in my anal sex workshops. (I had three planned during the trip.) People often ask me why I don't have a real person to poke during my seminars. In workshops with men and women of different sexualities present,

I won't do a live demo; it keeps the focus on the information and dis-courages creeps looking for a free show. I have let my fingers do the walking at some women-only classes and S/M conferences. The people who've volunteered to get done are always self-proclaimed backdoor betties, but when push comes to penetration, they get shy. Instead of being able to illustrate some in-depth techniques, I end up fitting half of one finger in a tight, stage-frightened butthole. Listen, it's hard to have your ass in the air in a room full of strangers and relax, and I know.

To demonstrate my tried-and-true techniques, I've been using a nifty little male masturbation tool called the FleshLight. A sleeve of a super-real-feeling material that sits in a plastic silver container with a screw-on top, it's meant to look like a giant flashlight (hence the name), in case you leave it lying around and your mother finds it. The FleshLight comes in four varieties depending on the opening you want: vagina, mouth, generic slit, and butt. Practical and portable, it's my ass in a can, and it does me just fine. Alas, my little assistant was sitting back home in America, and I had no idea if I could find a replacement in Canada. Even if the FleshLight was available up north, I knew from experience that the butt version (go figure) is the hardest to locate, so my chances weren't looking good.

A couple hours north of Toronto, we stopped for dinner in the small town of Barrie. Behind the restaurant's parking lot, I spotted an adult video store and decided to check it out. Hey, you never know. It had a pretty impressive selection of videos for a place that seemed to me to be in the middle of nowhere. As I was checking out the toy section, I spotted her. She was so big, she had her own shelf. Two round globes of ass flesh pressed up against the clear plastic window of the box. The Juli Ashton Ultra Realistic Pussy and Ass. I met well-known porn star Juli Ashton, a blonde all-American girl with real tits, years ago at the World Pornography Conference, where she spoke on a panel about the adult industry. I remembered her as bright, articulate, attractive, and genuinely engaging, and before me sat an exact, full-size replica of her ass. (It said so on the box.) Although it would be tax-deductible for me—I love my job!—this anatomical wonder came with a hefty price tag: $400 Canadian (about $285 U.S.). So I left the store empty-handed, and I decided I would attempt to get another butt FleshLight or something comparable once we got to Toronto.

Our first stop in Toronto was the girl-positive sex-toy store Come As You Are, where I had two workshops scheduled; it reminded me very much of New York's Toys in Babeland—clean, well-lit, full of high-quality products chosen with women's pleasure in mind. Hardly the place I could ever find Juli Ashton's ass, which I could not stop thinking about. I relayed my dilemma to Cory, a worker-owner from the store, who turned out to be a thirteen-year veteran of the sex-toy industry. This high-strung, fast-talking bundle of efficiency made several calls on his cell phone, and within twenty minutes, he turned to me beaming and matter-of-factly announced, "I can have Juli's ass for you in two days."

Forty-eight hours later, Cory hand-delivered Juli's ass to me at my hotel room, just in time for my workshop later that day, when I proudly displayed her, spanked her, and slid my lubed-up fingers in her. I even put a butt plug in that sweet hole between her cheeks (after proper warm-up, of course). Juli's ass brought a (w)hole new dimension to my teaching; people who've seen my workshop before told me they actually got turned on when I demonstrated penetration techniques on Juli's ass. Nearly everyone wanted to come up and touch her. (Her pussy's pretty great, too, and she even has a G-spot!)

Canadian laws are so obsessed with the degradation of one human being by another—depictions of sex combined with bondage or one person peeing on another are against the law—and yet you can purchase a woman's pussy and ass, without the rest of her body, without a face or a brain, for a few hundred dollars. It's enough to make a radical feminist's head explode. To some men, Juli is just a new-fangled blow-up doll. To antiporn feminist Andrea Dworkin, she's a misogynist toy that encourages violence against women. To me, she's the ass and pussy that have changed the way I teach people about anal sex. Thank you, Canada!

There's No Place Like "Oz"

Lots of gay and lesbian viewers are wetting themselves over the new Showtime series *Queer as Folk,* which follows the lives of fags and dykes in Pittsburgh. When it comes to the boys, *Queer as Folk* definitely gets it right, but sadly there are far fewer lesbians on the show, and the ones we do get are bickering, jealous bitches who just want to have kids and settle down. We've still got a long way to go. The show is being applauded for pulling no punches when it comes to the depiction of gay and lesbian lives. Words like *real, uninhibited,* and *gutsy* are simply euphemistic references to the show's explicit content—yes, they actually show you said queer people being sexual. In the world of gay TV, that's revolutionary stuff. On network television, while straight people routinely romp around in their underwear and grope each other, the supposedly slutty Jack of *Will and Grace* has never even been seen in bed with another man.

Queer people are starved for gay characters to be as sexual as their straight counterparts. Maybe you think I shouldn't complain because, after all, we did have Ellen. But Ellen never got remotely hot and heavy with anyone; she could have slipped her hand up a chick's skirt just once. Geez, she never even trimmed and filed her fingernails before a date. I'm holding out for the day I see Will butt-fucking a new boyfriend. Okay, maybe that is asking too much—I'll be more realistic—Will being butt-fucked by a new boyfriend. It's easy to work into the show: We see him rolling around in the sheets with some hottie, but as he grabs for more lube he notices there is a brand-new bottle on his bedside table, which Grace put there. (How and why she got it can be a subplot.) Or what about gay John, the receptionist on *NYPD Blue?* How come we haven't seen his bare ass next to another man's butt? We've seen everyone else's on the show. And John Goodman's gay character on *Normal, Ohio*—no, I don't particularly want to see his ass, but why can't he get a quick blow job now and then? Oh wait, that gay show's been canceled already.

So I thank the goddess for cable, where the possibilities for queerness and sex are seemingly endless. But with all the focus on *Queer as Folk*, I think gay viewers are missing the hottest gay show on cable television, and they don't even know it. It's called *Oz*, and it's a show about life inside the fictional Emerald City Unit of Oswald Maximum Security Prison. (C'mon, *The Wizard of Oz* reference should have given away that it's a big old queenfest!) I just got HBO, so I'm a latecomer to *Oz*, arriving in the second part of season four. What prompted me to check it out in the first place was actually *Law and Order: Special Victims Unit*. I've got a small crush on actor Christopher Meloni, who plays a detective on that show, and I recently read a blurb in *Out* magazine about him playing a gay guy on *Oz*. In general, we queers feel honored when heteros play gay, but I was more intrigued by a straight guy playing gay in a prison drama on HBO.

And Meloni has not disappointed me; in fact, he has exceeded my wildest dreams. Meloni plays Chris Keller, a convict in love with a fellow *Oz*-mate named Tobias Beecher. In a recent episode, Ronnie (played by the hunky, blue-eyed Brian Bloom), an old friend of Keller's, arrived at Oz. After Beecher had sex with Ronnie, a jealous Keller was determined to also get Ronnie in bed. Keller kissed Ronnie—and kids, I do not mean some tepid network television hug with a kiss on the cheek; I mean he kissed him full on the mouth, and if there wasn't tongue involved, well, these guys are even better actors than I imagined. Keller also got an intense blow job from Ronnie worthy of any top-rated scene in a gay porno. And to shove it in Beecher's face (not his cock, but the fact that he did Ronnie, too), Keller made a little gesture to Beecher across the prison from his cell in the middle of the night. No, it wasn't the middle finger. Keller dropped his underwear for this "fuck you," bent over, and spread his ass cheeks for his lover. Let's just say that this is an image I will not soon forget. As an actor, Meloni doesn't just have guts to play gay with such gusto, he's got balls, and an asshole, too. (I have seen them with my own eyes.)

Lest you think it's only love and lust behind bars, remember *Oz* is a prison drama. The amount of violence can be overwhelming and sometimes unbelievable—why do the prisoners have access to so many weapons?—and people die at an alarming rate. Some of the story lines are also over the top, and the "messages" can be annoyingly heavy-handed. But that's the idea—life inside is all black and white. And anyway, who cares? Guys are chasing each other around and fucking and it is my new favorite show! Unfortunately, after that great blow job, Keller breaks Bloom's neck before he comes (something about being ratted out to the feds). Meloni's character is not exactly the gay poster child, and I don't think the Gay and Lesbian Alliance Against Defamation (GLAAD) is gonna be running out and applauding a show where some of the men who like other men are also sadistic bastards.

But to me Keller is like the gay antihero. He's no role model or saint, but he's also no asexual Will, no nonthreatening Ellen. And I am telling you that for me watching *Oz* is like watching really good gay porn. Tough guys, danger, and violence mix with forbidden sex: sometimes forced, sometimes ugly, always hot. Watching *Oz*, I felt strangely like one of those gay male subscribers to *Playgirl*, ogling all the straight men, just wishing they'd fuck their buddies—and then they do! I swear the only thing that could make this show better would be if prisoners could break into song-and-dance numbers in Emerald City. But that's just my faggy musical-theater fetish talking. And that, of course, is an entirely different show.

Your Wife's Porn

Women are picky when it comes to pornography, as illustrated at a recent gathering where ten dykes watched *DreamQuest,* the splashy, expensive new feature produced by Wicked Pictures and Adam & Eve. Considering it was straight porn, these girls were much less squeamish about the excessive number of blow jobs than I had predicted. They did have plenty to say about manicures, penis size, and the presence of ponies. "I am very impressed—some actual muffdiving, not that fake, snake-tongue shit like in *Playboy*." "His dick isn't very big; I mean, in the fag porn I've seen, the guys are HUGE." "No no no! Look at her nails…she's not going to put them in that poor girl's ass, is she?… Yikes!" "Are those real? I think they're real. Yeah, real, definitely real." "I didn't know so many porn stars had their pussies pierced. Cool." "If I'm gonna look at cocks, I wanna see some unbelievably large ones. I have not seen one yet." "I thought the horses were great."

With the industry hype focused on its quarter-million-dollar budget (one of the most expensive pornos ever made), the producers of *DreamQuest* are hoping its time has come—time for a sex movie with big-time production values. (Unscripted, bare-bones pornos can be made for as little as $10,000.) A cross between *The Princess Bride* and *Debbie Does the Underworld, DreamQuest* is a romantic magical adventure starring Jenna Jameson as Sarah, a woman on a mission to save fantasy from the clutches of a Satan-like creature named Vladimir. On Sarah's journey, she encounters a spider woman and her slave, big-nosed trolls set on tripping her up and feeling her up, blond cock-sucking human candelabras, and glitter-dusted fairies wearing wings and G-strings. There's even a well-choreographed sword fight involving our lesbian panel's favorite character, Tundra. Clad in a silver breastplate and thigh-high boots that Xena would kill for and armed with two clear Lucite dildos that made us all drool, Tundra (played by Alexa Rae) proved to look the best, but fuck the worst. Once she had Sarah splayed out in her snowy lair, the ice princess's spectacular frosted eye shadow showed more promise than her pussy-pumping techniques. Luckily, Jenna took over, fucked herself with both dildos (one in each hole), and brought the scene out of its cold demise.

The feature's cinematography is not entirely consistent, but it is superior to typical porn in many spots, partly because it was shot on film, instead of video. The elaborate sets and makeup are effectively moody, the costumes detailed and sexy. The enormous cast of more than twenty top adult stars showcases the best of sex (the wildly orgasmic Teri Starr takes the cake and Brad Armstrong's cock), acting (porn veteran Randy Spears's hysterical scene-stealing), and that rare combination, a fucking thespian (Jenna!). Although the editing is top-notch, sometimes the pace lags, and more than once during our viewing, someone shrieked, "All right, already—get to the sex!" When they do get around to doing the deed, it's really hit or miss, and, for all those predictable cum shots, the sex was often anticlimactic.

So, does the Hollywoodization of smut make a better fuck flick? I suppose it depends on whom you ask. This new breed of porn-with-a-plot is intended for couples (read: straight women), and the formula is a simplistic view of Mars and Venus. Show enough sucking and fucking to appeal to the average guy (the easiest target). Soften said activities with characters, dialogue, and Hollywood finesse, so that these same guys won't be embarrassed to watch it with their wives. The notion that women may not just be unoffended but may also get off is a bonus. This new marketing strategy explains the emergence of a couples-focused genre that sometimes reminds me of romance novels in action. Although we poke fun at the bodice-ripping, Fabio-starring fantasies, they are the most mainstream form of a stroke book for women. Do you think it's their fascinating plots that make them bestsellers? Wake up and smell the pussy, folks. It's dripping wet from all the commotion between the pages.

I am thrilled that finally the industry is acknowledging women as consumers of porn, and making products that women won't simply stomach but actually might enjoy. This new crop of rentable romps and the wave of woman-friendly sex-toy stores may go together as well as garters and stockings. But here's my next question (a tricky one, I know): Is this what straight women really want? Some straight women have no interest in porn, plot or no plot. The publishers may deny it left and right, but I still believe that the only reason *Playgirl* stays in business is all those fags with straight-guy fantasies.

Back at our lesbians-watch-breeder-porn panel, Jane said, "Straight women want real characters and fewer blow jobs that last for an hour. Just a lot of the in-and-out doesn't do it for them. They want some context to their sex." "Het chicks don't want romance. They want to be fucked by a lot of different guys against their will," said Grace, one of the more jaded panelists. Of course, these two scenarios represent only some women's fantasies, and there is a whole world of possibilities in between. "I think they still might be better off with Femme," said Claire.

Femme Productions, founded by former porn star Candida Royalle, is a line of erotic videos "from a woman's point of view." Not feminist per se, and certainly not soft core like many assume they are, Royalle's videos are full of passionate sex focusing on women's pleasure and relating to the characters and story lines. Femme videos are some of the only videos distributed by a mainstream company that portray "internal" cum shots. That's right—there is no wacky splooging on her face or in her mouth, which is, of course, considered the Money Shot in almost all straight porn.

Money shot or no, we know that women have a very different relationship to visual pornography than men. Whether it's *Sodomania #27* or the new Victoria's Secret commercial with two underwear models suggestively dancing together in the desert, most of you guys are a piece of cake. Female fans are a lot more complicated—some like it nasty, some like it sweet (and plenty like it both ways!). Femme Productions paved the way for a growing list of movies for those girls who like a little conversation with their cock.

Panic in Pornville

John Ashcroft loves pornography. Sometimes, when he's in the mood to be by himself, he'll rent *Inner City Black Cheerleader Search* and have an extended self-loving session. He especially likes adult film star Midori and believes she gives the most enthusiastic blow jobs. Dick Cheney only goes for the girl–girl features; his library includes *Where the Boys Aren't*, *Shane's Slumber Party*, and his newest favorite, *Lesbian Survivor*, a spoof of the hit TV show. At Laura's request, George W. buys titles like *Debbie Does Dallas*, on DVD, of course, because of the bonus footage: George W. is intrigued to see what goes on behind the scenes. They watch a feature together on their big-screen TV, then retire to the bedroom for some spirited role-playing. Those white Dallas Cowboy cheerleader go-go boots Laura wears really get him going.

I wish.

In reality, since Bush was sworn in as president and put his extremist buddy John Ashcroft in the attorney general's office, word has it that the adult industry is having a collective panic attack. The main fear of pornographers is: Will they be targeted under stricter obscenity laws and antiporn legislation? Well, George W. did vow during his campaign to "vigorously" enforce federal antipornography laws. No surprise there, but his presence in the White House has some skin-flick producers running scared. Four of the biggest players—VCA Pictures, Vivid Video, Hustler, and Video Team—met with their lawyer, Paul Cambria, to discuss strategies. One unidentified company drew up a working list with Cambria of "Box Cover and Movie Production Guidelines." I like to think of them as the New No-No's. The list was subsequently leaked and appeared on a porn-gossip website in late January 2001 and then on the *Adult Video News* website. Here, in the italics below, is the list, followed by my blow-by-blow commentary.

No shots with the appearance of pain or degradation. No blindfolds. No wax dripping. No bondage or bondage-type toys or gear unless very light. No forced sex, rape themes, etc. No degrading dialogue, e.g., "Suck this cock, bitch," while slapping her face with a penis.

Thanks for the example, guys. These don't come as any big surprise, since, even when it is a consensual fantasy, bondage and other S/M combined with sex are considered potentially offensive. That's why, to stay on the shelves, most S/M videos have already done away with such cover images. But who wants to see someone whipped and degraded without then being fucked into oblivion?

No facials—body shots OK if shot is not nasty. No bukkake. No spitting or saliva mouth to mouth. No girls sharing same dildo in mouth or pussy. Toys are OK if shot is not nasty. No peeing unless in a natural setting, e.g., field, roadside. No squirting.

First of all, if the shot is not nasty, I don't want it. So now they want to limit the representation of bodily fluids. Since many women, including porn stars like Dasha, Alisha Klass, Ava Vincent, and plenty of others, ejaculate when they orgasm, is there the implication that these women are now not allowed to come on camera? That's one of the perks of the job, stupid!

No food used as sex object. No coffins. No mentration [sic] topics. No incest topics.

My condolences to necrophiliacs, vampires, and Barbie twins fans everywhere.

No two dicks in/near one mouth. (Notice that double penetration of a pussy or ass is still okay.) *No shot of stretching pussy.* (Luckily, Extreme Associates' *Planet of the Gapes* is safe—they only show gaping assholes.) *No fisting. No hands from two different people fingering same girl.* (Just when I was hoping that things would loosen up when it comes to sticking all five of your digits inside a girl's pussy—a depiction that has been taboo in videos for far too long—we're back to square one.)

And here come my favorites: *No male/male penetration. No transexuals [sic]. No bi sex. No black men with white women themes.* What kind of blatant homophobia, transphobia, and racism is this bullshit? So white men can fuck black women, but black men can't fuck white women? Whispered in a closed boardroom meeting, I'd definitely believe it, but who would put such a thing in print?

Remember, these activities aren't against the law to depict, but they may be considered obscene according to certain community standards. And this isn't Ashcroft's list—I shudder to think what might be on that. (Can you say, "No penetration whatsoever"?) Self-censoring themselves, the porn masters are anticipating what might get them into trouble during the Bush years, and will be shooting and packaging accordingly. Will there be antiporn witch hunts, prosecution, and legislation? You can bet on it. Do you think all the faith-based organizations funded by Bush's new federal program are gonna be opening up soup kitchens? Some of them are going to go after sex in the name of religious morality. Like Boy Scouts, these pornographers want to be prepared. They are some of the largest, richest enterprises, with the most to lose if they are prosecuted.

But some industry insiders smell a rat. The big studios are already pretty squeaky-clean, especially since much of their revenue depends on soft-core versions of their films being sold to adult-cable channels. These so-called new standards may be a way to further distance themselves from the more radical, independent (and less well-funded) "little guys" who push the limits in porn with extreme, outrageous, and, yes, potentially offensive material. (Does the title *Ass to Mouth* mean anything to you?) But good pornographer versus bad pornographer is a dangerous direction to go. In the end, they are all vulnerable to the sex-hating, censorship-loving right wing.

I'm going to go rent *Thighs Wide Open* before it gets pulled off the shelf of my favorite video store.

Behind the Money Shot

The Money Shot, a biweekly Internet television series from Carbon Based Films, follows the trials and tribulations of staffers at the fictional *Blue Movie Guide.* The series is touted—and it's not PR hype—as an insider's look at the porn industry. The show's creators got their material by profiling starlets and reviewing XXX videos for *Blue Movie's* real-life counterpart, *Adult Video News.* These folks know the secrets of Pornotopia because they watched the ins and outs in the flesh (or on tape) for a living. It may sound like a dream job to a porn fan, but *The Money Shot* tells a darker tale of a life spent pushing PLAY or PAUSE.

In the first episode's opening scene, two porn stars are going at it on a film set as the director looks on, barking commands. The moans and yelps of the stars are suddenly drowned out by the sound of a snoring guy in the corner of the room. Mr. Sleeping Beauty, identified as a *Blue Movie Guide* reporter assigned to cover the production, is one of the colorful yet terminally jaded writers on the show. Although it's an entertaining glimpse at what really goes on behind the XXX scenes, it's a curious one; I mean, how could a guy actually nod off while people are having sex a few feet away from him?

I don't think I am yet so disillusioned; however, I was wondering if George W.'s reign, new content rules set forth by some major porn producers, and general hysteria might indeed cause a visit to an adult film set to result in a catnap. My access to a Vivid Video shoot called *Sweet Desires* was the perfect opportunity to see for myself just what was happening in the unassuming suburban homes of the sprawling San Fernando Valley.

When I get to the set, I attempt to casually slip into a leather chair a room away from where they are shooting, but close to the video monitor. (It's no piece of cake to be inconspicuous, considering I'm the only woman in the vicinity wearing clothes.) Contract girl Kira sits naked on a marble-topped kitchen island. The twentysomething former stripper signed an exclusive contract with Vivid as soon as she entered the business two and a half years ago. With long legs and a tiny waist, big silicone breasts, and hair worthy of any shampoo commercial (the word *cascading* comes to mind), she's prime Vivid Girl material. Her creamy skin, the color of coffee with half a cup of milk in it, hints at some ethnicity (Hawaiian? Pacific Islander?), the only element keeping her from being a brunette Barbie.

Costar T. J. Cummings unwraps a pink condom and rolls it down his cock as Kira spreads her legs. I'm getting a cold ass just thinking about how long she's been on the countertop. Someone brings in a wooden step stool for him to stand on. (He can't quite reach the counter on his own.) T. J. slips inside Kira's pussy, and almost immediately he's pounding her hard. She makes a high-pitched noise every time he slams into her; it sounds like a word somewhere between "Ohhhhh" and "Help," and it makes the rather tame scene worthwhile for me.

One of the production managers leans over and says, "I love his ass. I'm not gay or anything, but that's a great ass."

Director Robby D laughs. He looks like he just came from winning an extreme skateboarding championship. I have to admit T. J. does have a pretty amazing ass—a tanned, muscled bubble butt, worthy of any A-list man-on-man feature. He looks like a gay porn star because, well, he's attractive and has a gym body, and dudes who look like him usually *are* gay porn stars.

"Wait, the condom's gone," a crew member announces. "The condom's not there anymore." It obviously came off and slipped inside Kira, who giggles as she tries to fish it out.

"That's why they call it a snatch," says one of the crew members. But Robby D actually likes to call it a *cookie,* which he does several times, as in "Put your hands on your cookie, Kira." I can't help it; all I can think of is Girl Scout cookies.

With a new condom on, T. J.'s cock has gotten harder and flushed a bright pink—now I see the logic of the color choice. He starts pumping away again, this time for only a few seconds before the DP (that's the director of photography, not to be confused with a "dp"—shorthand for double penetration) yells "Light!"

The c-light is a light shined directly on the action (whether you want to call it crotch or cookie or cunt). It helps us see the "c" better. Makes the "c" brighter. Like the spotlight on the diva at an opera, it helps the "c" to sing. I appreciate the light's direct approach to the "c." No fumbling around with the lights out. I wish I had a c-light handy sometimes, so I could see what I was doing. Now, the guy who holds the c-light, well, he's about as close to the fucking as possible without being in the movie (or in the girl's pussy himself). And his job is to follow the "c" with the c-light. Which can be harder said than done if the "c" is rambunctious, slippery, or dodgy. But Kira's "c" is well-behaved, docile, predictable enough to be easy to follow.

You may think that the c-light guy has a difficult task, but poor T. J. practically has to come on command. Male porn stars stay hard for a long time (could be a couple of hours) getting sucked and fucking without ejaculating. Then, the director calls for the money shot, and they've got to deliver. Luckily T. J., who's not on Viagra like many of his colleagues— "Hey, I am only twenty"—has no problem, and performs like a Boy Scout getting a merit badge. After he pops on Kira's tits, he tiptoes off the set to get dressed and hurry to another shoot. I see Robby D wipe the cum off Kira's breasts himself. What a gentleman, I think. Now that's a money shot.

Dyke Debauchery

Plenty of queer women work as porn stars, strippers, and sex workers, but a lot fewer of us are willing to fork over cash for cooch. Sure, we'll spend our savings on WNBA season tickets, but when it comes to sex, lesbians are notorious nonconsumers. We have one of the smallest selections of self-produced porn of any sexual community I know, only a handful of places where you can see lesbian go-go dancers, even fewer spots to see women strip for women, and no regular sex clubs of our own. So when I heard about a party that was going to feature live dyke sex performances, I was skeptical.

Any dyke sex event is like your wayward, fucked-up sister who never has her own apartment and always needs a place to crash. The bachelorette pad for the evening was a gay strip club in the Tenderloin district of San Francisco. Its giant marquee announcing the "All Male Revue" vibed with the night's performers, who call themselves the Gender Defiant Dykes for Fagdom. Faggy or not, we lesbos always have a cause, and this was a worthwhile one: fundraising for a dyke porno flick called *Debauchery*. There was another agenda as well, one that producers made clear by hanging simple white signs with bold black letters all over the place. The signs read: PLEASE FUCK. Encouraging.

Our vampy, andro-cyberpunk hostess, Trashina Cann, introduced the first act of the evening: a big-breasted butch in a tank top and a red-headed dominatrix who looked like a witch. Their performance was typical leatherdyke fare: Butch cuts femme's clothes off with a knife, femme sucks butch's dick, and they fuck in various positions. The pair's number culminated in the femme's orgasm, followed by her "stabbing" her aggressor, with fake blood everywhere.

The main attraction was a bunch of five rowdy, raunchy construction workers perched on scaffolding, catcalling and generally behaving badly.

A daring femme appeared, prepared to scale the scaffolding, and once she began to wrap her long legs around the silver metal bars, she had my full attention. I thought that if the five really manhandled the girl, really fucked her up, it might get me raring to go. But I couldn't stop thinking the worst: These are dykes, and I'm in San Francisco, home to some of the worst performances, erotic or otherwise, I have seen in my life. There are probably just going to be a few blow jobs, a smack on the ass, and that's that. I am jaded and had no faith it was going to be any good.

The femme egged the boys on, daring them to jump down and get a piece of her. The first to take the bait was the hottest of the bunch, a black butch with a razor-sharp haircut and lots of swagger. When she unzipped her pants, I recognized it right away: Her cock was the rubber replica of porn star Sean Michaels's impressively large member. Thought number one: She's gonna start with that?

Oh, yeah, she started with it all right; a handful of lube, and the chick sucked that puppy inside her cunt like a Tootsie Roll. Reading the script of my dirty little mind, the butches all did her, sometimes one in her mouth and one in her pussy at the same time. Make no mistake: She was running the show, orchestrating her own gang bang, and it was fucking beautiful.

One butch had been playing with a major power tool the entire time, not between her legs, but a big vibrating drill that scared the shit out of me. Sure enough, she attached a pink sparkly dildo of considerable size to it, fired it up, and prepared to finish the girl off. This was no simulation; that tool vibrated like a jackhammer on speed and lurched inside her, and the chick took it like a goddess. She moaned and went nuts. Then, with four or five fingers inside her, she ejaculated so much squirt that audience members directly under the scaffolding most definitely got soaked. It was heaven. And it was history: Trashina reminded us that this was only the second occasion when female ejaculate had been spilled on the floor of this theater, the first being her girl-jizz from a performance during the first *Debauchery* party.

The show was over, but another question still loomed: Would dykes follow the pleas of the abundant signage and get it on? I was so jacked up by the performance that the PLEASE FUCK signs seemed to be speaking directly to me. I checked out the downstairs scene, a dark, cavernous maze of tiny video booths, a large room with a big-screen TV playing porn, a tiled room with several showerheads, and a brightly lit computer room for online chatting and cybersex. Although the theater's hot line had said that it was closed for a private party, men were still allowed to come in, and there were a few wandering around down there. At first I thought it was cool; they were just a bunch of fags, and maybe I would get to see some gay-boy action live and up close. But when I started to check out the guys, I remembered that all the men in a gay sex club are not necessarily gay; in fact, a lot of the dudes that night seemed more like married men who wouldn't mind getting a blow job from another guy. They didn't bug me very much, but I did wish they weren't there. (Especially since Trashina said that a mainstream adult company had offered her ten grand just to come film the show, and she declined. She emphasized that this night was *by* dykes and *for* dykes, so the dudes fucked with that a little.)

A door to one of the video booths popped open, and I spied a Latina woman and an African-American woman, both naked and sporting strap-ons, one with a thick dildo covered with a condom. They giggled, as if they had lost something. Then I was distracted by girls groping each other on the couch in one of the hallways. I saw a cute couple by the stairs, and the femme had her hand down the butch's pants. The elastic of her boxer shorts was visible, but the hand disappeared inside the shorts as the girlfriend writhed against the wall. Folks were being encouraged to head back upstairs for the corncob fucking contest, but I am sorry to report I missed my chance at vegetable stardom, as I got carried away in the shower room downstairs. I was just trying to set a good example for my dyke sisters.

Why I Love Porn

Porn is an aphrodisiac professor and an inspirational activist all rolled into one.

Porn turns women on. Over 40 percent of American women (that's over fifty million) experience some form of sexual dysfunction, and many have trouble getting aroused. For us, there is no magic blue pill that works like Viagra does for men. Watching people fuck on film can stimulate an important female sex organ—the brain—which has a direct line to the clit. When women like what we see, our bodies say so.

Porn teaches. We can all learn from porn, and I am not just talking about educational videos. Porn gives us ideas for new positions, new scenarios, and new techniques that can rev up our sex lives. The first time I saw starlet Ava Vincent in her self-proclaimed favorite position, "pile driver" (legs way over shoulders; think *Cirque du Soleil*), I knew I wanted to give it a try. I realize the dialogue can be cheesy and laughable, but sometimes it's really hot—if you've ever heard Jewel De'Nyle get her mouth going, you know what I mean. If you're a dirty-talkin' novice, steal the good lines from porn! Besides making you a budding phone sex seductress, porn can give you the words or the impetus to talk about something. Instead of having to describe it in detail (which may seem intimidating or impossible), you can simply point to the screen and say, "Baby, I want to do *that*."

Porn empowers. Now more than ever, there's porn that creates positive messages about sexuality, focuses on women's pleasure, and highlights real orgasms. Add to that the recent explosion of porn directed by women, porn starring sexually empowered women, and porn focused on women's pleasure, and you've got a powerful aphrodisiac. When I see a little piece of another woman's authentic sexuality, it's at once mesmerizing, reassuring, and magical. Sometimes, when an actress gives a certain look or comes like crazy, I see myself on the screen. Sometimes, I see pure fantasy: When a well-hung stud puts his enormous dick in a woman's ass, I soak my panties, even though in real life, something that big isn't gonna work for me. But fantasy is a crucial part of a healthy sex life for women.

Do I love all porn? Of course not. There's plenty that bores me, offends me, makes my feminist skin crawl. Bad porn cares less about everyone involved. Its formula reduces men's desires to "I want to come on your face," and it reduces women's desires to "I want to serve some guy's needs, and my sexuality doesn't matter." Sexuality for both men and women is more complex than that. Good porn makes men feel more comfortable with women. It helps them see how sexy foreplay is, that it's not just something they're required to do to get to "the main act."

The answer to the prevalence of crappy porn is not "all porn is bad" or "porn breeds violence." Compared to the United States, there are countries with tougher antiporn laws and higher rape statistics, as well as countries with less restriction on porn and lower rates of violence against women. There is no conclusive data on the correlation between pornography and violence against women. If we took away all the porn in this country, we would still have violence, abuse, and rape committed against women.

We live in a society in which we are relentlessly teased and tempted by sexual images. But the subliminal message is usually about buying stuff rather than actually getting naked and exploring pleasure. Quite a few Americans still have too many hang-ups and repressed ideas about sex to simply enjoy it. Watching porn can be a lesson in sexual honesty (especially the amateur stuff!). Good porn encourages sex to happen—with yourself, with your partner, or with your lover dressed as Shaft. When people are reduced to their body parts, and there's no emotional connection or mutuality, then porn is joyless and mean. But when it says to men and women, "Sex is a healthy, fun adventure," porn speaks the truth.

Sex Ed 201

Girls Who Squirt

Recently my friend Cooper looked quizzically at the bookshelf next to my bed. Pointing to the bulky pink plastic package nestled between a row of space-age sex toys and a box of baby wipes, she asked, "What are those for?"

Extra Large Underpads for the Protection of Bedding and Furniture. (You find them in the drugstore near the Depends.) I have only so many sets of sheets, so I need to be prepared for a gusher. Although they are intended for use by incontinent people, those in the know with bladder control keep 'em handy for girls who squirt—they make cleanup so much easier after an evening with a female ejaculator.

Have you ever had your hand inside a girl, fucking her really well, and all of a sudden she soaked the bed? Or maybe you discovered a larger-than-usual wet spot underneath you after a hot round of sex. Finding a woman's G-spot—the tissue of glands and ducts around the urethra called the urethral sponge—has become the hot sex act of the late '90s. You're definitely hip if you can locate the spongy sucker (toward the front wall of the vagina), then stimulate it and make her hum.

Many women find that if their lover puts pressure on the spot and presses and pulls just right, they can ejaculate. There might be a drizzle or a shower or—don't underestimate a high-pressure system—a torrential downpour. If you find the spot and make her ejaculate, you're on the cutting edge of New Millennium Sex.

The 1982 publication of the explosive book *The G Spot* put the spot and female ejaculation on the map. Subsequent books, videos, workshops, and sex toys devoted to the G-spot raised popular awareness about this erogenous zone. When I taught men "How to Drive Your Woman Wild in Bed" at the Learning Annex, half the group knew where the G-spot was and the other half had heard about it and were dying to locate it. There are even porn videos featuring squirting girls, and some starlets are known for their liquid abilities—notably Sarah Jane Hamilton, Alisha Klass, and Jewel Valmont aka Ava Vincent.

An innocent babydyke in college, I first heard of female ejaculation when Debi Sundahl came to campus to show her instructional video *How to Female Ejaculate*. I got the low-down on my G-spot that day and a lesson in the controversy surrounding the whole concept of female ejaculation. There are people who believe that it just doesn't happen (the same folks who believe the G-spot doesn't exist), that women are urinating, not ejaculating. But they're wrong. I was mesmerized by women jerking off, coming, and ejaculating onscreen. Yet another radical concept straight out of San Francisco: We girls can shoot our loads just like the boys.

It took a few years and another opportunity to see a woman actually do it—this time in person—before I started on my mission to learn how to ejaculate. I saw it live when I ran into my friend Kim Airs (owner of Grand Opening! Sexuality Boutique in Brookline, Massachusetts, and infamous girl shooter) in the bathroom at a sex party. She had just finished having sex with someone, and she said she was coming all over the place.

"Wanna see?" she asked, and I eagerly nodded.

She whipped out her own absorbent pad (a must-have accessory), spread her pierced labia, cocked her hips forward, and started shooting juice from her pussy. It was amazing to see her ejaculate so close-up, and she looked like a fucking goddess doing it—beautiful, powerful, sexy.

I decided that night I just had to learn how to do it. I was ready to rent the video again, take a workshop, invest in all those toys specially designed for G-spot stimulation. But there are some things you just can't plan. And you know, dear readers, how I love the unexpected.

Let me set the stage for my virgin coming, my immaculate ejaculation. Two of the hottest butches in New York requested my presence at a certain club in Brooklyn: Val, a stocky, mean-looking top who's been in the scene for twenty years and has the impeccable skills to prove it and who handles a flogger like no woman I have ever seen, as if it's a poised, powerful, poetic extension of her right arm. And her boy Red, named for her coppery razor-short hair, whose innocent freckles camouflage an intense tolerance for pain and torture. Red is one of the finest butches I have ever laid eyes on; she makes this femme bottom want to be a butch daddy just for her.

I leaned against Red's solid body, felt her rock-hard dick through soft leather pants as Val cut all my clothes off with her knife in a public scene at this club. I was flogged, had clothespins stuck up and down my back and ass, flogged some more, hooded, dragged to a truck, and driven to an unknown location. There were geography and music trivia questions answered incorrectly, punished with slaps and spanks. There were cocks and fingers shoved in my pussy, mouth, and ass. Red held me down while Val pierced my chest. It was a long, complicated scene full of pushing boundaries, initiation, and good old-fashioned fucking. I thought it was over as we all crashed in Red's bed in the early morning hours.

In the morning, I woke up on my back in between two hot butches. Heaven. Red had already shown me how to make her squirt and, in symbiotic lesbian fashion, she was gonna make me ejaculate. Red snapped on a latex glove and started fucking me with the same ferocity as the night before. Her energy and passion are boundless. She was working my G-spot with a definite mission and suddenly I got *that* feeling. It's a feeling I've had plenty of times during penetration and G-spot stimulation, a feeling like I was going to pee. I have always resisted the urge, held back, many times even stopped the action to run to the bathroom. More often than not, I wind up on the toilet with a trickle or no pee at all. So, I had that feeling as Red was working magic with her fingers inside my pussy.

"I feel like I'm gonna pee," I said.

"You're not going to pee," she reassured me. "Just let go." It was tough. I felt like I'd been practicing for years to hold it in for fear I would pee on lovers who weren't exactly the golden showers type. But Val was there in the bed, and Red was talking in such a sure, soothing way. We had been through a really intense scene, and I had a profound amount of trust for both of them. So I did what she said, and I let go.

Minutes later, I was coming. It felt like a different kind of orgasm altogether than I'm used to. I had that climax feeling, but instead of being followed simply by a rush and pussy contractions, I felt this warm wave run through my insides. It just took over, and I went with it. When Red took my hand and put it on the blanket underneath me, I was shocked. I made a puddle that soaked her beautiful black comforter. It seemed like an enormous amount of liquid to come out of my little body.

I gushed, verbally this time. "Oh my God! I did that! I've never done that before, it's so cool. How did you make me do it?"

She filled me on her secrets of an obvious expert, how she finds the G-spot, works it for a while, then reaches behind it and literally tries to pull the come out. She is a woman who knows how to ejaculate herself, and loves to make other women do it.

"Usually when women come, they make noise, they make faces, you can feel their cunts contract, but it's all an internal experience. When I make a woman ejaculate, it's a visible, tangible sign of her orgasm—I love it!"

I've been able to ejaculate twice since then. The hardest part still is getting that full bladder feeling and being able to push out rather than hold back. It was a life-changing event, and I look forward to perfecting this newfound trick. Kim, where did you say that you got those absorbent bed pads?

So, is ejaculatory fluid the stuff of revolutions? Definitely. No more griping from men that women fake it—here's that elusive "proof" beyond heavy breathing and squealing. And girls can do anything boys can do, better. I am hesitant to say it's radical simply because it's something men do. Yet, every woman I've ever seen ejaculate looks strong, fierce, in control of her pleasure and her orgasm. Female ejaculation represents yet another element in the endless ways women get off. Remember when clitoral stimulation first came into popular consciousness? It opened a whole new world of pleasure for so many women to whom vaginal penetration was nice but didn't drive them wild. G-spot stimulation and ejaculation can do the same thing.

Plenty of controversy and debate still surrounds female ejaculation. Where does the fluid come from? Ejaculate comes out the urethra, as detailed in *The Good Vibrations Guide: The G-Spot,* and opinions differ on whether the fluid originates in the bladder, in the urethral sponge, or a combination of both. This liquid has been analyzed by only a few scientists in the lab who've extracted it from women through a catheter, and by a whole lot of chicks in the bedroom who've sniffed the sheets post-romp.

Female ejaculatory fluid is considered to be sweeter and more manly than urine (it contains more glucose or fructose than urine, and a higher concentration of the prostatic acid phosphatase—previously thought to be only present in men's prostate gland secretions—than urine). Of course, there is so little research on female ejaculation that a lot of the phenomenon is still a mystery; imagine if scientists said, "We don't know exactly what's in semen, but it does seem to cause pregnancy." Researchers need to get on the ball and devote some serious time and money to studying squirting girls.

I've had plenty of opportunities to do field research in this area since the woman who taught me how to ejaculate became my girlfriend. She's made me a squirtaholic, and I've gotten a little obsessed with how many times I can make her squirt, how much I can make her squirt, and how far I can make her squirt (our personal best: four feet, from the middle of a hotel room bed to the TV screen on the dresser). I haven't gone so far as to collect her ejaculate in a jar. Give me time—it would be in the name of science.

The Art of Anal Fisting

"Anal fisting: party trick or real sex act?" A writer once posed this question to me during an interview. I giggled, but he did have a point. Most people think anal fisting is either a gay urban legend or a freakish sexual circus feat. Actually, it can be a real sex act *and* a party trick, if you play your cards right and know what you're doing.

So where does one learn the art of anal fisting? In Florida, of course, at Living in Leather, the 14th annual conference of the National Leather Association–International. The weekend offered S/M seminar staples: workshops, meetings, shopping, awards, and play parties. I had the honor of teaching two workshops: Anal Toys 101 and Anal Fisting.

Now, when I say the words *anal fisting,* most people's immediate reaction is a wide-eyed, half-terrified, half-titillated "Yikes!" Take a deep breath. (It's all in the breathing.) Anal fisting, also known as *handballing,* is the gradual process of putting your hand (and for very experienced players, sometimes your forearm) inside someone's ass. *Fisting* as a term is misleading since you don't go inside all at once like a punch; usually your hand is not in a clenched fist once it is in there. Gay men popularized fisting in the late '60s and '70s during the sexual revolution and founded private fisting clubs in major urban areas.

I've read and heard tales of these sex clubs, filled with hungry men, waiting slings, and cans of Crisco. Although it is an intense exchange of power between two people, fisting isn't exactly S/M. Because it is an outlaw sexual practice popularized by gay leathermen, it remains associated with and practiced by S/M folk, though not exclusively. Yet, like S/M, anal fisting explores and tests the farthest reaches of the mind's and body's inner limits.

Anal fisting is a rarity among women, even though vaginal fisting has been somewhat accepted. The vagina has long demonstrated its versatility, but sexual adventurers have paid so much attention to this one fabulously flexible orifice that they have overlooked the promise of the other. As a result, unlike gay men, women lack a history to hang on to like a sturdy sling, the legacy of fisting pros, and the role models to pass the skills from generation to generation.

I was scheduled to teach the anal fisting class with leatherman and leading handball expert Bert Herrman, author of the only book devoted exclusively to the subject, *Trust: The Hand Book*. He also publishes *Trust: The Handballing Newsletter*. Bert, a fisting legend, has been putting his hands in men's asses since I was in diapers. A true meeting of the minds *and* asses, the workshop in Florida proved to be a unique bridging of different perspectives, genders, and generations. In our introduction, when we talked about warming up for fisting, our differences were readily apparent. An old-school fister, Bert's into getting high on pot and poppers and stuffing gobs of Crisco, whereas I am into endorphin highs and a nice, thick water-based lubricant.

We viewed *Handball Loving*, which is unlike any video I've ever seen. Bert's approach to fisting is very spiritual; he sees it as a path to enlightenment and higher consciousness, a way to connect with a higher power and soul-bond with another person. He draws on Eastern religions, particularly the principles of tantric sex. In that way, he is at the forefront of future sex, incorporating spirituality into sexuality.

Then there is the simple amazement factor of seeing Bert with his arm almost to the elbow up his partner's ass, then later with both hands inside him. It really is a different kind of sex; yes, there's pleasure and intimacy and orgasm, but that's not all. Both men were transported into a deep trance, their bodies melding, their souls merging.

That night, after the workshop, I was inspired. I've been anally fisted before, but it was a long time ago and I wanted to do it again. My girlfriend and I had already decided to host a small sex party, a half dozen of us, in our room. I started with a medium-sized butt plug (appropriately called Voyager) in my ass, which I wore for a while, then switched to a larger, very thick red plug. Whenever that one slides in my ass, it feels too big at first, but inevitably I take a deep breath and in it goes.

When I felt like my ass was relaxed and ready for more, she put on a latex glove, slipped out the butt plug, and started working her fingers inside me as I lay on my back. I took lots of deep breaths, concentrated on relaxing and opening up. She eventually got all five fingers up to the final knuckles—the widest part of the hand, the dreaded sticking point. Totally turned on, totally amazed that there was so much of her in my ass, I tried to flip over on my stomach. "Whoa, whoa," she insisted. I was so absorbed I didn't realize I would've broken her arm if I continued to roll. I kept asking for more lube, but finally she said, "Honey, you have a ton of lube in your ass. There's just no more room."

We both knew that was as far as she was going. At that point, an orgasm doesn't matter because the experience is physically and mentally so intense and all-encompassing. She withdrew and we relaxed. We then enjoyed some cheese and crackers with our guests.

During the scene, I remembered Bert talking about what it feels like when you're all the way up to someone's transverse colon (beyond the rectum and descending colon). I realized I'm definitely a below-the-transverse-colon person. Even Buttgirl has her limits.

Bend Over, Boys!

Attention, all straight men! This is a call to arms. I know the secret to a better sex life. I'm willing to share it with you. There is something you need to learn how to do. Something that can transform your life. You must try it at least once; I am sure you won't be disappointed. You've got something to pick up from your gay brothers. And it's not just those fashion and decorating tips you marvel about on *Will and Grace*. Something your wives and girlfriends can be taught by their lesbian sisters. No, it's not a crash course in expert muffdiving. There is a craze sweeping the nation, and you oughta know about it. It's ass fucking—with you on the receiving end.

For many of you, your first foray into the land of anal penetration took place in a sterile white room, on a paper-covered table. Your proctologist squeezed a lump of K-Y onto his latex-clad hand and shoved his finger up your ass. It wasn't erotic, it didn't feel particularly good, and you aren't even attracted to the guy. (Okay, maybe you are, but that's another article.) All this happened five minutes after words like "prostate cancer" and "rectal exam" were uttered. Some turn-on. Now you know what we feel like at the gynecologist. Put this experience out of your mind—it was a medical exam. I'm talking about mind-blowing sex.

Check out the best-selling porn titles, articles in magazines from *Details* to *Redbook,* the sales figures of this columnist's book on the subject. It's as undeniable and obvious as tense sphincter muscles—anal sex has become one of *the* hot sex acts of the new millennium. And this time, it's not just for butt pirates. While they are getting their share of the booty, gay men have not cornered the anal market. It's a falsehood that *all* gay men have anal sex, and it's equally mythic that gay men have more anal sex than straight people or lesbians. In fact, that oh-so-traditional pairing of man plus woman may just surpass the man-on-man statistics in this particular, um, area. Butt-banging breeders may even throw their own pride parade. What will be the colors of the Anal Pride flag?

Every single day that I worked at the woman-owned sex-toy store Toys in Babeland, at least one heterosexual couple bought a dildo and harness for her to fuck him. Remember My First Pony, a sweet toy for little girls? Well, for these adventurous women and their partners, I recommended what I called "My First Strap-On"—for the ride of his (and her) life. It's a slim silicone dildo named Mistress, which I consider to be the best for virgin voyagers, and a simple functional harness. And, of course, I recommended lots and lots of lube.

The growing popularity of boys bending over was equally apparent in San Francisco at the sex store Good Vibrations. Jackie Strano, a salesperson for five years, and her partner, erotic writer Shar Rednour, were also inspired by the trend. The sexy duo teamed up with lesbian porn company Fatale Video to create *Bend Over Boyfriend,* the first and only sex instruction video all about women giving men anal pleasure. It stars author-sexologist Dr. Carol Queen (who has a doctorate in human sexuality education) and her partner, Dr. Robert Morgan, a sex educator and chiropractor. After a detailed anatomy lesson and hands-on demonstration by this real-life couple, two other couples try out their expert tips and techniques.

Bend Over Boyfriend was the maiden porno voyage of Strano and Rednour's production company, S.I.R. Productions (stands for Sex, Indulgence, and Rock 'n' Roll). The response to the video was unequivocally orgasmic. *Bend Over Boyfriend* was on the Good Vibrations bestseller list for twelve consecutive months and named the best-selling video of all time, until *Bend Over Boyfriend: II* knocked it off the list.

Bend Over Boyfriend: II, subtitled "More Rockin', Less Talkin'," leaves the educational details behind and focuses on five hot sex scenes of girls strappin' it on and stickin' it in. Dr. Queen reappears to show one daring couple the ropes, and her presence, in true porn fashion, leads to a raucous three-way. The video's got dirty talk, cross-dressing, role-playing, S/M, shoe licking, real couples who love anal sex, a butt plug with a horse tail on the end of it, and lots of other sex toys. In fact, one toy, called

Bobby Sue, should be credited as a star of the movie—it makes appearances in multiple scenes and works its ass off. Designed and manufactured by Vixen Creations, Bobby Sue is perfect for the job: a silicone dildo with a hollowed-out base. This little hole-in-one makes room for a vibrating egg, which in turn makes the dildo vibrate in his ass and against her clitoris. I just love sex-toy technology.

Since anal pleasure is still taboo in American culture, anyone who admits to being a backdoor betty is on the front lines of sexual liberation. As women, since we are already positioned as the receptive, penetrated partner, we need only reorient ourselves to focus on the *other* orifice. Men, on the other hand, are the penetrator, the active partner, the pencil to her sharpener. Straight men are coming out of their own closet (who knew they had such a fabulous one?), proudly saying (like they do in the video), "I want to get fucked in the ass!" and "I love getting fucked in the ass!"

These guys have gotten over their shame and fear and embraced all the ass has to offer: those nerve endings, that sensitive tissue, and the pleasures of prostate gland stimulation. A few inches inside the rectum and toward his navel, the "male G-spot" and a world of ecstasy await. Even a well-known television and radio personality admitted to all his listeners that he had experienced—and enjoyed—prostate stimulation. And this, my friends, is the stuff of revolutions.

Fear not: Women can get in on the revolutionary sexual equation too. In this new reorientation, straight girls can wield dicks (dicks—they're not just for dykes anymore!) and see how the other half fucks. As they try out the role of active penetrator, hetero girls can slip their tongues, fingers, and cocks inside their male lovers' bodies, learning how to give and get pleasure in a (w)hole new way.

So does this mean men are finally getting in touch with their "feminine" side? Yes and no. Yes, they can be the receptive partner, be on the other end of a hard cock for a change, and maybe get to know what it's like to give it up. But guys, you can take it up the ass and still be a man. So what are you waiting for? Straight men of the world, unite... and bend over.

Wetter Is Better

If I were stranded on a desert island and could have only one sexual tool with me, I'd have plenty to choose from: ben wa balls, candy-colored anal beads, ice-cream-swirled dildos, strut-worthy strap-ons, buzzing vibrators, and beefy butt plugs. Not to mention S/M gear like restraints, paddles, floggers, canes, nipple clamps, and many others. But the choice for me would be simple. I'd pick the one erotic aid that changed my sex life forever. It's clear, it comes in dozens of varieties, and it's lube.

In college, my girlfriend introduced me to the liquid powerhouse as part of our safer sex practice in the early '90s. Since we were using condoms, gloves, and dental dams, lube was—and is—the perfect partner for latex. But latex or flesh, I think lube makes every kind of sex better; after all, the wetter and more slippery all the parts get, the hotter the amorous rite gets. Doesn't everyone want a slicker hand job, a juicier finger fuck, a smoother rear entry, and a moister muffdive? Of course you do. I am still perplexed that there isn't a tube or bottle (or supersize pump) of lube on every bedside table in America.

In San Francisco recently, I got the chance to go inside a place most girls don't even see—a gay male sex club. Upstairs at this two-floor fuck palace was a room full of partitioned cubbies, some with vinyl-covered beds, another with a sling hung on chains. Mounted on the wall in each cubby were soap dispensers filled with something far more useful and appropriate than Dial: water-based lubricant. When I first spotted these perfect pumps, they reminded me of hotels that have dispensers in the shower of shampoo and conditioner. So clean, so convenient, so efficient. That's one of the things I love about gay men—they can be so direct. We're having sex and we need lube.

Their hetero brothers have a lot to learn, however. Many men resist using lube because they feel threatened by anything they perceive as a sexual helper. When a customer at Toys in Babeland chose to buy his wife a sizable vibrator, I suggested he also purchase some lube. He declined, insisting, "Oh, we don't need that. I can turn her on all by myself." This was a common exchange. I tried to persuade him gently, when what I really wanted to say was: Well, the fact of the matter is that she may be plenty turned on, but that doesn't mean she'll be slick enough to take that big vibe with ease. If she's not comfortable, chances are her pleasure will be compromised.

Women are often embarrassed or feel insecure about using a lubricant. We need to assure ourselves that using lube does not mean there is something wrong with us. In mainstream media, lube is marketed only to postmenopausal women, since many experience vaginal dryness. But lube is for everyone.

We are blessed with vaginas that naturally lubricate, but the truth is that some women juice up more than others, and for many women how much they lubricate is not based on desire alone. The time of the month, diet, general health, dehydration, exercise, stress levels, medications, and other factors all affect how damp your panties get. In other words, you could be totally aroused and still experience vaginal dryness.

A little lube is all you need to be ready for action, to make penetration smoother and easier, which will leave you feeling more relaxed and sexy in the long run. Many women still silently endure pain, friction (not the good kind), and irritation from penetration without proper lubrication. And if your partner has a larger than usual basket, well, good for him (or her) but maybe not so good for you. Lube will help you make good use of the average to the ample, rather than feeling overwhelmed and impaled. And as for anal penetration, well, you cannot do it without lube. So anyone wanting to bury the bone in a girlfriend's backyard had better grease it first.

Remember (okay, it was before my time, but *you* remember) when all we had was gooey K-Y Jelly? Here are the best things K-Y has going for it: You can find it in any drugstore (and maybe even the in-laws' medicine cabinet) and it will do in a pinch. But K-Y was developed with medical exams in mind, not a rockin' carnal marathon, if you know what I mean.

So, just put that K-Y in your natural disaster emergency kit along with the flares and canned food.

Along with the K-Y, many people use vegetable oil, Vaseline, baby oil, moisturizer, or Crisco. Another woman came into the store asking what she could do to give her husband a really good hand job. "We use lotion, but it dries pretty quickly." Not only will lube work better, but it's safer for him to fuck her after she works him with her hand without the risk of sticking lotion in her pussy, where it doesn't belong. Oil-based lubricants like those mentioned are difficult to wash out of the vagina and can be a breeding ground for infection. They also break down latex, so they're not condom-compatible. Leave them in the kitchen and bathroom, where they belong.

Then get yourself to a cool sex-toy store and marvel at the eye-popping number of different lubes to choose from. Silicone-based lubricants are the newest on the market. Brands like Eros, Eros Woman, Wet Platinum, and ID Millennium boast the most slippery ride of your life, and it's true—lubes made of silicone stay wet for a very long time, sometimes longer than you want them to. Because you can't wash them out, you have to wait for the body to naturally flush the lube. They are safe to use with condoms; however, they have been shown to ruin some silicone sex toys.

Nonstaining, easy to clean up, and available in several textures, water-based lubricants are condom-compatible and safe to use. They're made with a variety of ingredients; the main one in most is glycerin. For a thin, liquidy lube that mirrors pussy juice (making it great for vaginal penetration), try Liquid Silk, Astroglide, Probe Light, Slippery Stuff Liquid, Lube de Luxe Liquid, or Eros Woman Water Formulation. For a thicker, gel-like lube especially good for anal penetration, I recommend ID, Maximus, Slippery Stuff Gel, Wet, and Probe Thick and Rich. Don't worry, guys, all of these can be used to jerk off, too.

Flavored lubricants allow you to butter her muffin with everything from mouthwashy mint to lollipop strawberry. Women sensitive or allergic to glycerin or especially prone to yeast infections should avoid the flavors and stick with glycerin-free lubes (like Slippery Stuff,

Liquid Silk, and Maximus). Many of the lubricants are also available with Nonoxynol 9 (shown to kill the HIV virus), but many women find that they are sensitive to this chemical and develop irritation, burning, itching, and even infections.

There's a lube out there for everyone, so get over your insecurities and get some.

The Five-Finger Club

Have you heard about the study that claims people who are gay or lesbian have shorter index fingers than straight people? One might conclude that it gives us a disadvantage in reaching the G-spots or prostate glands of our lovers. But I see it as a bonus: The shortcoming makes room for the other four fingers! After all, when you think of hand balling someone's butt, you think "gay men." Likewise, fitting all five digits into a hungry hole is automatically associated with lesbian lust.

When I was a babydyke in college, vaginal fisting—penetration with your entire hand—was definitely the hip sexual activity among queer girls. In the late '80s, I remember budding sexpert Susie Bright's vulva-stretching *On Our Backs* article about it, and more than one homemade sapphic porno capturing the delicious deed on video. Girls who fuck girls are always devising ingenious new ways to give our pussies pleasure, since we have not one but two little kitties to make purr. When one woman fists another, it is a defiant act—bold, outrageous, boundary-busting. Oh, and it feels great, too.

But fisting is not just for muffdivers anymore. More and more hetero-sexual couples are getting into the experience. As a man with his finger on the pulse of sexual trends, *Taboo* magazine editor and S/M porn producer Ernest Greene is a big fisting fan: "I was introduced to it by a bisexual woman. I think it's a woman-driven development in sexuality. Women like to explore the range of possibilities their bodies hold."

Fisting is yet another example of hets having queer sex, which is always a good thing. Another hand man, Bryn Pryor, editor of *Adult Video News*, says: "I first did it as a teenager, encouraged by my girlfriend, who knew what she wanted and told me to do it. I did it before I even knew there was a name for it. You can feel every movement that your partner makes."

Men who fist discover they have an important sex tool (other than the obvious one) that can show their partners a good time. And let's face it, as women get older, especially if they have kids, everything gets bigger. Girls, instead of dishing out cash for misogynist cosmetic surgery to tighten your fuck-hole, simply encourage your sweetie to give you a hand. It's also a perfect antidote to men's size anxieties: You guys might be limited in what's between your legs, but I bet you've got big mitts. If you come and she hasn't, or she wants to come again before you're ready for round two, slip inside her in a different way and listen to the sound of one hand clapping. Sounds a lot like an orgasm. Now, fellas, if you do want to give your girl the five-finger discount, I suggest lots of lube, patience, warm-up, and communication.

At a private sexfest I witnessed last year, Ernest Greene put his large hand inside a fierce, ballerina-bodied woman with fiery red hair; after several orgasms, she actually rotated 360 degrees around his fist—an unbelievable party trick. The acrobat turned out to be porn star Chloe, a fisting diva who's out to change the world's view of this sacred act. "It gets me off better than anything else," she says. "You just can't be any fuller than when you have someone's entire hand inside you. It's also emotional, even spiritual for me. It's the only act that can actually move me to tears, but they are good tears."

Last year, Chloe was caught at the center of a porn industry minis-candal involving her favorite fetish. While filming *Tampa Tushy Fest* for producer Seymore Butts, Chloe and costar Alisha Klass got very hot and heavy. Alisha had always wanted to try fisting and knew that Chloe was the perfect teacher. Alisha ended up with both her hands inside Chloe's cavity and Chloe's hand inside Alisha's ass. "I made the choice to include the scene," says Seymore Butts. "It was real, spontaneous. Both of them were so into it." Butts knew he was taking a chance. You see, industry custom firmly places fisting among unacceptable acts—along with pissing, sex with bondage, enemas, and other fun stuff. You can put four fingers inside a woman, you can put a dildo the size of a tree in her, but you can't slip that thumb inside under any circumstances without putting the film's distribution at risk.

But Seymore decided to go for it. The scene was clearly not a coercive or degrading exploitation of two drugged-up naive girls off the street. It was a spirited expression of sexuality between two of the best and brightest in the business. After some retailers panicked about the content, Seymore offered them the option of replacement without the fisting segment. Only 3 to 5 percent of the tapes came back.

"I think I did a service to show people a new form of pleasure," Butts argues, "one that hasn't been represented in adult video since the '70s. I believe people do learn about new things from porn. The scene won two major industry awards, which is validation that we did a good thing."

In an industry where some videos depict thirty men ejaculating on one woman's face, girls being double penetrated, and other unconventional activities, why is fisting considered obscene? "People think of it as violent, that it hurts. But it can be a slow, loving, consensual experience on the woman's terms," says Chloe. "I think the word *fisting* misleads people—this is not the *Fight Club*."

Chloe's latest attempt to push the envelope is her starring role as a fisting guru in *The Fist, the Whole Fist, and Nothing but the Fist* (Elegant Angel Video). Chloe decided to do the film because she believes there isn't enough information out there: "People come to me all the time—other actresses, crew members, fans—for advice and suggestions. They want to try it, but they want to do it right." In the video, she leads twelve female porn stars (seven of whom had never been high-fived on the inside) through the basics of technique and safety. By the end, ten of the women get vaginally fisted, and actress Felicia Ann also takes a hand in her ass.

The jury is still out on the distribution issues, whether enough retailers will agree to carry the video and if it will sell. I have a feeling it will, since audiences are starved for information on the subject. Greene applauds the effort: "Like S/M, fisting has moved inward from the fringe to the mainstream to become part of the menu of sexual activity. When there is more depiction of it, there's a greater understanding and a greater interest in the practice itself." For Chloe, the video was mission accomplished: "It was amazing to witness—to see these women getting off in a way that I have been personally getting off for years. It was one of the biggest thrills of my life."

My Tantra Mantra

At one of my sex workshops, I overheard a bright-eyed young guy, a dead ringer for *Felicity* star Scott Speedman, ask, "What's tantric sex?"

His friend, a strapping Canadian, replied, "Oh, that's where you have sex for a really long time and don't get off."

I saw the opportunity to educate these hetero hunks at an impressionable age to consider that sex can be something more than the ol' wham-bam. "Well, you may not get there by the traditional route, but you certainly do get off. It just might not be in the way you think," I suggested.

Lest you think that these two were all beauty but no brains, let me reassure you that these misconceptions about tantra are pretty common. Before I knew anything about tantric sex, I had some bizarre ideas in my head of what it was all about. Tantric sex is what I always imagined Dharma taught Greg, ancient secrets no corporate lawyer could ever resist. The first image that sprang to mind was of two people in an uncomfortable yoga position, breathing deeply and meditating on sex, but not actually having it. That didn't exactly sell it to me. Or I pictured having to channel some Eastern god while I had my fist in my girlfriend's pussy, a tall order for a girl who's easily distracted. Then there was this vague notion of partners creating and exchanging sexual energy with each other. That just befuddles this particularly grounded Taurus—I still don't even have the chakra thing down pat.

In tantra, sex (like all other aspects of life) is sacred, and sexual energy is considered to be our life source. People fuck to connect with each other and a higher power; they channel sexual energy to reach greater consciousness and enlightenment. Unlike Western sex, tantric sex is not just about pleasure and orgasm; in fact, tantric lovers prolong the experience, often having multiple orgasms, in order to focus the ecstatic energy. Guys especially, if you want to learn how to be multiorgasmic, tantra is one way to get there. When some people think of tantra, they associate it with *The Kama Sutra,* the classic eighth-century Indian text that teaches sex as an avenue to spiritual bliss. The connection between tantra and *The Kama Sutra* is that both come from ancient Indian teachings. Let me tell you that *The Kama Sutra,* which has been published in various translations, is not a breezy beach read. (Thank the gods for *The Complete Idiot's Guide to the Kama Sutra,* but where is *Tantra for Dummies?*)

Even with an ancient, impenetrable erotic manual and a bit of confusing spiritual mumbo jumbo, something continued to intrigue me about tantra, and I wanted to know more. Then, there was Madonna on the cover of *Rolling Stone* with a bejeweled bindi on her forehead and henna-stained hands alluding to her discovery of Eastern spirituality—had she ditched her material ways to dabble in Hindu nooky? If Madonna could go tantra, maybe I could too.

There was still one sticking point: Tantric sex reminded me of people in Northern California who smoke too much pot, burn too much incense, and have way too much time on their hands. How are all the latte-addicted, Palm Pilot–carrying, hyperactive New Yorkers ever gonna reach a higher level? The answer came to me last Sunday in the form of spiritual leader, sex educator, and one right-on hip chick named Barbara Carrellas. Carrellas concluded her series of tantric sex workshops at Toys in Babeland by teaching a practice of her own invention—urban tantra. She calls it "a conscious sacred sexuality for a kick-ass environment," and urban tantra is where Eastern sensuality meets Western S/M on a street corner in a rough part of the city. Carrellas's form of tantra helps us shed the armor we wear to survive our fast-paced, high-stress lives and reconnect with our erotic selves.

Her incorporation of S/M elements into conventional tantra makes sense to me, since I have seen people practice S/M who are clearly on some sort of journey. When my girlfriend gets flogged, she looks like she's flying, and the scene definitely transcends the traditional concept of two bodies doing things to each other. It's this look she gets in her eyes, the way her breathing changes, the way her body reacts to the intensity of the feelings.

Carrellas, our blond tantranatrix, took us through several exercises—one where I got to blindfold my partner and feed her strawberries and chocolate. ("Don't just taste what you are being fed, actually become it. Notice something that you hadn't noted before about what is in your mouth: its sweetness, sourness, temperature, or texture.") Another exercise directed us to pick a nearby toy to help waken our bodies. I selected a vibrator shaped like a gun that had an exceptionally strong buzz, and my girlfriend chose a rubberized billy club. The idea was to stimulate our bodies and give feedback to each other about what we liked. Our final exercise had us breathing in tandem, rocking back and forth, and then simultaneously holding our breath and tensing all our muscles. When we let go, we were light-headed, much like that postorgasmic blissed-out feeling.

Since the workshop, I have read *Sexual Energy Ecstasy* and *Tantra: The Art of Conscious Loving*, watched *Tantric Journey to Female Orgasm*, and surfed over to a tantric website. Each writer and practitioner has a different take on tantra, but there are shared themes. The concept that sex is a significant, powerful force is what appeals to me most. Western culture denigrates sexuality and relegates it to the margins of our lives. Family, relationships, career, and spirituality are prioritized, and sex is seen as an added bonus to the important things in life. When the power of sex is acknowledged, it's used by the advertising industry or Hollywood, but only as a means to sell more stuff. The idea that sex could be channeled to transform your life is what tantra is all about. But the funny thing about tantra is that there is no one-two-three how-to guide. It's not as much about learning techniques or skills as it is about reorienting your beliefs and ideas about sex.

Yes, I am just beginning to figure it all out, but watch out—I'm definitely getting tantric on your ass.

Ass Licker

"Will you sign it to me 'from Ass Licker'?" asked a woman with an accent, as she handed me my book to autograph.

I must have given her a quizzical look, because she went on to explain:

"I'm Irish, and back home, we call people who suck up 'ass licks,' but when I say that here, everyone looks at me as if I'm crazy. It's one of my favorite expressions, and for you, well, it means something entirely different now, doesn't it?" Yes, it does.

Analingus, commonly called "rimming," is the oral caress of the new millennium. Once *Sex and the City* aired its "tuchislingus" episode, we could no longer deny what was on the minds of ordinary folks everywhere and, more importantly, what was in their mouths. Many people love the simple pleasure of having their ass licked or licking a partner's ass. If you've never given it a try, you are definitely missing out. Because the anal area is so full of nerve endings, even the tiniest sensations can register like juicy earthquakes on the rectal Richter scale. From two warm globes to the crown jewel, there are a million little folds and crevices to find back there. To lick or be licked? I say: Go both ways. (But then again, I say that about a lot of things.)

A tasty treat in and of itself, a rim job can also be a prelude to anal penetration. Many people put their mouths where the money is in order to introduce someone to the joys of backdoor pleasure. Once you've had the tongue, you might be apt to consider some more. I know plenty of girls going down on their men as a first step toward transforming them into bend-over boyfriends. And, men, if you'd start your quest for her ass with your mouth (instead of your cock), you'd probably get a lot farther.

Personally, I like a smooth-as-silk hole, whatever its gender may be, so I can feel each and every inch with my tongue. As I have previously revealed, I like to shave my own ass, sans mirror, and I am happy to take a blade to someone else's to maximize pleasure for both of us. By contrast, I recently spoke to a reporter (who was supposed to be pumping me for naughty details) who confessed he "loves when a woman's pubic hair extends back and up the ass crack." Translation: He likes hairy bungholes. And I say, good for him! I know he's not alone in seeking out the perfect backdoor bush.

Fur-loving or not, some folks may feel especially anxious about rimming because of the association between the asshole and defecating; we learn at an early age that if something is dirty or smells bad, we shouldn't put our mouth on it. You are not alone if your fear of shit prevents you from exploring this taboo love, including being tongue-tied when it comes to your sweetie's ass. Porn star and anal queen Chloe says in my video *The Ultimate Guide to Anal Sex for Women,* "Get over your fear of shit!" Honey, I second that emotion, but I realize it may be easier said than done for many folks.

Fear no more—Buttgirl is here to calm the masses and those reluctant yet potentially eager tongues of yours. First, a brief anatomy lesson about what lies beneath the boxers. You may imagine your tongue to be a foot-long warrior, but in reality, it cannot reach past the anal canal. It certainly can't get anywhere near the colon, which is the storage facility for what you're afraid of. If you are a generally healthy person with good bathroom habits, then your butthole is almost as clean as a garden-variety vagina, which many of us lick with desire and enthusiasm. Having an enema before your friend's tongue goes in there will also, well, clean things out.

To be completely safe, you can slap a barrier between tongue and tush. Originally designed for use by dentists, dental dams are squares of latex that safer-sex practitioners have co-opted for use as oral-sex barriers. Because they were not developed with sex in mind, dental dams can be too small and too thick to be ideal. Glyde-brand dams are a larger, thinner version designed specifically for oral sex that do a much better job. Also keep in mind that the plastic wrap you probably already have in your kitchen is not just for leftovers; try covering someone's privates in Saran

Wrap and go to town without having to hold the dam in place. Safe, hands-free ass licking at last!

My favorite trick is to take a nonpowdered latex glove, cut the wrist off, and slice it up the pinky side. Then I stretch it out and put my tongue in the thumb hole—it's like a minicondom for your other little soldier, affording you way more sensation than you get while lapping at a piece of plastic.

I know some of you are saying, If I can't have direct contact, I don't want any at all; and for those of you opposed to latex-covered lust, you need to assess the risks. If you are wandering the outer perimeter, and your partner has recently emptied her bowels and washed the area, then you can count yourself relatively safe. If, however, you are doing what I call "diving for pearls," then you have a greater chance of coming into contact with bacteria and trace amounts of fecal matter. As the licker, you can be exposed to STDs, including HIV, as well as hepatitis, which has become a serious health concern. On top of that, if the owner of the ass being licked has a gastrointestinal bug, you could pick that up as well. If you and your partner have both tested negative for disease, then just a hot soapy shower will ensure that your anal romp will be nothing but good clean fun!

When I kiss someone's ass, there is no mistaking my intentions: I am using my mouth to bring about a state of nirvana. And I am not alone in my tongue-in-cheek endeavors; I believe that butt munching is on the rise, and with good reason. See, it used to be that only gay boys were the analinguists (or at least they were the only ones admitting it), pushing and probing that little pucker with wild abandon. But why should fags have all the fun? As I've long believed, the asshole is the most democratic of all orifices—we all have one! So, why not put lips to rump with your fellow countrymen?

The Female Hard-On

Several clean, well-lighted, sex toy stores around the country sponsor a National Masturbate-a-Thon each year. That's right—instead of walking or running, participants gather pledges and collect cash for each minute they spend pleasuring themselves. All proceeds from these jack- and jill-off fests go to sex-positive organizations. Parties to celebrate participants who "came for a cause" are inevitable, and I attended one where I found myself on the dance floor sandwiched between slices of sexy, sweaty, horny girls. As the band belted out a Joan Jett song ("Do you wanna touch? Yeah! Do you wanna touch? Yeah! Do you wanna touch me there? Where?") girls were bumping and grinding with gusto. Strangers rubbed their drenched bodies up against mine, fingers stroked my flesh from every direction. It was a wild, wild night.

Although I was riding the high that came with the knowledge (and firsthand experience) that sex in the city is thriving, my spirits were slightly dampened because I had just read a *Newsweek* cover story called "The Science of Women's Sexuality." Next to a photo of a woman in the throes of passion were the words "Searching for the Female Viagra: Is It a Mind or Body Problem?" Fueled by the success of Viagra in treating male sexual dysfunction, scientists have turned to the sexual problems of women. But what promised to be an informative article turned out to be a muddled mess that reinforced just how little scientists know about women and sex. I found it especially telling that the report was written by a man.

The bad news is that in the most recent study of the effects of the super blue pill on women, Viagra was no more successful than a placebo in women with a wide variety of sexual dysfunction symptoms. We've given all the men supercharged erections, but haven't had any luck when it comes to women's erotic woes. Forty percent of American women experience some form of sexual dysfunction. It's actually a bigger problem than it is for men (30 percent suffer from some form of dysfunction), and yet all the money and research has focused on the boys. In part, this is typical of a misogynist industry that has always geared research toward males. But there is another reason that the fairer sex has again gotten the short end of the stick: Men's sexual problems (including erectile dysfunction) just seem much easier to solve than the complex, layered issues surrounding women's sexual dysfunction.

Concerned that medication I was taking was diminishing my libido, I queried my doctor about it. He asked if I could still get turned on and come, to which I replied yes, but I was worried that my sex drive had nearly disappeared. "If you can achieve orgasm, then there is no sexual dysfunction." Gee thanks, doc. I tried to explain that even if Tom Cruise walked in with his flight jacket from *Top Gun,* a freshly shaved asshole, and a raging hard-on, I just wouldn't feel anything. Even if Nicole Kidman joined him—with a huge strap-on between her legs, nipples perked up like minitorpedoes, and a double-ended vibrator with unlimited juice—still nothing. Now, if neither member of this supercouple—nor both—can get my juices flowing, well, something's wrong. Isn't it? According to this doctor (and plenty of others), no.

The doctor's dismissal of my problem is symptomatic of a medical industry that not only is clueless about women's sexual dysfunctions, but barely knows what's going on with female sexual function. The truth is, there are many different forms of female sexual dysfunction. Some women have little or no desire to have sex. Others have trouble getting aroused or can't get turned on at all. Others cannot achieve orgasm, and others experience pain during sex. Some women have a combination of these symptoms. For me, while on this medication, after we got into it and I had my tongue on Tom's butthole and Nic's slim fingers in my pussy, I'd get into the groove and shoot my load. I'd just have trouble getting revved up in the first place.

On the subject of the Big O, the *Newsweek* article was even more infuriating. Pondering the evolutionary benefits of the female orgasm, a pull quote teases—"One possible theory: orgasms in women have no function and are just a developmental vestige, like male nipples." First of all, why are we wasting time, money, and column inches on debating the importance or necessity of the female orgasm? It's just more misogynist bullshit, if you ask me. (And on the subject of male nipples, try telling all the men who appreciate having theirs tweaked and squeezed and clamped that they have no function.)

To understand why some of us have an easy time of it and others don't, we first have to understand sex and girls: female sexual anatomy (folks still can't agree on how big or far-reaching the clitoris is); desire and the experience of arousal and pleasure; the complexities of the female orgasm; plus, the emotional and psychological aspects of sex and how they play a role in arousal and satisfaction. You see, we don't even have the 411 on this stuff, so how can we expect to figure out how to fix the leak when we don't know how the plumbing works in the first place?

I will say it again—we need more research, folks. There are promising options on the table beyond Viagra: other drugs that work for men being tested on women, several creams designed to increase blood flow to the vagina and clitoris, a testosterone patch that seems to increase sex drive but has problematic side effects. The most interesting little item in the *Newsweek* article was a new, recently FDA-approved device called EROS-CTD, designed to pump blood to the clitoris. Reminiscent of a penis pump, which gets blood flowing and pumps up a man's erection, the EROS-CTD is basically a clit pump. It reminds me of a butch dyke I know in San Francisco, sex educator Karlyn Lotney, aka Fairy Butch. Fairy Butch has an innovative technique for clit pumping in which she employs a penis pump to make her clit (temporarily) the size of two short fingers—her own female hard-on. Whoops, there I go: describing female arousal in men's terms, but the truth is that the tissue is the same, and we do get hard-ons, too. The frustrating thing about this doctor-approved, by-prescription-only sex toy (which costs over $300 and isn't covered by most insurance) is that it's an FDA-approved vibrator (and a pretty lame one at that). Many women don't know they can get more powerful vibration for a lot less money and no magic script for as little as $12 at a sex-toy store. Forget fighting with your HMO, and get thee to a sex shop, pronto!

Pump Up Your Clit

For years, the penis pump has been a sex toy for boys. While the devices are available in several different styles, the Dom Perignon of penis pumps is the Millennium Pump, a handheld contraption with assorted sizes of detachable plastic cylinders. The bottom of the cylinder creates a vacuum seal around the base of the dick, and with each squeeze of the pump, suction and pressure increases, and blood rushes to your chubby. Part of the pump's appeal is its multifaceted personality. Slip your cock into its cylinder, and this baby can get you up and help you stay that way (who needs Viagra?). The advantage of a detachable cylinder is that you can pump up, then detach the pump, leaving the pressurized cylinder on. It will also suck you off better than an ambitious intern. It may even give your hot rod a lasting boost—some guys who pump up on a regular basis report permanent increases in length (research has shown that pumping can stretch an internal ligament up to two inches).

I must admit that I am jealous that such a multitasking toy only works on men. Why can't *I* indulge in the pleasures of a tight seal and the suctioning ability of a Hoover? Thank the goddess, lesbian ingenuity has struck once again. In yet another step toward equal orgasmic rights, women have commandeered something originally intended only for phallic pleasure and transformed it into a tool of pussy power. Using the same pumping mechanism, and replacing the penis-sized cylinder with a smaller one (originally intended for use on nipples), chicks have created the Clit Pump.

I first took the Clit Pump for a spin when my friend Sarah brought one with her on a recent visit. When she took it out of the plastic bag, I admit that it didn't put me in the mood right away. It appeared complicated (a pressure gauge that looked like it belonged in the Tour de France, not my bedroom), clinical (tubing attached to a cylinder three and a half

inches long with a five-eighths-of-an-inch diameter), and a little intimidating (a brass pump with a metal handle reminiscent of hedge clippers).

"Drop your drawers," she said in her thick English accent.

I did as I was told, and soon she was rubbing a handful of ID Glide
on my "bits" (the English have such bizarre words to describe anything
sexual) and lubing up the inside of the cylinder as well. I slid my clit, its
hood, and part of my inner lips into the cylinder, then pressed the rim
firmly against my skin.

"Try to create a perfect seal so that the vacuum action will work,"
recommended Sarah.

Pump in hand, she squeezed once, and I felt a pull, as if a suction cup
was on my clit. She squeezed again, and blood rushed to my pussy,
making it throb. Squeeze number three, and I looked down to see my clit
red, swollen, and filling half the cylinder. It looked huge.

I suddenly remembered the first time I saw porn star Sydnee Steele
on the set of an adult film. Like all women, when the juices started flowing, Sydnee's clit grew. But she had one of the largest I've ever seen—I
was captivated by her juicy pussy and full, luscious clit that could fill my
entire mouth. I recall being super turned on but also really envious. It
would be so cool to have a really big clit. (See, guys, you are not the only
ones who can be obsessive about size.)

With Sarah's hand wrapped firmly around the pumping mechanism
and the cylinder fused to my pussy, I was well on the way to a bigger clit
(at least temporarily). As a bonus, not only was it big, when I took the
cylinder off, it was supersensitive. One touch of a vibrator, and I was in
outer space. I was raring to go in five minutes flat!

Scientifically speaking, it makes perfect sense that the same pleasure
principle can be applied to both cock and clit. Even though we have been
conditioned to think that penis is to vagina as yin is to yang, that's entirely
incorrect and has kept all of us in the dark about women's pleasure. The
fact is that the clitoris (not the cunt) and the penis are very similar in
structural design: Both are made of erectile tissue, both fill with blood,
swell, and harden during arousal. Before you reach for the pump—well,
before you touch another clit (your own or someone else's), you must read

Rebecca Chalker's fantastic new book *The Clitoral Truth: The Secret World at Your Fingertips*. Chalker details every last millimeter of the clitoris. While it is similar to its penile counterpart, it's much more than mini-manmeat.

Which is good news for butches and other genderbenders. Karlyn Lotney, a San Francisco sex celeb and advice columnist also known as Fairy Butch, details the ups and downs of clit pumping in her book *The Ultimate Guide to Strap-On Sex*. One of the most knowledgeable and experienced pumping aficionados, Lotney says, "Some female-bodied people such as transmen and stone butches who do not identify with their female genitalia find that oral sex is transformed after clit pumping; because the size of the clitoris may increase dramatically, fantasies of fellatio are easily accommodated." Lotney has even pioneered a technique of penetration with a cylinder, but don't you dare attempt it without carefully reading her tips and caveats first.

Before you accuse me of penis envy (again), let me assure you I am smitten with my new toy not because it makes my clit into a cock, but because it shows me yet another incredible thing my body can do. I love new gadgets and gimmicks that get me off! The Clit Pump is an expensive little gift (around $90 for the pump and the cylinder) but I say it's a better stocking stuffer than that scooter you were gonna get.

Sex Nerds

I was a total nerd in high school. Maybe you can't tell by looking at me now, or maybe you've known all along. Yup, a straight-A honor student, the pet of many teachers, editor of the yearbook, all with an awkward fashion sense and the dreaded glasses. They weren't black-rimmed or Coke-bottle thick, and I never wore a pocket protector or belonged to any *Star Trek* role-playing club, but my IQ and my suburban high school caste system nonetheless rendered me a nerd. Let's face it, in high school, nerds are not sexy.

As an adult, I have attempted to reclaim my nerd identity, make it my own, refashion it, and flaunt it. People who've seen my anal sex videos tell me, "You look like the bookish girl next door, but you fuck like the chick from the wrong side of town!" I'm glad that people appreciate me as a smarty-pants, even when my pants are off. It's time for more nerdy sex kittens to strut their stuff on- and offscreen. I want people to see all the geeky girls (and boys, for that matter) in a new light. I want everyone to know that teenage geniuses into biology become scientists who discover things like Viagra. That shy boys cut from the football team grow up to be porn stars. That girls who favored Shakespeare and drama club over *Seventeen* magazine and cheerleading can spin a hot erotic role-play scene that will knock your socks off. And that's very sexy.

I've got some sisters for the cause doing a damn fine job representing nerd girls. For example, NakkidNerds is a website dedicated to sexy nerds, describing them as "smarter than your average porn stars." Chloe, the mistressmind behind the site, says, "I wanted to capture the girl you see in the back of the class sitting there reading her book, not paying attention to anybody." The models are all self-proclaimed nerds, with Chloe vouching for them (there is no accompanying Mensa documentation). Their goal is to offer both their mams and their minds, but I'm still hoping to log on one day to find below some cutie's shot a link to her genetics dissertation. What is it about nerds that some of us find so sexy? Their intelligence, of course, but it's more than that. I like the contradiction: Geeks are not supposed to be wild in the sack. I'll take someone with a well-developed brain over a muscled body any day. If you think it, I will come.

I was in sex nerd heaven when I attended the 2002 Society for the Scientific Study of Sexuality Western Region Conference in Manhattan Beach, California. The Society (called Quad S for short) is made up of doctors, psychiatrists, psychologists, sociologists, sexologists, sex educators, researchers, and other academics dedicated to the pursuit of knowledge about all things sexual. They're folks who put their brainiac ways to good use so that we know more about human sexual functioning, have a better understanding of erotic desires, and see the shifting paradigms of sex throughout history. Fuck, so that we can get laid better and more often! These are the teenage nerds all grown up (sure, some still have bad fashion sense and awkward social skills), and they're on an erotic education mission. Look past their buttoned-up images, and they're in the laboratory "observing" female Japanese macaques (a kind of primate) having sex with other female Japanese macaques. Hello! Can anyone say girl–girl action? They are "measuring" rapid ejaculation patterns in men who orgasm quickly. Or they are "researching" women who sell their panties on the Web. Imagine if Bill Gates's passion in life weren't computer software, but countertransference, and he gave a talk entitled "'I Have to Suck His Balls to Calm Him Down': Countertransference Disclosure vs. Countertransference Interpretation." Are you with me?

You may think that going to a sexology conference couldn't possibly be as stimulating as hanging at a strip joint or watching an S/M performance, but it absolutely can. Each fascinating study I heard about conjured up another study I wish I had the funds to support. Dr. Anne Lawrence, both an M.D. and a Ph.D. (but whose real double-threat is her great style and nice legs), reviewed her research on "Satisfaction and Regret Following Male-to-Female Sex Reassignment Surgery," and found that the happiness of MTFs depended a lot on the success of their surgeries. Since female-to-male transsexuals have fewer surgical options than their tranny-girl counterparts, I wonder what a similar study of FTMs would yield. Carol Cassell discussed the ways in which teenage girls learn about sex and their sexual role models in the media (Buffy the Vampire Slayer, Britney Spears, and Brandy). In her talk about doing therapy with polyamorous clients, Joy Davidson noted that there is very little research or literature about polyamorous people, which means that psychologists often have no understanding of nonmonogamous lifestyles beyond swingers (and, by the way, there isn't a heck of a lot of research on swingers, who aren't simply spouse swappers, but negotiators of just one kind of open relationship). And I still want a comprehensive study of women who ejaculate. All the studies are inherently political because they seek information about fields about which there is far too little knowledge, especially female sexuality and sexual minorities.

Don't forget, there was also the sexy-nerd star factor, with so many of the leading people in their fields all in one place—like Eli Coleman spilling behind-the-scenes secrets from the Surgeon General's Report on Sexual Health; sociologist Judith Stacey fresh from her appearance on the gay parenting *Prime Time* episode with Rosie O'Donnell; and Beverly Whipple, incoming president of the World Association for Sexology and coauthor of the groundbreaking book *The G Spot*. Nerd hotties with advanced degrees and sex on their brains everywhere I looked! Imagine the bragging rights I'd have if I could say I went to a sex conference and found Beverly Whipple's G-spot? I didn't, unfortunately, but there's always next year.

Ponies, Puppies, and Perverts

I Was a Pro-Dom Virgin

As the elevator door slides open on the top floor of this ordinary office building in the Flatiron District, the reception area looks like the lobby of a small upscale hotel. Lushly decorated in shades of burgundy, hunter green, and other inky hues with well-polished dark wood furniture, the room has a sexy, gothic quality. I am at Pandora's Box, one of New York's finest dungeons, to schedule a session with a professional dominatrix.

"Do you know what you have in mind?" asks Lara, one of the managers.

"I was thinking about some bondage, flogging, and maybe play piercing."

"Hmmm..." she responds. "I am not used to women coming in here and knowing exactly what they want. Usually if women come here at all, it is with their husbands—reluctantly."

She gives me a big leather portfolio that has photographs of all the house Mistresses. I look through the pages of women in full dominatrix-ware, stylized settings, dramatic poses. I was expecting that there would be more to go on: some sort of bio of each of them, a list of their specialties, a brief missive, something to give me a feel for their individual personas. But, for the most part, I only have photos. I am reminded that this profession is geared toward men as I search to no avail for the fierce butch top. There is lots of lipstick and over-coiffed hair and cleavage—I mean, some of the Mistresses look downright *girly,* which isn't my thing.

Amidst all the femmey drag, I seek out the ones who look tough. Lara tells me that one of my choices, Isabelle, is also a manager and will be working tomorrow.

"She may be able to take a break to do a session, but you'll have to call tomorrow."

There is a flurry of activity in anticipation of a big client who's due to arrive, so I hang around for a while, hoping that some of the women will come in and I can check them out in the flesh. When Mistress Sydney walks in, I know right away she's the one. When Lara introduces us, she immediately tops me as she tells me to do something. She also seems genuinely eager to do a scene with a woman. It's true that probably all the women would do a scene with another woman, but, as you can imagine, some would be more into it than others.

Lara gives me a copy of the extensive information form that all clients fill out, the house keeps on file, and the Mistress reviews before each session. There are the rudimentary questions about medical problems, experience level, and pain tolerance. One section asks me to rate my interest (from 0 to 5) in various activities and the intensity level (light–medium–heavy) I'd like to experience: spanking, flogging, caning, bondage (rope), bondage (other), slapping, humiliation, public humiliation, sensory deprivation, blindfolds, hoods, gags, mummification, straitjackets, wrestling, foot worship, kicking, nipple torture, golden showers, enemas, hot wax, rubber toys, forced feminization, cock and ball torture, play piercing. The next section is a list of role-playing options to check: student/teacher, mommy/child, abductor/abductee, nurse/patient, trainer/dog, mistress/slave (and some others I can't remember because I wasn't really into that part). The final section is what you'd like your Mistress to wear: leather, latex, PVC, corsets, high heels, boots, no shoes, gloves, medical, uniform (specify). When I am finished with my form, it's all there on paper—all my desires tabulated and rated. No one has to do any guesswork, not even me. I return it to Lara, who gives me an appointment for the next day.

When I arrive for my session, Isabelle greets me at the door. I recognize her from the portfolio, though she is much more beautifully striking than in her photos. Tall and slender with chin-length golden hair, she looks refined, assured, experienced, and a little severe. She's dressed in a black suit, whose jacket is classic and tailored, though the skirt is more daring—short, slightly shimmery—and her long legs are emphasized by super-high patent leather heels. She would make a perfectly demanding teacher or a strict equestrian trainer with a serious riding crop. My fantasies are already in full swing.

As I tour the different rooms, I am struck by how elaborately and thoughtfully each one is decorated and equipped. The "Role-Play Room" has lots of different enclaves: the colorful, majestic carousel horse (for mommy/kid scenes) and a vanity and mirror, with drawers of cosmetics and wigs (good for cross-dressing and "forced feminization"). The "Classroom" has a blackboard and little desks with attached chairs, and around the corner is a black vinyl bondage table leaning against a wall full of whips, floggers, canes, and leather restraints. The "Versailles Room" is actually two rooms decorated in the style of 18th century French aristocracy—lots of plush couches and chairs, an ornate chandelier, a throne-like chair on a raised platform fit for a queen. It reminds me of an upper-class ladies' boudoir. The next room is "The Dungeon," which is pretty self-explana-tory—wooden stockades, a bondage table, a wrought-iron cage, an eerie-looking coffin, and some sort of saw horse apparatus. The temperature feels noticeably cooler in "The Dungeon" than in the other rooms.

Mistress Sydney's long, curly hair is pulled back loosely, and she is dressed in an outfit similar to the one she wore when I saw her last night—black silky, clingy pants; high heels; and a black lace bustier. She has off-white chiffon skin and dark, perfectly lined lips.

"Hi, how are you?" she says, pleased to see me, smiling genuinely, holding my questionnaire in her hand.

"I'm nervous," I admit.

She reviews my questionnaire with me, asking me a question every now and then, commenting, nodding, taking mental notes.

"So, you'd like a *little* public humiliation, right?"

"Um, yeah…" I giggle. When someone whispers in your ear, "I bet you'd like to have my friends watch me spank you and see what a hungry slut you are," that can be hot. But in this context, it felt too matter-of-fact, de-eroticized, businesslike.

"Now, what about humiliation in private?"

"Well, I like to be told what to do, given orders, disciplined. I suppose it's more discipline than humiliation. Sometimes I can be a wise-ass and need to be put in my place."

"Very good." Pause. "What kind of sensory deprivation do you prefer?"

"Blindfolds, mostly, I guess. Maybe a gag, but not a hood or ear plugs."

She nods, then reads aloud to herself. "Play piercing, good; 5 for slapping, good; hot wax, you're not really into."

She reminds me that penetration and sexual acts of any kind are illegal and not part of the services provided. She tells me that my safeword is "mercy," but I must use it properly, as in "Mercy, Mistress, please."

"Would you like to have an enema to start?" she asks. Now, she doesn't know I wrote a book on anal sex, so this question immediately makes me think she's got me pegged. I agree.

She leads me to the "Medical Room," where our scene will take place, which is mirrored on all four walls and the ceiling. A white vinyl table sits in the middle of the room with white leather restraining straps, white leather wrist and ankle restraints, and metal stirrups at one end. Glass shelves with glass jars of medical paraphernalia line one wall. In the corner stand a tank of oxygen and an IV stand. A white leather hood hangs on a hook to the left of the sink. There are white cabinets everywhere. She tells me to get fully undressed, and she leaves the room.

So there I am totally naked, surrounded by my reflection, already feeling at a disadvantage. When Sydney returns with a handful of floggers and a paper bag stuffed full, she tells me to get on my hands and knees on the table. She fills a clear IV bag with water and I feel tubing slide inside my ass. She's careful, gentle, and the water pressure is very low. But I quickly feel myself filling up, and I say something to that effect.

"You can take it," she says, reassuring but firm. "Hold it like a good girl."

And I do until I feel like I am going to burst and say, "Mistress, I feel like I have to go." She instructs me to walk naked through the lobby and to the bathroom. When I return to the room, she tells me to bend over the table with my ass in the air.

"I'm going to invite my friend, another Mistress, in here to spank you."

I can't see who comes in with her, don't want to turn all the way around to try because that would be disrespectful. I imagine that it's Isabelle. The second Mistress runs her hands up and down my back and legs. She slaps my ass and her touch is firm, deliberate. They talk about me as the spanking continues, and Mistress Sydney tells me that I am being punished for not taking the whole enema bag. She also tells me that I better take the spanking and not make her look bad in front of another Mistress. The spanking gets progressively harder, and they talk about how, when the second Mistress starts to hit me with more force, I let out a squeak.

"I like that sound she makes," cackles the second Mistress. "I want to hear it again. This little bottom of yours is adorable and so sweet, Sydney."

My ass becomes so raw and the smacks feel so intense that I am convinced that she must have switched to a leather paddle at some point. She can't possibly hit me this hard with her bare hand. Mistress Sydney then ties my hands with rope and some very skilled knot work.

When she is finished with the knots, she says, "Ask nicely for more. I know you want to."

I think I am nearing my limit, so I say, "Please, can I have a *little* more, Mistress?" They both giggle and tell each other how cute and well-behaved I am (as if I'm not even there). Then Mistress Sydney unties my wrists and tells me to turn over and lie on my back, and I am staring at my naked body in the mirror on the ceiling. I also see then that it is not Mistress Isabelle who's been making my ass cheeks burn, but a Mistress I saw last night; she was in a white latex minidress and nurse's cap carrying a black medical bag. I also recognize her from the big leather book: It is Mistress Maxim, whose nickname is Mad Max. She has a mane of red hair the colors of Cajun seasoning, dark lips, and a sinister look in her eye.

"Have you ever played with clothespins?" Mistress Sydney asks.

"No," I answer honestly.

"But you can take them, can't you?" It's sort of a rhetorical question.

Mistress Sydney tells me to spread my legs, then they both go to work on me. I feel fingers squeezing sections of my pussy lips, then the pressure of a clothespin clipping the flesh. As more clips are added, the sensations build until I am overwhelmed with stimulation. I can't tell exactly what's going on, what they are doing to me. Four hands travel over my labia, my opening, my bush, my asshole. When they brush against a clothespin, I feel a surge in my pussy. They seem to be nudging the clips one at a time, then a few at a time, until I am reeling from the feelings.

I feel a clothespin press on my clit, then another. I feel the wooden clips pinching little pockets of flesh surrounding my asshole. The clips are adding so much pressure to my clit, I feel like I am going to explode. I imagine that they are sliding clips inside me, in my pussy and in my ass, and once they are inside, they press the ends together and I feel two wooden pegs open, filling me up and stretching me at the same time.

"Mistress Sydney," I say, "may I come, please?"

"Yes, you may," both Mistresses answer in unison.

When my breathing slows down, Mistress Max starts to take off the wooden clamps; as each one comes off, I feel a seething pain in my pussy. They comfort me, tell me I'm a good girl, tell me they know it hurts, that it hurts the worst when they come off. When the last one is off, Mistress Max cups my mound in her hand. I feel like I need an icepack or a cold compress or something, but when she takes her hand away, it feels a lot better. Mistress Max leaves the room, and Mistress Sydney stands above me, strokes my head, talks in soothing tones.

When I come down from the high, she is still there.

"We didn't get to do everything on your list, but I hope you enjoyed your experience."

I sit up, still naked and dazed, and blurt out a million questions. How did you get into this? How long have you been doing it? How long have you worked here and where else have you worked? What do you like and dislike about it? What's the difference between topping a man versus a woman?

"Send all the lesbians you know to me," she says, and she is sincere. I *do* think that a session at Pandora's would make a great gift for a friend. I tell her that if I get a good royalty check soon, I will definitely be back to see her. And next time, I can leave my notepad at home and concentrate on her sumptuous breasts spilling out of the bustier and her voice, stern but warm.

But the more I think about the session, the more I realize that it was exciting and fun and interesting, but it lacked something. It was ultimately superficial, the antithesis of intimacy, though I know it is hard to create intimacy on the spot and with a time limit. Taking someone to bed for the first time can be risky—you have to figure out what makes them purr, and vice versa—but that kind of dangerous vulnerability can be really hot. Since everything was articulated on paper beforehand, my Mistress had knowledge about my desires, but she didn't have any *context* for them. She knew I "needed" discipline because I told her I did, which is nothing like the moment when a top puts me in my place in a scene because she has watched me out in the world and knows just what I need. A girl with instinct and courage (but no questionnaire) can push my buttons, hit a nerve, and drive me wild. And for that woman, I will gladly submit. Mercy, Mistress, please.

Sir, Yes Sir!

Have you ever fantasized about being shouted at and humiliated by your commanding officer? I'd always found that exciting until, on the Discovery Channel, I saw *Marine Corps Boot Camp*, a brutal documentary that made the role-playing too real. Rules, self-sacrifice, discipline, power dynamics, and testing the limits of the body and mind—it was all so clear to me: The military is the ultimate sadomasochistic scene! While such a scenario scares wimps like me, it leads other girls to soak the crotches of their BDUs (battle dress uniforms). A few of the proud militaryphiles have used that frothy fuel to create the Dyke Uniform Corps (D.U.C.).

Comprising four founding generals, privates, and recruits, this is the only group of its kind for women. The D.U.C. is united by a love for dress blues, discipline, and demerits. "What I like most," says General Butch, "is the camaraderie, the integrity of our members, the encouragement to lead my own disciplined lifestyle. What I like about uniforms is the sense of belonging in the military that I never got to experience. I like creating and wearing a proper uniform, feeling the preciseness and power."

I met Generals Butch and Blade when I trained as a recruit at the New York battalion (which, incidentally, is a ranch house in a Long Island development).

"Sir, this recruit is reporting for duty as ordered by the General, Sir." I stood at attention (or at least at my interpretation of attention as described in my orders) in front of General Butch, a strong, solidly built dyke with a handsome face and steely eyes. She looked at me completely deadpan with a mixture of ambivalent affirmation, delightful disdain, and hunger. I felt myself get weak in the knees. Maybe this was going to be more fun than I thought; I could feel my clit jump at the possibilities.

Listen, this girl can get off just by uttering the word *Sir,* and women in uniform make me melt, but this adventure was a lot more than that.

Clad in the authorized D.U.C. recruit uniform—black BDUs, white T-shirt, black combat boots—I was about to go through dyke boot camp, and I was scared. Terrified. As I stood at attention, General Butch corrected my posture, fixed my hand position, and proceeded to dole out a slew of demerits for all my violations: a leather belt instead of regulation web belt, white shirt not well ironed, dog hair on the pants. I could tell she loved every minute of correcting me.

"Do you know how I work off demerits?"

"Sir, no Sir."

"With a cane, recruit. Do you like canes, recruit?"

"Sir, no Sir." In fact, I hate canes. How did she know that? Man, she was *good*.

"Well, I do, recruit. I like them a lot."

General Blade looked on as General Butch continued to taunt me. General Blade is the strong silent type; she sat by quietly, her salt and pepper hair trimmed neatly under her beret, her sinewy body still beneath her perfectly pressed uniform. That quiet demeanor can be even more intimidating than the aggressive one, and I knew they called her Blade because she likes to play with knives.

I was definitely on foreign soil: the turf of butches who play with other butches, drop-and-give-me-twenty-you-sissy territory. A place no femme has gone before. I immediately had flashbacks of high school gym class and the ex–drill sergeant who led us through a regiment of exercises every day. As the most nonathletic person I know, I dreaded gym class and especially the exercise drills. I can't even do a push-up, and I knew that was not gonna help me out with the D.U.C. Training sessions are usually personalized for every recruit, and the Generals knew I was a bottom and a girl; training programs are also designed for tops, lest you think that they just recruit bottoms to push them around all day. Of course, some of us like to be pushed a little.

Since I didn't have brawn on my side, I worked the brainy angle, carefully researching and memorizing all there is to know about the D.U.C. Of course, my memory of everything I'd read went out the window as soon as General Butch began barking orders at me; there was definitely a part of her that tried to intentionally trip me up so that I could be penalized for it. The D.U.C. mission statement seemed easy to remember: "The Dyke Uniform Corps is a private association of women of honor, integrity, and discipline whose mission is to share a common interest in the wearing of military and law enforcement uniforms in the leather, S/M, and fetish communities." But, try saying that over and over while being carefully scrutinized and intimidated, doing sit-ups, push-ups, and pull-ups, running up and down stairs. Try reciting it correctly and perfectly without fucking up. And fucking it up—well, screwing anything up, really, or just looking at the general was cause for a boot in the back during push-ups, face down on the floor smashed into the carpet, and other demeaning, compromising positions. Okay, you're right, I enjoyed the punishment, but I was still trying to do a good job.

In the tradition of true brotherhood and teamwork, D.U.C. Recruit M. J. had traveled all the way from Rhode Island to attend my training and assist me. She was a cute boydyke, all butch-tough on the outside and soft-sweet on the inside, with a bleached blond flat top and impeccable manners. All the makings of a well-trained service bottom, and the Generals were lucky to have her. She was in charge of teaching me to salute and about face. For about face, she told me I pointed my toe too much ("like a dancer or something"), and my salute wasn't sharp enough. At one point, she tried to show me what I was doing wrong, but gave up when she said, "See, it should be like this, but you're doing... well, I don't even think I can do what you're doing." When I gave my first salute to General Butch, she who never cracks a smile burst out hysterically laughing. I salute like a girl, they said. Yes, I was definitely the dyke Private Benjamin, but, unlike Goldie Hawn, I was determined not to cry. And I didn't; I lifted my head high and got through it all. The running, the orders, the questions, the leg lifts, the sit-ups, the quizzes. I was down on the floor with my face smashed into the carpet so much I got rug burn on my forehead. On top of all the physical demands, there was nonstop quizzing on D.U.C. knowledge. Imagine if Regis Philbin ordered you to do wind sprints, then asked the million-dollar question.

After my pathetic showing on some piece of gym apparatus I couldn't even identify, let alone conquer, I found myself once again on the floor, this time face up, with the general pouring Powerade down my throat (the highlight for me because, besides the humiliation, it reminded me of a golden shower scene). Okay, so I liked that part. I was beginning to realize that my little turn-ons are like drooling over a UPS uniform for a Ken doll compared to the turn-ons of the women in the Dyke Uniform Corps. This recruit was definitely rethinking "no pain, no gain."

In the D.U.C., military rules and regulations are a big part of the allure; plus, hierarchy and power structures are eroticized to the full extent of the law. Perfect for perverts into orders, authority, and, of course, a woman in uniform. And they do not fuck around when it comes to uniforms. As part of becoming a private, recruits have to assemble an ensemble of their choice, and learn each detail about it, including the branch of service, the type of uniform, and the meaning of all the stripes and badges and buttons. Recruit M. J. taught me about her uniform, as well as several brought out by General Butch—Air Force ceremonial blues, Army mess whites, Navy dress whites, Marine mess dress. It was a collection so impressive it made this femme's vintage-gown fetish look novice. The women of the D.U.C. take their fetishes very seriously, and when they don the uniform, they become true-blue members of the Corps.

It does not escape my feminist eyes that the institutions the D.U.C. emulates and fetishizes are patriarchal, homophobic, and antipeace. Is it subversive for these women to reenvision the military on their own terms? By exploring the subtext of dominance and submission and eroticizing the power dynamics of the military, they create their ideal fantasized world. It is an elaborate one, and it is their own. They are unabashed fans, not critics, of the armed forces.

General Butch: "There are some current military and ex-military who might have feelings about a bunch of S/M dykes who are not military wearing a uniform. Our response to them is that we endeavor to wear and instruct people on the wearing of a correct military or law enforcement uniform and hold it in the highest respect. We honor those who wear them to defend our country and our safety." I could almost see the stars and stripes billowing in the wind behind her, but who cares? She sure does look hot in that uniform.

Pervy Ponygirl

A sexy pair of Fluevog boots called Grand Nationals started it all. The name pays homage to the breathtaking, determined, cross-dressing Elizabeth Taylor straddling an enormous galloping horse in *National Velvet*. What young girl didn't want to be the tomboyish Taylor, tough enough to tame an animal several times her size? Before puberty, most girls would rather have a pony than a beau any day. I was no exception, and, already exhibiting my ambitious nature, I was not content to collect plastic horses. By the age of nine, I was riding every day and competing in horse shows. Sociologists theorize that the female fascination with all things equine has something to do with controlling our own budding animal sexuality. For me, the relationship between horse and rider was magical, intense, and very powerful, but never consciously sexual. Did my early experiences in the saddle make me a pervert?

Let's return for a moment to one of my adult fetishes—shoes—and the Grand Nationals. You might know them by their other name: They're called "hoof boots" after their high carved heels, cleverly shaped like cloven hooves. Both names are actually misnomers—horses don't have cloven hooves, animals like goats do. But imprecise metaphors be damned—the first time I slipped these black beauties on, I was transformed. Soft, dark leather ends just below the knee; delicate lacing runs from midfoot all the way up the side of the leg. They would look and feel a lot more like the boots I wore as a rider if it weren't for that hoof heel, which makes one feel more ready to be ridden. Standing up in them for the first time, I felt my center of gravity shift—my whole body pitched forward, tits jutting out front, ass sticking out back. I bought them at once, and when I showed them to The Cowboy she encouraged me to debut them at the ball, aka New York Gay Pride. They inspired our first foray into ponyplay.

I slipped on the boots. The Cowboy tied an elaborate body harness on me with crimson-colored rope she'd hand-dyed. She circled my breasts with rope and threaded it between my legs, where it rubbed in all the right places. She lubed up a plastic butt plug attached to a real horsehair tail and slid it inside my ass, tying knots here and there to secure it in place. The last touch was a metal bit covered in black rubber, which she placed gently in my mouth.

I trotted down Fifth Avenue with The Cowboy; actually, I was an English pony, though she was a Western trainer, handling me with reins she attached to the bit. At first, the whole thing was pure dress-up. Really, all I fetishized were those fabulous boots. As we went along, I found myself getting into the ponygirl role. I liked stamping my hooves, snorting, and pulling on the reins to get The Cowboy's attention. She even made me whinny a few times. At the end of the parade, a young man introduced himself to me and said that he was a ponyboy. I later learned that he was Ponyboy Silk, a major player in the ponyplay scene. I felt guilty, as if I had appropriated the horsey fetish only for fun, still convinced that I was not a true ponygirl really into ponyplay.

Ponyplayers are a unique subset of the BDSM community: men and women who are into either being human ponies or owning, training, and riding human ponies. Once clandestine and underground, in the last decade these kinky folks have come out of the stable with their own events, etiquette, and brand of eroticism. Katherine Gates extensively documents ponyplay in her book *Deviant Desires: Incredibly Strange Sex*. With respect and a subjective yet nonjudgmental approach, Gates delves into a world of cart ponies, two-legged and four-legged ponies, and the trainers who handle, ride, and show them: "Outsiders usually assume either that it's about bestiality (absolutely not!), that it's about degradation of the pony, or that the owners routinely whip the pony as part of the play. I suppose a few players feel that it's some kind of humiliation, but the vast majority are quite proud to be ponies."

This particular fetish seems to be as much about the gear as it is about the horse–human connection. Some of the equipment is borrowed from the horse world, like saddles modified to fit human ponies; tails made of real horse-hair; metal and rubber bits; and horse brushes and grooming tools. A cottage industry has formed to cater to ponyplayers, manufacturing bridles for humans, custom-designed corsets and body harnesses, and other solutions to the fascinating challenges of transforming human hands and feet into hooves that are practical and functional.

The erotic elements of ponyplay depend on the people involved: Some get turned on from actually being ridden or from riding a human pony, a fantasy reminiscent of childhood piggyback rides. Others like to transform into an animal, shedding the pressures of humanity for a while. Serious ponygirls and ponyboys might spend an entire weekend at a retreat or a horse show without walking upright or speaking, sleeping on straw and eating from a feedbag. All this may sound freaky, but one of the leading couples in the scene that I met were downright normal.

At the 2000 International Ms. Leather Contest, I attended a ponyplay workshop given by Paul and Emily Reed, who publish the magazine *Equus Eroticus*. Emily, whose ponygirl alter ego is called Frisky, took the reins in the class and covered everything from grooming and handling to training and showing. A bubbly, zaftig redhead, she talked about how she likes to fasten bells to her tail so that she jingles as she moves. Wearing the tail really puts her in "ponyspace." Her love of being a ponygirl was sweet, genuine, visceral; when she talked about her fetish, she did not come across as sensational or weird.

What appeals to me about being a ponygirl is that it is an interesting twist on dominance and submission. In a traditional Master/slave relationship, the slave is completely submissive to the Master. In ponyplay, the top trains, rides, controls, and maybe even owns the human pony, but the ponygirl also has a will and personality of her own. Ponygirls can be stubborn, frisky, aggressive, shy, playful—they can disobey or give in to their animal instincts, and that's all part of the play. Like their animal counterparts, human ponies are seen as majestic creatures not simply to be tamed or subjugated but to be respected, admired, and adored.

I suddenly have a craving for a nice big carrot.

Me, My Panties, and the Mayor

After spending six hours in relentless traffic in a car with an engine on the brink of overheating and without any air conditioning to drive to a place that is supposedly three hours away, the last thing I wanted was to put on leather. But when I arrived in Providence several hours behind schedule, that was exactly what I had to do: squeeze my perspiring self into a black and red leather corset, leather skirt, and lace-up knee-high boots and walk onstage to emcee the 2001 Ocean State Leather Contest.

You may be thinking: a leather contest in Rhode Island? How many leatherpeople can there be in the smallest state in the country? The answer is plenty, and what they lack in numbers, they more than make up for in passion. The Ocean State Leather Contest is much like other competitions around the country, from New Jersey to New Mexico. Local members of the S/M community vie to earn the title of Mr. Ocean State Leather (for men), Ms. Ocean State Leather (for women), or Ocean State Leatherboy (who, incidentally, can be of any gender, since being a "boy" in the world of dominance and submission is more a state of mind than a set of chromosomes). The contest is also a fundraiser for Enforcers RI, the gay and lesbian leather organization that produces the event and donates all proceeds to local AIDS groups.

All contestants are interviewed by a panel of judges, perform a fantasy onstage, and model their best full leather, "hotwear," and "cruisewear" (which has nothing to do with kinky shuffleboard on the lido deck of The Love Boat—think *cruise* as in cruising for a hot daddy, a submissive girl, or whatever turns you on). Before you start picturing a shallow, Miss America–style popularity race about who is the best looking or has the flashiest outfits, let me assure you that leather contests have a rich history among S/M folk, as they promote leadership and service in the community, and as such are taken very seriously. Winners at the Ocean State meet go on to perform various tasks throughout the year, including judging other local competitions and representing Rhode Island at American Brotherhood Weekend, a national contest that crowns its own American Leatherwoman, Leatherman, and Leatherboy.

For such a small community, I was impressed with the ambitious production of a two-night contest and struck by how closely queer men and women worked together to make it happen. Meeting former and current title holders from places as close as Boston and as far as Denver, as well as this year's contestants, gave me an overwhelming sense of how being accepted by a community really does change people, inspiring them to give back and serve as role models for the next generation of leatherpeople.

I, too, felt compelled to give something to this vibrant community. As my co-host and I were encouraging people to buy raffle tickets as part of the fundraising efforts, I got the idea that I would auction off my panties. (Well, it was for a good cause, after all.) I started the bidding at a modest $10, and pretty soon the price for the small piece of fabric covering my pussy and ass was up to $100. Needless to say, I was a little surprised. Then came questions from the potential bidders. How long had I been wearing them? Since about ten that morning, with plenty of sweating (remember all that traffic? Well, it made my pussy pretty ripe). Could the winner not only have the panties but take them off me? Sure. One zealous leatherfag generously shouted out, "One-fifty!" and I was beginning to think that he'd be the one to walk away with my pussy-juiced panties. But the dykes in the crowd pulled through, pooling their resources rather than bidding against each other, and came up with $200. Then a pack of them—including a broad-shouldered woman with a buzz cut, a boyish blonde in head-to-toe leather, and a cute butch in a naval uniform—jumped onstage, seductively lifted my leather miniskirt, slipped off my satiny black Victoria's Secret bikini, and then exited to cut them up for souvenirs. I was more than happy to surrender my panties to a bunch of dykes for charity.

By the time the next night rolled around, I eagerly slithered into a supertight pair of leather pants (sans panties this time); by then, emceeing seemed like a piece of cake next to watching contestants work their butts off. Every time I looked backstage, there was a flurry of leather jockstraps, chaps, and bizarre props (including a box of Dunkin' Donuts and a *Star Wars* light saber) for the fantasy segment of the competition. For her fantasy, one woman transformed herself from a junk-food-eating housewife in curlers into a whip-toting dominatrix. One of the "boy" contestants began her fantasy being pushed around by a top in a military scenario, which transformed into a playful romp with children's toys used as S/M implements. Her excitement was infectious, and she was rewarded with the Leatherboy title.

After leather sashes were draped on all the winners, a surprise guest arrived to make a brief speech: Providence Mayor Vincent "Buddy" Cianci Jr. Never in a million years would New York City's Mayor Giuliani even consider showing up at a leather contest to support the queer community, let alone be as gracious as Mayor Cianci was. A staunch supporter of the community (racketeering, schmacketeering, his indict- ment and subsequent conviction have yet to overshadow his gay-positive attitude), the mayor used the word "transgendered" so many times that I wanted to marry him. He giddily asked if one of the drag queens (B. B. Hayes, who performed earlier in the evening) would do a special number for him, and she obliged. When the clock struck 2 A.M., everyone headed to a local club for an after-party of S/M play. I thought New York was the city that never sleeps. I could barely keep my eyes open, but couldn't resist watching some hot scenes to finish off the weekend. The folks in Providence really know how to show a leathergirl a good time.

Wide World of Water Sports

"Are you kinky?" I asked a model at a photo shoot when she bemoaned not having a girlfriend. A reluctant matchmaker, I didn't want to point her in the direction of paddles and spanking if she was looking for candlelight and cuddling. "I haven't had a lot of experience," she admitted, "but, yeah, I'm kinky." She paused for a moment. "Oh, but I'm not like *golden-showers kinky*." The room went silent. I looked at the group: a photographer, an assistant, a girlfriend, and me. I knew for a fact that *at least* three out of four of us had indulged in and enjoyed the world of piss play. Are we really that kinky? Not anymore.

Golden showers is a term once exclusively employed by leatherfolk to describe taking pleasure in pee. Golden showerers fetishize the feel, the smell, the taste of piss; they enjoy the erotics of pissing on themselves, pissing on others, or being pissed on. Once confined to the world of S/M, water sports have made a splash in wider circles. Even actress Kate Winslet let her yellow nectar flow for the camera in *Holy Smoke*. She seemed to really enjoy doing the scene, as she giggled about it during an interview on *The View,* and don't give me that crap about *acting*.

My friend and piss maven Gigi says she first got passionate about pee when she was suffering from severe allergies and someone recommended urine therapy. For three months, she drank eight ounces of her morning's first release, and she says her health dramatically improved. During her treatment, she became obsessed with her pee, filling the bathtub with it, she says, and rubbing it all over her skin. Gigi can ejaculate, so she is accustomed to spraying lovers with bodily fluids, and piss play takes it one step further: "I like peeing on my lover because I consider my urine sacred, healing fluid."

Gigi's transgendered boyfriend George enjoys being the recipient of Gigi's golden potion: "I like it when I look up and I see the expression on

Gigi's face—her dominance and the sensual release. I also like the sensation of being peed on, the warmth of pee splashing on me, and I like the
taste." And how does urine fare with the taste buds? "Gigi is a vegetarian
with a very clean diet. Her piss tastes great, like tears and vegetable soup."

Gigi and George are not the only ones dabbling in between-the-legs
dribble. Water sports have become a stroke-book staple. *Penthouse* was
perhaps the first mainstream porn rag to feature pissing pictorials, and it
opened the floodgates more than two years ago. A *Penthouse* spokesper-
son acknowledged being at the forefront of presenting the practice, but
declined further pro-pee public comments, saying the magazine was wary
of the topic in deference to distributors. In the November issue 1999, two
of the three spreads show women peeing on themselves, on each other, or
on their male partners. And February 2000's edition displays a woman
streaming on her hunky partner. Several magazines have followed
Penthouse's lead.

Peeing has become so popular with the readers of the fetish magazine *Taboo* that it has dedicated the spring 2000 issue to April showers,
featuring pissing in every pictorial. "Letters in favor of golden showers
have poured in," editor Ernest Greene says, "whereas much fewer anti-
pee comments have dribbled in." Greene believes that *Taboo* has made
water sports more publicly visible and helped break down some of the
shame and silence. So, what's the turn-on that has created this new urine
nation? Greene has a mouthful on the subject:

"It's the allure of the unfamiliar—readers are always looking for
something they haven't seen before. I believe the curiosity factor plays a
role, too: Men are getting to look in the girls' room *finally*, and see how
everything works down there. There are also, of course, sadomasochistic
undercurrents to piss play. For the top, pissing on someone can be a ter-
ritorial assertion of dominance, and for the bottom, receiving and/or con-
suming pee is a demonstration of submission. There's also just the sensual
aspect of it: It's hot and wet and nasty all over."

In San Diego, an organization called the Waterboys is dedicated to
man-on-man pee lovers: "One of our missions from the very beginning
was to destigmatize water sports and give guys the chance to explore this

wonderful erotic activity," says cofounder Dan G. "Now, everywhere you look, people are wearing yellow hankies [the S/M community symbol for golden shower lover]." Dan's company has a website and publishes the quarterly magazine *Waterboys,* which in its fifth year has 2,300 subscribers. Waterboys also hosts monthly piss-play parties in the Los Angeles area for several hundred men. From his golden empire, Dan philosophizes about the increasing popularity: "As gay men get older, we tend to be creative and want to experience new things, expand our sexual repertoires. And with water sports, we can do it in a safe way."

Splash Alan, a contributing writer to Waterboys, says, "Piss is sterile. As long as you don't have any urinary tract infections, your urine is safe. Hell, back when I was a navy corpsman, we were instructed to always try and keep open battle wounds to the abdomen moist. If water wasn't available the instructions were 'piss on the battle dressings before application to the wound.' What more can I say?" According to San Francisco Sex Information, urine isn't necessarily sterile, but it is very clean as far as bodily fluids go, even cleaner than spit. Peeing on someone or in someone's mouth is relatively safe; being peed on or in can be safe, with a few exceptions. Hepatitis B, cytomegalovirus (CMV), the genital herpes virus, chlamydia, and gonorrhea may be present in the urine of a person infected with any of these diseases, says Dr. Beth Brown, a physician and advice columnist. Therefore, if infected urine comes into contact with broken skin, transmission and infection can occur.

Swallowing urine that is infected with CMV, chlamydia, or gonorrhea could theoretically lead to infection. There is no evidence of HIV being transmitted through urine. The American Liver Foundation's Hepatitis and Liver Disease Helpline claims that peeing on someone or in someone's mouth cannot transmit hepatitis A, B, or C. Certainly, there is mixed information out there about the safety of golden showers, mostly because of a lack of research. I have a simple solution. Let's drop our drawers and open our mouths in the name of science. Who's with me?

Leather Puppy Love

My girlfriend and I just returned from LeatherFest XI in Palm Springs. Yes, I slipped on my tightest leather pants in 113-degree heat. It may sound insane, but that didn't stop us and about five hundred other leatherfolk from spending Labor Day weekend sweating in the desert. There were the usual offerings—more than sixty-five workshops covering topics from temporary piercing to body punching, plenty of shopping in the vendor area, a huge dungeon with separate spaces for men only and women only, a human pony show, a gala dinner banquet, and even an intensive Boys and Girls Academy, to which people had to apply to get in. But the best part of the event by far was that producers, the San Diego–based BDSM organization Club X, reserved the entire Riviera Resort and Racquet Club, creating an unparalleled Club Med-with-whips-and-chains atmosphere. Normally when I attend an S/M conference, we all have to "behave" in public and deal with the "regular" folks in the elevator who are more often than not horrified, titillated, or both.

At this event, everyone could be themselves, which meant there were bottoms proudly displaying bruises and lash marks on nearly every part of their bodies, submissives wearing collars into the pool, more uniforms and leather swim trunks than I've ever seen near a hot tub, so many hankies in pockets you would have thought it was required dress code, and even a woman slinking around in a cat costume. I would not have been at all surprised to see a slave girl eating out of her Master's hand from under the table at the hotel restaurant. Apparently, neither would the Riviera staff, since not a single eyelash was batted in my presence for the entire weekend (which was a good thing, since there is no group that appreciates—and over-tips for—good service like kinky people, for some of whom service is not only an important part of their fantasies, but a way of life).

In the midst of this surreal place, I developed a newfound canine fetish after attending a workshop given by Master Michael and jefpup. The two men created an ingenious website devoted to the niche of the S/M community that likes puppy play, where owner-handlers and human puppies role-play doggy scenarios. I expected a typical workshop; you know, put the puppy on a leash, play fetch with the puppy, reward the puppy with bones. Myths were dispelled (people into puppy play are not into bestiality), tips dispensed (a shallow bowl is easier for a human puppy to eat from), gear rated (wrestler knee pads for comfort and durability), and techniques taught (vanilla wafers make great training treats). But in addition to all the tricks of the trade, Master Michael offered a deeply personal, intimate perspective on human puppy play. Taking care of a human puppy is just as much work as watching over an animal rescued from the pound, though the owner gets a break from it when the human puppy has to, say, go to work. (Hey, I've got an idea: Anne Heche and hubby should try parenting a human pup before their little one arrives—you know, to work out the kinks.)

Master Michael had two very well-behaved pups to demonstrate ways of moving (hands and knees versus hands and feet) and obedience trials. The puppies also got a chance to speak "out of their puppy head space," and expressed a desire to let go of inhibitions, to take a break from the stress of the real world. What would it be like to have your existence revolve around getting your ears scratched, chasing a ball, and curling up at your owner's feet? Human puppies like to simplify their desires and motivations as they embrace the side of themselves that acts solely on instinct; they also get to sniff people without being called crude. As I watched a puppy in the audience wag his tail, drink water, and lick his owner's hand, it made a lot of sense. All the yoga and meditation in the world might get you to a relaxed state, but maybe puppy play is simpler and quicker. It was one of the most thoughtful, playful, and sane BDSM workshops I've ever attended (and I am not just saying that because the facilitator at the electricity-play workshop mildly electrocuted herself by accident the next day).

Allowing someone to explore aspects of themselves and be rewarded for good behavior with petting and snacks may be fun, but what's erotic about it? For some, it is pure role-playing with no erotic component, because when a pup is a pup, there is no sexual interaction. The idea that someone relies on you to feed and discipline them can be another twist on dominance and submission and a turn-on in and of itself. For others, the pup is always a human pup capable of frisky human sexual behavior with other pups or their owners. It inspired me to consider putting a certain boy I know on all fours just to see where his wet nose would nuzzle first. Woof!

Pierced for Pleasure

If the thought of a simple flu shot makes you dizzy, I warn you: Take a deep breath before you dive into this particular adventure. My friend Sherry and I perform fetish shows together, and she has a knack for getting me into all kinds of kinky situations. She called me one day and asked if I would pose for the flyer for the next party. The theme: "Pleasure in Pain," a night when the folks from Pleasurable Piercings would be on hand to do some complimentary clit and nipple piercings.

Almost a decade ago, before there were body piercing shops all over the country and supermodels with pierced noses, I got my naval pierced at the Gauntlet in L.A. I liked that I had added something to my body, adorned it, and changed it. But I also loved the ritual itself. There is nothing like that moment when needle pierces flesh, and I yearned to re-create it. That was also the year that I spotted a woman with multiple piercings, wings tattooed on her back, and a purple hanky in her back pocket. She was working a supermodified body before it was so hip, and I immediately consulted my copy of *Coming to Power* to find out what her hanky symbolized: play piercing. I was intrigued.

Since then, I've had other permanent piercings as well as some of the temporary variety. During scenes where I've been pierced, the most I've had is about ten needles in my chest, and they were enough to send me into endorphin outer space. When Sherry asked me to be pierced and photographed, I knew exactly who I wanted to pierce me: Val, the trusty butch top who co-topped me the day I learned to squirt.

We met at Sherry's studio in Brooklyn, and Red (the hot butch who taught me how to squirt) came along to hold my hand. Red actually despises needles, so she carefully positioned herself behind me where she could hold my arms, whisper in my ear, and give me moral support. Val laid out the disposable needles with the care of a hand-blown glass collector handling her most precious pieces. I asked her about all the different colors, and she explained: the clear ones were 25 gauge; the blues 22 gauge; the yellows 20 gauge; and the pinks 18 gauge. Remember: the smaller the gauge, the bigger the needle.

"I don't want any pink ones—that's way too big for me," I told her.

She replied, "Okay, no pink ones." She told me to take my shirt off as she snapped on a pair of bright teal rubber gloves.

She rubbed down my chest with alcohol, looked me in the eye with alarming concentration, and told me to take a deep breath. The first needle felt good—a brief prick, then a smooth sliding underneath my skin as the needle penetrated me. I looked down and there it was, a sharp and shiny point that disappeared into a strip of raised skin and then was capped with a blue plastic tip. It was on my chest, above my left breast, and soon had a twin on the right side.

Val continued moving down my chest, inserting needle after needle. There were some that were so smooth, they slid right in with a sensation very much like a finger in a wet pussy. There were some that were slower or deeper and made me squeeze Red's hand really hard as she whispered in my ear, "That's a good girl. Breathe. Deep breaths. There you go." There were some that made me scream, a combination of intense pain and ecstasy. Val convinced me that the pink ones weren't so bad, but they were pretty mean, and as a pink needle went in, I was sure I couldn't take another one into my body. She'd let me regroup, then turn to the ever-diminishing pile of needles, choose one, and pierce my flesh again. And again.

During the piercing, Sherry snapped a bunch of shots, including some of me screaming and hanging on to Red for dear life. She was surprised about how the scene was going; she'd seen me take ten 25-gauge needles without even a gasp. But by the end of this scene, there were only a few needles left on the counter. There were 42 in my chest—plenty of them were pink—21 on each side running from below my collarbone to the bottom of my rib cage.

When all the needles were in place, Val ran a piece of dental floss underneath the ends of the needles on both sides. Then with a piece of metallic red cord she laced around each end of the needles, and criss-crossed over to the other side until my chest was laced up like a corset. The cord pulled the needles in toward each other, causing a new, different sensation. I don't remember much about the photo shoot itself; I was so high at that point, I was in my own world.

By the time I had them all in, I was so juiced up that I felt like I could keep them in forever. I looked in the mirror finally and was actually amazed at the sight. They looked beautiful, and I felt so tough for taking them. I had small red dots on my chest for about a week, and the marks linger still, though they grow fainter every day. I'm still amazed that I did it, but I did, and I've got the pictures to prove it.

Finding My Inner Dom

She glides to the front of the room as twenty-five pairs of eyes follow her. My gaze is first drawn to her brimming breasts, which spill out of a jade green brocade corset. Making her generous curves even more pronounced, the corset hugs her waist close and tight like a possessive lover, eventually giving way to a long black slinky skirt. The skirt reveals only creamy white ankles and feet propped up in six-inch spiked patent leather heels. The black heels shine like her shoulder-length ebony hair, cut with sharp Betty Page bangs. The bangs frame her black cat-eye-shaped glasses. What a study in feminine detail and finesse! I feel honored to have the chance to learn from her.

The center of attention is Midori, instructor of "The Art of Feminine Dominance," a class she teaches around the country. She is also known as Mistress Midori to her clients—she works as a professional dominant, splitting her time between San Francisco and Washington, D.C. To fans, she is FetishDiva Midori; she appears in photographer Steven Diet Goedde's sumptuous book *The Beauty of Fetish* as his compelling latex-clad muse as well as in S/M movies like *Dark Paradise* and *Cruel Beauty*. She also goes by the title "Ma'am" to her flock of loyal submissives, slaves, and houseboys.

Lately I have been interested in exploring my dominant side in a sexual context, which made the $25 admission to Midori's class a not-to-be-missed opportunity. (I say "in a sexual context" because I am a bossy, aggressive top all day, but not usually with my lovers.) As someone who has experienced the power of a dominant partner, I am always in awe of what it takes to be a successful top. I am also fascinated by what makes a dominatrix a dominatrix. Some women can simply walk into a room and instantly command your attention, your respect, your submission. What is it about them? Can anyone do it? Is it something you have inside you or can you learn to do it? I looked to Midori to find the answers.

Midori's approach to feminine dominance is careful, thoughtful, intelligent, and fascinating, as clear as her voice but also as mysterious as her smile. First, she encouraged students to free-associate to the words *femme* and *feminine,* and the responses revealed how complex the expressions (and the roles) are for women today: warm, curvy, fragile, seductive, powerful, nurturing, sensuous, lipstick, nails, garters, delicate, bitch, manipulative. Then we brainstormed the word *dominant*—decisive, intense, manipulative, insensitive, mean, powerful, nurturing, forceful, painful, strict, in charge. Some terms appeared on both lists, and some seemed to contradict one another.

Speaking of language, I asked Midori why she calls herself a professional dominant and not a dominatrix. "For me, *dominatrix* sounds harsh and reminds me of porn movies. *Dominant* is a gender-neutral term and works better for me. Dominatrix is a profession or a performance, whereas dominant is a state of being."

Midori has her own definition of what constitutes beauty. It's not custom-designed sexpotwear, manicured nails, Gucci shoes, or perfect hair and makeup (though she does have all those, and then some). Beauty is confidence, grace, posture, and presentation, says Midori. So how does one go about finding her inner dominatrix? Midori has two methods for discovering the goddess within. "Outside-in" involves dressing the part, then doing the part—putting dom on like a costume, then acting accordingly. Midori recommends finding your own fetish object or objects that get you into femme dom—a particular pair of boots, a certain lipstick color, a leather bustier. She likes to make a ritual of becoming the femme dom to delineate herself from the everyday world. "Inside-out" is a deeper, more difficult path to dom, which reflects her emphasis on probing inward for that inner dominant, nurturing her, channeling her, then letting her come out and play.

One helpful way to find the femme dom in you is to search for dominant female archetypes with whom you identify. In class, we were asked to list women of mythology, history, and media that we can identify as female tops. The group nominated Joan of Arc, Helen of Troy, Medusa, Queen Elizabeth, Bette Davis, Marlene Dietrich, Marilyn Monroe, Mae West, Xena, and Madonna. Then there are pure archetypes: the exacting ballet teacher, the strict governess, the severe Mother Superior. Take a little from each archetype you identify with, then mix it up with role models from your own personal history. Midori told us about her grandmother, how she always had a quiet dominance that instilled in Midori a sense of respect and a desire to always please her. It rang true for at least one student, who commented that she'd tried to be dominant with her lover before, but it didn't work out: "I did what I thought I was supposed to do, rather than what I wanted to, rather than being me."

Midori appears to live quite a charmed life, and I asked her, "What's the best thing about being a dominant?" She said it depends on the relationship; sometimes the dynamic is limited to sessions of play, other times she is in role with someone twenty-four hours a day. "I like to have control," she says, "but it is also the mutual satisfaction my partner and I get out of the power exchange." As a top, she sees herself as a leader, parental figure, nurturer, mentor, and role model.

Even enlightened, feminist chicks still struggle against the tradition of socializing women to be quiet, passive, submissive, and gentle. Midori's class was like a consciousness-raising seminar where women were encouraged and empowered to find the inner "she who must be obeyed"—to acknowledge her, feed her, celebrate her. To find that spark of dominant fire inside us and stoke it. Every woman should take a class on how to be a dominatrix—to learn how to tie up her lover, stand up for herself, get what she wants, and celebrate her power. I can't wait to take my own inner dominatrix out for a spin.

Looking for Mommy

"From this moment on, you will address me as Ma'am," I said.

"Yes, Ma'am," he said, head bowed, eyes lowered.

It seemed like a simple process: directing my boy to call me Ma'am. Master and Sir were all wrong for my particular gender expression. Mistress sounded too much like a professional dominatrix, which I am not. So I chose Ma'am, to signify my role as Top, to reinforce the power dynamic between us. To remind him each time he says it who's in charge. The first time my boy slipped, I was tucking him in bed for a nap, stroking his head, reassuring him that his painful headache would subside. He mumbled in his sleepiness, but we both heard it: Mom. Don't think I hadn't noticed that Ma'am is very close to Mom, a title with which I never identified. But Ma'am was quite distinct from Mom, so I never worried that either of us would confuse the two. When the word slipped out of his mouth (was it inevitable?), it didn't ring in my ears like nails on a blackboard. It didn't make me wince or shock me. My lack of negative reaction was more surprising than any other response could have been. In the context, feeling loved and cared for, his verbal gaffe fit, for both of us. I had to admit to myself that there was a little bit of Mom in Ma'am.

When I revealed the slip, and my subsequent realization, to an ex-lover, she *was* shocked, saying, "You? A Mommy? I cannot see *that* at all...." But I could, and my boy did, and even I entertained the idea of moving beyond the occasional language trick and embracing the Mommy in me fully.

For BDSM practitioners, there is age play, and then there is incest play, and both freak out most nonkinky people. People want to deny that young people have sexual desire and agency. Some won't admit that an age gap can be a fetish, a turn-on, especially when it's between consenting adults. We are often criticized and dismissed as chicken hawks and pedophiles: Throw *them* to NAMBLA and disassociate from them entirely. As a society, we want to condemn sexual abuse, and people see age play and incest play as a form of eroticizing it, and therefore glorifying it. But this jump ignores the fact that people who do this kind of sex play are consenting adults who explore the forbidden, sexual undercurrents of family, that what we do is fantasy, and that fantasies often don't reflect or jibe with our socially conscious politics and humanitarian values.

I am what you might call an S/M geek: When I get a taste for something, I study it diligently. So naturally, after my boy called me Mom, I began hunting for Mommy erotica, Mommy scenes, Mommy seminars, Mommy role models, Mommy websites. What did I find? Daddy, Daddy, Daddy.

Among queer leatherfolk, Daddy is arguably the most popular archetype around, and he is seemingly everywhere. Daddy workshops and panels are regularly offered at leather events; Daddy erotica and pictorials are found in gay and lesbian porn magazines; the popular erotica anthology *Doing It for Daddy* and the popular lesbian porn video *Dress Up for Daddy* pay homage to the adored subject with words and images; Daddy T-shirts, buttons, and bumper stickers could outfit a small nation. Search queer personals for the word *Daddy,* and you'll have plenty of potential dates to choose from. There are leatherdaddy contests around the country, and, in San Francisco, there's even an annual Dyke Daddy Contest.

The Daddies I know are a diverse bunch, but several common characteristics are evident: They are strong, warm, nurturing individuals with the ability to rule with an iron fist (or a velvet glove). They are often leaders, teachers, confidantes, mentors, and disciplinarians. Daddy can also be the patriarch of an extended leather family network, the one who makes decisions and keeps all its members in line and content. Daddy is an inclusive, expansive role. He easily crosses gender and sexual orientation lines: There are gay leather Daddies, female-identified Daddies, dyke Daddies, trans Daddies, and heterosexual Daddies. So why all the Daddy worship?

Gay men popularized the role of Daddy as gay leather culture formed. Taken (somewhat) literally, Daddy was a way to signify the importance and prevalence of intergenerational relationships: Older men brought younger men out of the closet, into the BDSM scene, and showed them the ropes. Daddy and boy delineated not just the obvious parent and child roles, but Top and bottom, teacher and student. Experienced players took younger ones under their wing, taught them S/M history, etiquette, and skills. For leatherdaddies, this process was one of looking out for, protecting, and raising newborn leatherboys.

The desire to be a Daddy or have a Daddy is deeply rooted in the psychodynamics of the traditional nuclear family structure. Many people grow up in homes with physically or emotionally distant fathers, or absent and unknown fathers, or other kinds of unavailable fathers (probably more than with these same kinds of mothers). The absence of the father, literally or symbolically, or the lack of a strong relationship with him, creates a longing, an intense craving, desire, and need to bond and connect with Daddy. As adults, we may seek out lovers and partners who remind us of our fathers, represent the father we never had or knew. For some people, the role of Daddy may be a chance to start from scratch; he can be whatever they want to make him. Maybe he's two parts imagination, one part reality, or 100 percent pure made-up character. If Freudians (and other schools of psychologists) put on their leather chaps for a moment, they'd conclude that for gay men (and straight women too), one's father was the first object of affection, thus Daddy is a deep instinctual desire from childhood. It's taboo among some leatherfolk to openly admit that we use BDSM to work through our personal issues, to rewrite our family dynamics, to heal broken relationships...but we do.

As with many other aspects of BDSM, lesbians often rely on gay male traditions to structure our relationships and communities: We borrow directly from them or we adapt certain elements of their culture to fit ours. We've adopted many of their leather contests, their protocols, and their roles. Thus, our embracing of Daddy seems perfectly, well, natural. So where is Mommy in this patriarchal lovefest? Although Daddy has no problem crossing gender lines, there seem to be few if any Mommies in gay male communities. (Notably, straight people engage in a fair amount of Mommy role-play, and it's most commonly a way to explore infantilism [being a baby], humiliation, spanking, and discipline.)

In theory, Mommy may have different qualities and a unique history compared to Daddy, but she is just as significant, if not more significant, a figure in everyone's life. No matter what your sexual orientation is, Mommy is every child's first love, first object of devotion, and the center of the universe. With our mothers we are often at our most vulnerable, needy, and searching for limitless love.

Although it may not be as well documented as it is for gay men, lesbian intergenerational relationships are an important way that culture and community are passed on from one generation to another. In Catherine Reid and Holly Iglesias's anthology of mother stories by lesbians (which are not specifically erotic, though some have sexual content), Mommy is *Every Women I Ever Loved,* which gets us back into those Freudian chaps again. In *Loving in the War Years,* Chicana lesbian Cherríe Moraga tells the story of her mother's jealousy of her lovers and Moraga's admission about their intense bond: "I know how strong your love is. Why do you think I'm a lesbian?"

Mommy is a role that can be specific, meaningful, and rich territory for lesbians. Whether or not you believe that Mommy was the first love/lust object for lesbians, she was undoubtedly a caretaker, nurse, teacher, mentor, disciplinarian, and seminal figure in their lives. So why then are there so few examples of Daddy's female counterpart in the world of queer kink? I have considered that Mommy/boy or Mommy/girl is as common as Daddy play in practice, but there should be some cultural evidence, and there is practically none: only a handful of references to Mommy in workshops or writing, and only one Mommy contest (the San Francisco Dyke Daddy/Dyke Mommy Contest in 1996). I can't go to a leather event without being surrounded by dark green hankies everywhere. The hanky code, first created by gay men to signal their sexual roles and interests (and adopted by dykes and even some straight kinky people), has expanded into as many as eighty different colors and patterns listed in various hanky codes. The dark green hanky worn on the left means you're a Daddy, and on the right, you're looking for a Daddy. There are hankies to represent everything from fisting and foot fetishes to navel worship and sailor lovers, yet nowhere have I ever seen the hanky code for Mommy.

The proliferation of deadbeat dads aside, it cannot be that all of us had wonderful mothers with whom we had perfect relationships—no scars, no issues, no stuff to work through. It cannot be true that none of us identified with our mothers, desired our mothers, or longed for a maternal figure in our lives. Not only is there a shortage of Mommies, there also appears to be a shortage of lesbians looking for Mommy. I've never heard the complaint "Damn, there are way too many boys (or girls) and not enough Mommies." Because of her significance in our lives and the unspoken desire that underlies a lesbian's relationship with her mother, she may have reservations about making Mommy the dynamic the subject of erotic play. Is she too intimate, too powerful, too strong an archetype to play with, to embody, to desire? Do we have a fear of the maternal figure?

Another reason for all the missing Mommies could be some form of misogyny and gender double standards at work. Daddy's reign as top erotic role choice reflects a tendency not only to eroticize and sexualize the father (and all things he represents) but also to empower him over the mother—the paternal as powerful and seductive, the maternal as meek and less desirable. It's an interesting metaphor in the context of parenting roles in American society: Mommy does all the hard work, while Daddy gets all the glory. Yet mother gets her own brand of praise: Mommy is honored, romanticized, held up as the giver of life, but why is she off-limits when it comes to S/M and sex?

To track the Mommy archetype, I turned to popular culture (which is modern-day mythology), where there are some pretty dismal examples. Like the detached, unavailable mother played by Allison Janney in *American Beauty*. The overly involved, doting mother from *In the Bedroom*. Fiercely protective mothers who turn psychotic in *Serial Mom* and *The Hand That Rocks the Cradle*. A controlling, domineering, obsessive mom as in *Gypsy* or *The Positively True Adventures of the Alleged Cheerleader-Murdering Mom*. Cruel, abusive matriarchs in *Cinderella* or *Throw Mamma from the Train*. Let's not overlook all the representation of mothers of serial killers: They not only house their sociopathic sons, but are clueless, are in denial, are overly protective, or have unnatural relationships with them. And, of course, the Mother of All Mommies: *Mommy Dearest*. Faye Dunaway's portrayal of Joan Crawford is not merely a queer movie buff favorite, but the single most popular reference to a mother in film of all time. A TV movie about a young woman who falls in love with a murdering boyfriend is brilliantly titled *Mother, May I Sleep with Danger?* The question reveals much about the power of the mother: to dictate behavior, to listen to her instincts and protect loved ones from harm, to permit or deny sex.

In the introduction to the anthology *Doing It for Daddy*, Pat Califia discusses the power of Daddy as it relates to masculinity:

> The essence of masculinity is the choice to be gentle even when one is stronger than others; to care for one's dependents and nurture the young; to devise rites of passage and train our charges to pass through them successfully; to help those who are in trouble; to work hard and perform well; to provide food even in time of scarcity; to deal with problems or emergencies in a courageous and effective manner; to mount a defense, and, if necessary, get hurt or even die in the process of protecting the people who are dependent upon and helping you.

Although Califia associates all these qualities with masculinity, I argue that they describe an ideal Mommy. The postmodern roles of Daddy and Mommy are less distinctly defined than they have ever been. Breadwinner, caretaker, disciplinarian—these could describe either or both parents. Gender roles have become more fluid, blurring the distinctions between mother and father. My notion of what makes a good Mommy is informed not by the 1950s *Leave It to Beaver* mom, but by a postsexual-revolution feminist single mom with a career. Likewise, this shift in parenting roles has affected how dykes fashion their Daddies; in some ways Daddy has become highly maternal.

The most thoughtful, complex look at Mommy/boy play between dykes is Karen Everett's deeply personal film *Sweet Boy*, where she explores this intense dynamic. The woman who plays Mommy in their scene admits that she is drawn to the boy's total surrender because it is a reflection of a part of herself she cannot access: "Your vulnerability is a reflection of my own.... I am given an opportunity to see myself, my vulnerability in the softness of your gaze, so I may love and honor this part of myself." Ultimately, the boy (played by the filmmaker herself) struggles when their affair ends abruptly, then learns both to grasp the mother/child dynamic within herself and to mother herself.

In my life, Daddy is more mythic, a romantic figure visited during school breaks and summers full of shopping, movies, theater, dinners out—the perfect full-service resort vacation dad with no rules, no real-life challenges or interruptions. Because I was raised by my mother, there was always longing associated with Dad: He was just out of reach, mysterious, slightly distant (if only literally); he could be a stranger. Mommy was as real as it gets: curfews, rules, holding my head while I threw up; fighting about friends, dating, money. She lived with me longer and knew me better than anyone else. Catherine Reid writes in the introduction to *Every Women I Ever Loved: Lesbian Writers on Their Mothers*, "From our mothers come most of what we know about love and touch, about caring and connection." But that's not necessarily the case for all of us. As I was growing up, my father was sensitive, nurturing, affectionate, more of a traditional Mommy than my mother, who was stoic and emotionally distant. Paradoxically, it was my dad who taught me what little I believe I know about mothering.

For me, role-playing the mother–child relationship and bond enables me to explore some of my deepest emotions—unconditional love, undying support, nurturing—as well as affords me an opportunity for honing my abilities to impart whatever wisdom, values, and ethics I possess to another human being. Ironically, many of the dyke Daddies I know also embody these qualities, but they do so in the role of Daddy. If the choice were simply about gender, then there would be a relatively equal number of Mommies and Daddies. It's clear that more butches are more likely to choose Daddy, while femmes more often choose Mistress, Lady, or Ma'am as their preferred role and title. Perhaps many of these Daddies are, by popular definitions, really Mommies, though they don't consider themselves as such. Or is it merely a matter of language? Language, the words we choose to name ourselves, is undeniably an important tool in the creation of queer and kinky identities. But the title Mommy, and all that accompanies it, seems much more taboo than Daddy.

Parental role-playing can be extremely emotionally charged and intense. As we re-create the family in a new way, we acknowledge that these roles are magnetic and perhaps inescapable; we consciously embrace their significance rather than blindly ignoring how central these early relationships are to our adult connections. When I am Mommy to my boy, I am caring, supportive, and nonjudgmental. I offer him guidance, teach him based on my life experience, offer him new opportunities. He is one of those fresh-faced leatherboys, just discovering a world of kink, all that it has to offer him, all that he has to give back. I am his mentor and teacher, and he is my student and muse. I take care of him, hold his hand when he's frightened, and let him go to facilitate his journey of independence.

For me, Mommy is laying down the law, being a role model, sharing my knowledge, looking out for my boy. Being Mommy is also about responsibility—he trusts me to take care of him, to watch, nudge, and sometimes push him as he grows. For my boy, Mommy is about asking permission, about doing what he's told, about respect and reverence. He wants to be a good boy, wants to please me, and his wide-eyed innocence is a precious gift. When I place the collar around his neck, I often say, "Welcome home," because for us, the dynamic *is* our home. We are at home in our respective roles, at home in our skin, at home in the world. Mommy is that home—a safe harbor for us both, a place of comfort and stability.

The erotic component is deeply rooted in the power dynamic between us, as well as in the dominance of Mommy. He doesn't call me *Mommy* during sex per se (that's not our kink), but in fact my Mommy qualities underlie our sexual play. The fact that we have sex at all breaks one of the oldest taboos. Technically, I am not old enough to be his mother, but when I imagine he's sixteen, I am. Or sometimes I am someone else's mom, sexually initiating him, showing him how to please a woman. Mommy/boy play is about the power each of us has: mine the power of wisdom, experience, years of lovers, and his the power of youth, idealism, innocence, eagerness to soak up every sensation and every minute like a superabsorbent sponge. When he places himself in my hands, shows me his deepest needs and secrets, his submission is a cherished gift, and I marvel at his ability to give it to me.

More than knives and needles, Mommy is definitely edge play for both of us. Mommy is simultaneously sacred and scary. She is a place I do not always want to go, a person I never thought I could be, a primal urge I cannot always control. What is most terrifying to me is that there is a boy who brings all this maternal magic bubbling to the surface. That there is a Mommy somewhere inside me. That I have the ability to reach her and reveal her to another person. As I play and am Mommy to him, I also delve into the dark, scarred territory of my own experience of being mothered. In the process, I reimagine my own mothering. I discover the mother I wish I had as a child but never did, and I *become* her. I see the Mommy he desperately needs, the Mommy I longed for, and the Mommy I want to be for both of us.

The Unbearable Queerness of Being

My Gay Boyfriend

After I heal from a breakup, I find it hard to plunge back into the dating pool. It's like getting up from a comfortable chair where you've found the perfect position, you stretch your legs and, reluctantly look for a different place to sit. Many years ago, after ending a two-year relationship, I was happily professing to everyone that my new sexual orientation was not queer or bi, but simply first come, first serve: Whoever had the guts to approach me, regardless of gender or sexual orientation, would get me. Sure, I was single and randy, but more importantly, I was flexible.

At a queer writers event, a gay guy I knew introduced me to his ex-boyfriend. We clicked immediately; soon, we were watching movies, going shopping, and having marathon meals where we'd tell each other about our sex lives in exquisite detail. I loved hearing about man-on-man action, and he was clueless about what dykes did in bed, so it provided endless entertainment for us both. He was charming, funny, and hot, and while I've got a thing for fags, this fag definitely liked boys. He never even hinted about being attracted to women. Although I am confident that I can per-suade people to play for the other team, I was content with our friendship.

Months later, he made a pass at me, kissing me deeply on the lips. Startled, I broke the embrace (not before getting a little tongue action) and said, "Um, what are you doing?"

"Kissing you," he smiled broadly.

"But you're gay!" I retorted.

"So are you," he returned, unflinching. "You of all people should understand that sometimes our desire isn't stuck in one place, Miss Don't Fence Me In. I seem to recall someone claiming that she was first come, first serve." I scowled, but he did have a point. He touched my hand, and said, "Do we really need to talk about this? I think you're sexy and I want to kiss you, okay?"

"When was the last time you were with a woman?" I asked (already knowing the answer from a previous conversation).

"Um, like eight or nine years ago or something, but don't worry, it'll come back to me."

"That's not what I mean! I mean...." He cut me off with another delicious kiss, and I decided to shut up.

The first time we had sex it was like being dropped into one of my favorite gay porn movies starring him as the hunky leading man. The way he undressed me, the way he moved into my body, the way he held his cock in his hand: confident, defiant, seductive. And his dick! The first time I saw it, eyes popping out of my head, I blurted, "Wow, the gay boys must love you!" All the fag personals I'd ever read had dick size featured prominently, and his dick was, well, quite prominent. That virgin encounter was definitely a fag smut flick, but then, what did that make *me?*

In high school and college, I was a total fag fucker (not always literally; think "star fucker"). Many of my crushes were on boys who fucked boys or boys who wanted to fuck boys. No surprise: Lots of dykes and fags are attracted to each other before they come out; we are drawn to one another by what we assume is desire, but it's really the connection of being queer, which is buried or still unknown to us. My attraction to gay men had another significant element to it: My dad was gay. The idea that I was into fags didn't take thousands of dollars of therapy to unravel, and I can hear the collective yawn of Freudian analysts everywhere. Being with my gay boyfriend as a way to directly enact the father fantasy. Fuck the unconscious, let's wake her up and really do this!

When we got together, I thought: Finally, perfect—a fag. We'll have so much fun together! Well, it turned out he wasn't even my kind of fag. He didn't like musical theater. He didn't get what all the fuss is about Judy Garland and Barbra Streisand. I could let go of his lack of interest in old-school gayness, because I thought, I'll be getting all the anal sex I could ever want! And not nice, well-paced anal sex, but "throw 'em down on the bed and fuck 'em like you mean it" anal sex. (Clearly, I had watched way too much gay porn.) But his first instinct was *not* to throw me down on the bed and fuck my ass with unimaginable aggression and fury. I begged him to fuck me in the ass, and he always replied, "I can do that with the boys; your pussy is what I want because that's the rare treat."

Besides my pussy, one of my gay boyfriend's favorite things to do was have anonymous sex. He trolled gym locker rooms, public restrooms, and bathhouses looking for lust. He was always safe, so I didn't worry about him. He'd come home late at night, smelling clean from a recent shower, and crawl into bed with me. I would make him tell me all the details of his encounters. *What was his body like? Did he have a big dick? Did he talk dirty? What did he say? Who made the first move?* I lived vicariously through him, his adventures my voyeuristic thrill. Sex with him after one of his tales was always a little bit nastier and more frenetic.

No one knew exactly what to make of us. People assumed he was gay and I was his fag hag friend, or they'd read us as straight, which freaked us both out.

"Oh, so you're both bisexual," people would conclude.

"No, he's gay and I'm a lesbian." I would usually introduce him as my fag boyfriend, and I could see everyone trying desperately to process that phrase and then respond appropriately. We met a guy at a party once, and after explaining our situation, he was mesmerized.

"Wow, that is so cool," he said. "You're the future!" Apparently we were the very *near* future, because we took him home that night.

Eventually, we went our separate ways. As a poster girl for polymorphous perversity, I never thought my own assumptions about gay men, gay sex, and gay nonmonogamy could be challenged, but having a gay boyfriend did just that. Every day with him was like that first night: a big spoonful of my own medicine. And swallowing it was a whole new experience.

The State of Lesbian Sex

It used to be that lesbians found sex the old-fashioned way: They went to bars, met each other, dated, fucked, and moved in. Dykes still keep cheap beer and U-Haul stock prices steady, but the bar scene is now only one of many ways to make a lust connection.

Contrary to the claims of pop psychology, not all women are drawn to dating, emotional connection, and sex in the context of a relationship. Some, perhaps many, are looking for a quickie, a group grope, or a voyeuristic thrill. But in the past, there were few opportunities for those desires to be explored. That is what has changed. Cyber connections, erotic videos, and women's parties have created a new public space for lesbian sex. And as these venues arose, so did dyke desire.

In part, this is a generational shift. The New Lesbian comes out at a younger age, and she's much less likely than her elders to settle for butch or femme. To her, gender presents a range of possibilities. She might call herself a boi, a girlfag, or a genderqueer. She has an ISP right out of the womb, she's the head of the gay–straight alliance in high school, and she majored in queer studies at college. Feminism, gay liberation, the sex wars of the '90s, and technology have produced more confident and experimental women ready to claim and celebrate their sexuality. The who (a stranger), what (one word: strap-on), when (on the first date), where (at a sex party), and why (cuz we're horny) of lesbian sex have definitely changed.

And, lest you think this is just happening in a small circle of downtown dykes, check this out: Women's S/M play parties, sex clubs, and bathhouses can be found in San Francisco, Los Angeles, Seattle, Portland, Philadelphia, Baltimore, Atlanta, Boston, Dallas, Austin, and even Washington, D.C. The sap is up and spurting.

But you don't have to leave the comfort of home to flirt, date, seduce, and fuck complete strangers. Technology has made new kinds of erotic relationships possible through the Internet, digital photography, and video. Dykes troll the chat rooms and personals of America Online, Nerve.com, PlanetOut.com, and Butch-Femme.com looking for love or lust—or both. Dykes engage in virtual relationships, sex, and S/M online, with the option to meet in real time.

A few years ago, two brainy, ballsy broads formed S.I.R. Video and jump-started the barely existent lesbian porn scene. Shortly after, Fatale Video, the most prolific lesbian porn company, which hadn't released any fresh dyke product in nearly a decade, reemerged with an annual Amateur Lesbian Porn Video contest. Fatale now distributes its first winner, *After School Special,* created by a bunch of New England dykes with a video camera and a taste for homemade smut. Add to the mix SexPositive Productions' *Please Don't Stop,* by and for lesbians of color; Austin-based Passion Fruit Video's *Home Cookin'* and *Gallery Erotica;* indie flicks like *Alley of the Tranny Boys, Girl King,* and *Sugar Sweet,* and we almost have a shelf full—hey, that's a lot for us—of unabashed, authentic queer sex.

The growth of community-created smut is undeniably significant. Dykes have claimed new technologies to produce our own images for ourselves. They are very different from mainstream/hetero images of "hot girl–girl action," in which big-boobed chicks with alarmingly long nails touch tongues and moan softly but never really fuck. Great dyke porn is more than a show for men. Not only is it a source of sexual validation, information, and inspiration, but it has a 69 effect on lesbian sex: Dykes inspire porn to get made, and porn inspires dykes to get laid.

Another sign of erotic evolution is the dramatic increase in lesbian public sex. Dykes into S/M and public sex now have several parties to choose from in New York, including those hosted by the Lesbian Sex Mafia and DUMBA, along with two monthly gatherings, X Party and Throb (which I co-produce). X-Party and LSM are heavy on the leather and whips; Throb is less exclusively devoted to kink. Notably, there is no dyke sex venue open seven days a week. We take over het or gay-male spaces for one night only. It's not liberation, but it's better than longing.

So, if you build it, will they come? The answer is yes, with some coaxing. When Throb first began, we often had to plant "ringers" at the club: These were not-so-shy friends who'd arrive early and do their thing to get the party started. It's a time-tested formula: Once a few people get down to sucking and fucking, others feel like they have permission to let loose as well. But it's still a challenge to get women to fuck in public.

Most women, however liberated, need lessons in sexual assertiveness. We have social baggage that prevents us from objectifying other women, whether they are strippers or potential sex partners. Anonymous encounters can also be a tall order in the lesbian community. No matter how large a city you live in or how far you travel outside your own social circle, it's still a game of six degrees of separation between you, your ex-girlfriend, and her new mate.

We've learned a lot from gay boys. For years, we not-so-secretly envied their pornos, their cruising rituals, their bathhouses, their promiscuity, their ability to have raw, blatant, unencumbered-by-emotions sex. Red, Throb's other producer, recently teamed with Michael (of the infamous Meatpackers parties) to create an all-genderqueer sex party once a month called Spam. At the inaugural bash in February 2002, Michael observed, "All the men are silently cruising or fucking, and all the women are talking. Men aren't used to there being any talking in a sex club"—and women aren't used to *not* talking.

It's a matter of training more than anything else. We seldom wink, drop our drawers, and jerk each other off. Spam has created a public space for a back-and-forth dialogue between queers about sex, which, from what I've witnessed, may take the form of a dyke fucking a gay boy in the ass or a fag getting his first mouthful of pussy. Building community alliances has never been so challenging.

But bonding has its limits. While the clothes check is a staple in gay sex clubs, most dykes won't take it all off. A butch with the perfect leather chaps to highlight that big bulge, or a femme with a breast-for-days nightie, would be offended at the thought of stripping down. That's partly because of female body issues, but more importantly because what we wear is a critical part of our gender and sexual expression. Unlike with the boys, our cunts alone don't dictate whom or how we fuck.

Maybe we can learn from gay men how to cruise and follow through. Maybe we can teach them to talk with their mouths full. In the future, perhaps lesbians will have our own 24/7 sex dens and gay men will be the ones taking notes.

Electric Shocks/Lesbian Cocks

"Closer to God" by Nine Inch Nails blared in the small, smoky club as I slinked down the bar, dressed in a black latex minidress shined to the maximum extent of the law. Everywhere I looked there were butches in suits, leatherdykes, and lingerie-clad girls. Teasing the crowd, I toyed with the zipper of my dress, which ran from my cleavage to between my legs. Finally giving in to them, I stripped down to nothing but my seven-inch heels. A fire-engine red dick in a red sparkly harness stood at attention between my legs. Gigi appeared in a black vintage bustier and Catholic schoolgirl plaid skirt. She kneeled in front of me, took my dick in her mouth. Her perky bobbed hair bounced freely as the red cock disappeared in the *O* her lips formed. I pushed her back, grabbed the cock, pulled it out of the harness. Then I dangled it enticingly in front of a cute cowboy from the audience, who graciously began to suck it. Gigi handed me an identical red cock, this one rigged by her with a metal wire running through the middle of it. The tip of the wire was covered in alcohol-soaked cotton. I slipped it through the O-ring of the Wonder Woman harness. With the strike of a match, the end of the cock burst into flames. Then she got down on her knees again. In one motion, she deep-throated the cock, swallowing its flaming head to the amazement of onlookers.

Her fiery red hair is a perfect match to her fetish—Gigi loves fire. And the hot blow job number was just the beginning. Later, she used two wire-and-cotton torches to seductively run flames along her arms and stomach. She deep-throated the torches, just like the dick, all to Eartha Kitt purring, "I'd rather be burned as a witch, then never be burned at all...." She told me that the torches actually do scorch her, proudly showed me the little red bumps forming on her sensitive, creamy freckled skin. She smelled vaguely of burnt flesh.

The fire was just a prelude to another sizzling act: electricity. I've only done electricity play once, with a TENS unit (an electronic device that sends currents through the skin to stimulate sensory nerves in the skin). Medical TENS units were originally designed for people suffering from certain injuries and chronic pain; kinky people have borrowed them for their tingling sensation. The TENS unit, even in the context of a scene, still reminded me too much of my trips to the physical therapist as a child equestrian with bad knees. I've never played with Violet Wands before, but you know I am always game.

The Violet Wand certainly is violet, but not much of a wand. It looks more like an old-fashioned set of clippers, with a hole at one end for various attachments, an on/off button, and a dial to control the intensity of the charge. Funny how there was no indication on the dial which way was up and which way was down—a masochist must have thought of that.

Like the TENS unit, Violet Wands were developed as a medical tool, but it's not clear what they were supposed to cure. Most of the attachments are glass, gas-filled bulbs (in the shapes of a pronged rake, a medium and a large glass ball, and a silver-dollar sized knob). When the bulb comes in contact with the skin, a glowing violet spark appears (that's how it got its name). As the bulb gets near, the spark jumps from the bulb to the skin, and you feel a hot, buzzing, tingling kind of shock; if it is pressed against the skin, the violet spark still happens, but the shock is gone. There is another attachment that you tuck into your clothes and that turns *you* into the voltage conductor—the spark comes right out of your fingers and shocks whatever you touch.

Gigi liked the rake attachment with the three prongs, and Rachel opted for the small knob that looked like a vibrator attachment. I went for the large glass ball, which looked like a crystal ball or one of those static lamps. We ran a shock down arms and legs, zapped nipples, even sent some voltage to clits and pussies. It felt like a quick shock and prickly heat on the skin, or, when you dragged the wand, a buzz dragging across flesh; to me, it had all the erotic charge of running into a bug zapper. But the party-goers were really into it, so we encouraged them to join in.

When one girl got her hands on the wand, she enticed her cohorts to try it out. Another woman, rumored to be a lesbo virgin, pulled her pants down as two goth girls went to town—one wand on her nipples, another on her clit. She gasped and groaned with each zap. Two other women pushed their shirts up, ready to try the fascinating feeling. It all broke loose then: women with shirts slid up, nipples poking out of bras, pants pushed down, undies shed, bare skin glowing and sparking. There were hands on breasts, wands on hands, fingers brushing across stomachs, buzzing and zapping, legs intertwined, and violet sparks flying everywhere.

These sizzling scenes—oh, and so much more—were captured on film. Unfortunately, what was the high point for me of an outrageous evening didn't even make the final cut. But those are the breaks when you're only the subject—or object—of the game. This particular game is known to all you TV viewers as *Real Sex*. When an HBO producer first approached me about doing a segment for the cable network's documentary-style show, I had mixed feelings ("Hooray! Mainstream media attention!" and "Yikes! What am I getting myself into?"). Of the few episodes I'd seen, one—the piece on porn star turned performance artist Annie Sprinkle— was smart and sexy. Most were goofy (like the so-called "masturbation club meeting," which looked more like a bunch of swingers to me) or blatantly salacious (clips of author Lou Paget's workshop on how to please a man featured repetitive images of women practicing blow job techniques on lifelike dildos). One was simply ridiculous: The story of a couple who together have "sex" with the high-priced, custom-made "Real Doll" was cheesy and obviously staged with actors.

While the producer was interested in documenting (as documentaries do) some "real" aspect of my sexuality, she definitely had her own agenda when it came to the focus of the story. Of all my interests that we discussed in preliminary meetings—anal sex, S/M, porn for women, lesbian gender identities—she seemed particularly focused on my casual mention of dykes and strap-ons. She zeroed in on that topic as tenaciously as my Boston terrier pulls at the leash for a stray chicken bone on the street. As a lesbian herself, she loved the idea of explaining the complexities of the sapphic sausage and putting those ugly penis-envy myths to rest once and for all on national television. Her phallic preoccupation ruled, and by the time the cameras were finally rolling, my friend Gigi and I were hosting a lesbian strap-on party, playing with electricity (which neither of us really do), setting stuff on fire (which Gigi loves to do), and giving sound bites about why we love cocks. Ah, the magic of television!

Before you think I was railroaded into this exposé like some *Real World* cast member prodded into a temper tantrum, Gigi and I did get to squeeze in a few of our own fetishes. We wooed the crew early in the day, and after seeing two girlie girls like us, I think they expected our friends to show up for the party later that night wearing G-strings and pumps. Since both of us adore butches (and believe that positive representations of them are sorely missing from mainstream media), we packed the club's audience with some fine examples of female masculinity, much to the complete confusion of the entire crew. Instead of lipstick and push-up bras, they got chaps, three-piece suits, and crew cuts. I could see the marketing team months later wondering just what they had on their hands. I mean, a show about lesbian cocks is one thing, almost palatable and certainly titillating when those plastic penises are strapped to super-feminine women. But when we match tomboys and women who look like men with the not-so-gender-neutral attachment, we've got a horse of a different color on our hands. Is Middle America ready for butch dykes in a show about lesbian cocks?

Well, they'd better be, 'cause here we come! The best part about doing the HBO special was the chance it gave me to make a little history: When will I have another prime-time opportunity to educate the masses about a particularly crucial but mostly misunderstood aspect of lesbian sexuality like strap-ons? Dildos, in one form or another, have been part of lesbian sexuality for a long time. During the '70s and the dreaded Sex Wars among feminists, dildos were considered by separatist and antiporn crusaders to be representations of penises, and therefore literal tools of the patriarchy. Never mind that they felt really good sliding inside our slick pussies—their shape and all its implications made them more politically incorrect than shaving your legs. Today, we're thankfully past all that, and dildos are one of many different sex toys available to women of all sexu-alities. From the most realistic peckers with balls, circumcised heads, and veins to lavender goddess and kitten dildos, there's something for every-one. We don't need a man to get some dick, and hey, we can actually have as many cocks—from slim and curved to thick and meaty—as our little cunts desire.

A long way from those days of dick-bashing, lesbians now have much better relationships with our penile friends. We embrace our cocks, reclaim our cocks, and, yes, wear our cocks out in public. Dykes are finally proud to say, Yeah, I've got a dick; actually, I've got several. Sometimes I want it to be real; sometimes when I am wearing it, I imagine it *is*. Other times, it's simply another pleasure tool to get the job done, and I'm happy to toss it on the shelf after it's served me well. And the idea that anyone, regardless of gender or genitalia, can have a cock has the poten-tial to definitely shake things up. It makes those of you equipped with one at birth seem so…limited. You've just got the one. I've got an entire drawer full of them.

Queer Co-Ed Lust

As the daughter of a gay man, and as a girl who likes to fuck women who look and act like gay men, I am way beyond a typical Oedipus complex. Besides, a traditional Freudian analysis of my penchant for faggy dykes just doesn't cut it; I am much more intrigued by the myriad of ways in which queer men and women define, create, imitate, and challenge each other's sexual identities. Every day, I see examples of gay and lesbian sexual imagery overlapping, intertwining: butch women who look like they've leapt off the pages of a Tom of Finland book, well-groomed gay men on Fire Island dressed like preppy lesbian lacrosse players, leatherdykes who belong in *Drummer* magazine, and leatherdaddies who should be in the lesbian porn mag *On Our Backs*. Often, our sexual personas and practices seem to tango perfectly with each other.

If fags and dykes have so much sexual culture in common, then why aren't there more mixed sexual spaces for queers? Don't get me wrong— I'm not totally against segregated gender territory. I think that women-only and men-only events can be useful at times (though, more and more, a vocal transgendered community is problematizing the very notion of "same-sex space"). In New York, there are so-called "pansexual" parties, but unfortunately, what pansexual has come to mean on the East Coast is far different from its West Coast definition of all genders and sexualities; a pansexual event in the Big Apple is ostensibly a heterosexual event, where many queers just don't feel comfortable.

I've asked around to gauge interest in a girl–boy sexfest. All the dykes I know are gung ho to see fags fuck, which doesn't surprise me since so many of us are gay-male-porn watchers. (A chance to see it live? I'm there!) Plus, dykes have so few spots to have sex that we'll gladly share one with our "brothers." Men, on the other hand, have no shortage of locales to have public, anonymous, or casual sex, including sex clubs, bathhouses, and cruising areas; they don't necessarily need or want to share. But there is a far more insidious issue that keeps us apart. Most gay men have little or no interest in seeing women fuck or even having them around while they do. Too many gay men are still on the "Ew, pussy! I don't even want to see that!" train, first stop gynophobia, last stop misogyny.

Is it too much to ask for some boy–boy cocksucking and girl–girl muffdiving under one roof? And not just where the boys and girls tolerate each other's presence, but where we actually support and celebrate each other's sexuality? I was beginning to think that New York just wasn't ready for my radical vision yet, until I went under the Manhattan Bridge in Brooklyn. DUMBA is an artists' collective–cum–queer housing cooperative in a loft in Brooklyn's DUMBO district. The collective hosts a sporadic queer sex party called "The Lusty Loft." I had the pleasure of attending one about a month ago, and was pleased to see my dream in action. Lots and lots of action.

In a maze of rooms small and large, people danced to a DJ in the biggest open space, ate vegetarian food in the kitchen, and generally behaved like people at a typical party. But walk deeper into the loft, and you'd see this was no regular Saturday-night soiree. I spied a hot gay couple in a small mirrored room just beginning to undress each other. When I went to the bathroom to pee, I saw two guys fucking madly in the stall shower across from the toilet, and I suddenly wished for a larger bladder. Everywhere there was groping, kissing, fingering, sucking, and fucking. Boys watched girls and girls watched boys in a kind of queer erotic nirvana that was truly blissful.

Now, I did notice that most of the group had several characteristics in common: They were young (was anyone there over thirty?), queer (I seriously doubt anyone would use *gay* or *lesbian* to describe themselves), radical (with clearly antimainstream, punk-rock, anarchist aesthetics and politics) genderfuckers (boys with lipstick, girls in drag). Young, queer, radical genderfuckers for whom the term *opposite sex* was practically meaningless.

The star attraction of the party was the "Interactive" room, a small space furnished with a bed and wired with multiple surveillance cameras.

Several feet away, anyone could watch what was happening on a dozen small screens that showed the scene from multiple angles. For a change, it was not being broadcast live on the Internet or recorded to be sold to underground amateur porn collectors. It was only there for a moment of exhibitionism and voyeurism. I watched two tattooed chicks get it on, followed by a threesome of older men, then four men, then two women whom I immediately wanted to make porn stars. (It's hard to keep my capitalist tendencies in check sometimes, even in such an anticonsumer space as DUMBA.)

A lusciously big girl was on her back, knees up, pumping her hips against her lover, a punk-rock chick who rode atop her, reverse-cowgirl style (on top, facing away from her). Both of them were gyrating frenetically, and at first I assumed that the bigger one was wielding a strap-on, but upon closer inspection, I realized: Look, Ma, no straps! It was another fifteen minutes before they became unglued long enough for me to see that they'd been riding opposite ends of a clear jelly double-dong. It was the kind of sex toy I always see in pornos that makes me think, "Does any real person ever use one of those things? And more importantly, does it really get anyone off?" Well, these two broads were apparently hell-bent on answering my question with a lively demonstration that screamed, "Yes! Yesss! Yessssssss!" to my query. They worked that dildo in an ingenious way I've never witnessed, partly because of the unique position (I assumed they had done it before), mostly because of the sheer enthusiasm behind the task.

Standing next to me, eyes glued to the glowing screen, one queeny guy said to another, with giddy excitement in his voice, "Oh, I hope she ejaculates—she's a big ejaculator, and she can squirt like nobody's business. It's so cool!" So few gay men even know that women can ejaculate, and I don't know many that would care about, let alone applaud, such a talent. That kind of talk just warms my heart and makes me think there is hope for all of us not only to get along—but to fuck side by side.

Queering the Swing

The last swingers party I went to was about four years ago in a converted office space of an industrial park outside Boston. While I did finally hook up with an attractive professional couple, I wasn't dying to become a regular in that world. Swingers seemed too straight, too male-dominated, and too suburban to intrigue me. I never thought of the current generation of wife swappers as queer or kinky enough for my tastes. Recently, I was invited to a swingers' party in a suburb of the city I was visiting, and decided to give "the lifestyle" (as those in it like to call it) another shot.

When my boy and I drove through the gates of the property, the parking lot was full, so we got a spot far away from the main house. When I stepped out of the car, I heard the unmistakable crunch of gravel beneath my feet. Great, I thought, a lot full of rocks and me in my six-inch patent leather stripper shoes.

"The gentlemanly thing to do would be to carry me all the way to the door," I said to my companion.

"How about a piggyback ride?" he replied.

So I hiked up my dress around my hips, jumped on his back, and wrapped my legs around his waist. I prayed the whole way there that we wouldn't run into anyone—a piggyback ride was not my idea of a good first impression. Inside the heavy wooden front door, I informed the guy at the front desk that we were guests of the couple who had invited us.

Swingers parties allow only single women or couples to attend, and by swinger definition a couple is a man and a woman. This was an interesting dilemma since my date was a tranny boy. I hadn't bothered to inquire on the phone about the policy for tranny boys and the women who love them—I was pretty sure there wouldn't be one. I thought we would arrive and present ourselves as we see ourselves. The manager looked at my boy's ID for quite a while, maybe because he looks 17 (he's 23) or because the first name I used to introduce him does not match the one on his driver's license or because the gender on his ID would technically make us a dyke couple, which we are not.

"It's $60," he finally said. We were in.

A short fellow wearing gray silk pajamas was our designated tour guide, and we followed him to the dining area (where, under a table, two men were being treated to after-dinner blow jobs), which was just past the dance floor. A single guy with a guitar and a laptop belted out covers of everything from Stevie Wonder to ZZ Top. We proceeded on the tour. The place was packed with people ranging in age from twenty to sixty, who looked like they could be at my cousin's wedding, with one important exception: The women wore peekaboo teddies and garters, and some of the men were in towels. Those towels were for the indoor pool (too chilly to take a dip in the one outside), where several naked folks frolicked, and the nearby Jacuzzi, so full it looked like there was more flesh than water in the tub. We passed a locker room, a fireplace with people lounging around it, and a large sectional couch facing a wide-screen TV playing porno. The size of the house was impressive, and its modest, resort-like decadence felt warm, inviting, and very conducive to sexual play. These people were obviously serious about swinging.

We stopped at a spiral staircase, where two signs read NO STREET CLOTHES and NO SINGLE MEN. Our guide explained that no strip-down was necessary since we were on a tour. We headed up the stairs, and walked past room after room, each with mattresses, most with piles of people going at it—tangles of breasts, hands, asses, cocks, all moving to the sounds of grunts and groans. Now we're talking, I thought to myself.

"No unaccompanied guys are allowed up here, so," he turned to my friend, "you can only come up here with her or another woman." We both nodded to convey our understanding.

"But, if you wanted to bring, like, five guys up here to do them all, well, you could do that, as long as they *all* stayed with you at *all* times." I smiled. "And if he had to go to the bathroom, he could go up here, but then he would have to make a beeline right back to you, no wandering around by himself." I loved these rules: It was as if we were on some island of Amazons where men weren't allowed to roam free. Works for me. Who said swingers weren't into dominance and submission?

After our tour, we went up to the balcony that overlooked the dance floor to indulge in some old-fashioned voyeurism. There was plenty of tits touching tits, but absolutely no man-on-man handling—not surprising since in most swinger circles, there's a double standard about homo desire. Well, they may be uptight about men boinking each other, but they have no qualms about nudity. As the night went on, everyone became half-naked or completely bare (hey, it does take the guesswork out of the equation), and we felt like the most overdressed couple there. I would have been up for swinging with someone while bringing my friend along and explaining, "He's shy, he just wants to watch," but it seemed like all the sex was going on in that third-floor area, and up there you had to be pretty much naked. What's a girl and her tranny boy to do?

To avoid looking like the tourists we were, I decided to borrow from two lovely ladies we watched earlier in the evening and give my friend a private lap dance; this way, I could also shed some clothes so that we wouldn't look so conspicuous. I proceeded to shimmy around, teasing him with my ass and peeling my dress off slowly. Then I knelt down in front of him and told him to take his dick out. I'm rarely on my knees in front of my boy, but in this case, I firmly believe that when I have my boy's cock in my mouth, he's at my mercy, not the other way around.

"Um...."

I suddenly remembered that I hadn't given him explicit instructions about what dick to wear to the swingers party. "What color is it?" I said.

"Black," and we both giggled. I was up for the challenge. I unzipped his fly, felt for the silicone cock, and carefully slipped it out the front hole of his boxers. I wrapped my hands around the base and, in one full swoop, slid my mouth down his dick until my lips met my hand. I decided it would be all about the sleight of hand—hand slides up as mouth comes up, hand slides down as I swallow. Several people started to watch us, and no one seemed particularly alarmed; they just saw a head bobbing up and down in some guy's lap. His body tightened in a familiar way, and I knew he was close. I picked up the pace, and his hips started to buck into my face. "May I grab your head, Ma'am?" he was panting. I nodded. His fingers splayed around my skull, he squeezed my head once, twice, then he came.

I had to pee, so I went to the bathroom, and when I came out, a group of men had descended on my tranny boy. I immediately panicked, thinking that our cover might have been blown, but instead they were merely trying to take him under their wing and show him how it's done. I feared our true identities would be discovered—spies in the house of heterosexuality. But they were just chatting him up, showing the new guy the ropes, and winking a little to acknowledge that he just got blown. If they only knew.

I Fucked a Straight Girl

My girlfriend had a reputation for throwing wild parties. Well, wild S/M play parties for women. When we decided to start a new party together, we wanted to expand the crowd to include not just the hard-core leatherdyke set, but also kinky girls and transpeople of all kinds: folks into a variety of turn-ons in addition to S/M, like public sex, anonymous sex, voyeurism, exhibitionism, and role-playing. We both loved the idea of one place where S/M players would flog and cane alongside vanilla chicks sucking and fucking—everyone getting it on in their own particular way. We wanted to see the cross-pollination of perversion: those nonkinky ones who came for the sex and ended up in bondage, and those rarely seen out of full leather regalia, butt naked with ass in a sling and legs in the air. But one phenomenon developed that we never expected: Every month, a few straight girls come to the party. I don't mean bi girls with boyfriends or even bi-curious ones, but bona fide, self-identified straight girls. I can spot 'em a mile away. We make a point to give all newcomers a tour, explain sex party etiquette, and answer questions. So when I spotted a preppy-and-potentially-het girl pair at one party, I asked the requisite newbie question: "How did you find out about the party?"

"We read about it in *Time Out*. We know it's for lesbians, but we didn't think anyone would know. We left our guys at home tonight. We wanted to see what this was all about."

"Great," I said in my most encouraging tone.

"I'm Jennifer and this is Ona." I looked them both over. Jennifer was a well-groomed slender woman with light brown hair, a recent manicure, tasteful makeup. Ona, who hadn't said a word, had shoulder-length blonde hair, wore black jeans and a black silk blouse. They were both attractive, but my gaydar didn't even hum. I had to give them credit for coming. It's not only a testament to the fluidity of female sexuality, but also an example of how acceptable it is for straight women to check out lesbians as compared to straight men (I haven't heard of any who go to gay male sex clubs just to "check it out"). I encouraged them to watch the action, then politely excused myself. As I made the rounds from the door to the dungeon and back again, I passed them a few times—they were glued together.

Hours later, the place was packed with more than eighty women, and I had lost track of time, between unclogging the back toilet and searching for a missing sharps container so that someone could do a piercing scene. In the play space, I ran into two butches who were focused on a corner, drooling over something or someone. I walked over and turned around to get a better look. Much to my surprise, there was Ona stripped down to her birthday suit lounging in a leather sling. Her friend was nowhere to be found. The shirt I met her in didn't do justice to her full breasts, and I would never have expected what I saw when I looked below her tits: an exquisitely shaved pussy. It was a top-notch job, and I knew she didn't get it at an Upper East Side salon like her friends.

"Beautiful shaving job—you did it yourself?" I respect a woman who's willing to groom her own twat. I walked closer, and her eyes met mine.

"Um, yes," she said, looking as if she's never been asked that question before.

"Gillette Mach 3?" I continued. She looked stunned.

"How did you...?"

"It's the only razor I use on mine. What kind of shaving cream?"

"None." And I swear she batted her eyelashes at me.

"Have you ever had sex with a woman?" I asked her point blank.

"Well...." I reassured her with my eyes that I already knew the answer. "No," she finally said softly.

"Well, I'd love to be your first," I said with my best femme swagger. She giggled. I reached over to the table next to the sling, snapped on a latex glove, and poured some lube onto my hand.

As I worked a finger inside her cunt, she felt wide open. "Has there been someone in here before me?" I teased. She blushed and giggled again.

"Well, my boyfriend and I had a quickie before his physics class this afternoon." The idea that this college dude had fucked her just hours before me got me really turned on. I wasn't quite sure why, but I decided to go with it.

"Does he have a big dick?" I asked, as I slipped two more fingers in her hungry hole.

"Yeah, I mean bigger than average." She cooed as I found her G-spot and worked it while my thumb rubbed her clit. She moaned.

"What about his hands?" I said, adding more lube, then sliding a fourth finger in easily.

She gave me a puzzled look, part dazed from confusion, part blissed out from the pleasure.

"What I mean to say is, well, I have very small hands. There are some things girls do better than boys." I got a rush just thinking about what I was going to do to her. "Have you ever been fisted?"

"Oh, no.... Um, no, but—oh, that feels so good," she was totally high. One more shot of lube, and my thumb left her clit. "Put your hand there," I told her, and she didn't miss a beat. I slid my thumb up against my other fingers. Slowly, I pushed her tender insides. She took a deep breath. "Good girl," I whispered, and I pushed into my wrist. She yelped, and her hand began moving faster on her clit. She made a squeaking sound, then took another deep breath, and screamed at the top of her lungs. Usually, straight girls don't even catch my eye, but I'm glad I made an exception for this one.

Cherry Popper

Based on my experiences of the last six months, you'd think I was chasing down the title of Anal-Fisting Cherry Popper (AFCP). I don't know if there is someone out there already considered (albeit unofficially) AFCP, but I think I am in the running to dethrone whoever it is. Since I teach anal-pleasure workshops around the country, I've, naturally, had requests for classes that cover the whole, um, hand-chilada. In the name of sex education, I get a good manicure, pack my bags, and travel to new cities, where I lecture on safety, preparation, and the wonders of there's-no-such-thing-as-too-much-lube. But talking tips and techniques doesn't always do justice to this five-finger subject, so, when possible, I also perform hands-on (more like hands-in) demonstrations. And lately, I have been on a roll.

To many, Anal-Fisting Cherry Popper might sound like a homo porno series, conjuring images of Crisco-coated arms disappearing into hairy buttholes as deep trance music plays in the background. That's because dipping into the bunghole is most often linked with gay leathermen—after all, they popularized hand-in-the-butt love in the '70s, and have been its main practitioners and teachers ever since. But the rest of the world has caught up with queer boys with short nails, and there is much more interest in this subject from folks who don't even know what a red hankie in your pocket means. Case in point: I mostly teach and demonstrate on heterosexually inclined women and men, as well as lesbians.

Since I don't have an anal-fisting demo bottom who travels with me everywhere I go (résumés for such positions gladly accepted!), I must rely on the kinky kindness of strangers in most cities where I teach. The usual scenario goes something like this: I tell the organizer of my workshop that I need a volunteer for either of the two classes I teach, "BDSM and Anal Play" or "The Art of Anal Fisting." I arrive in the city and, if I'm lucky,

I get the chance to meet and talk with my willing ass-for-hire before my workshop. More often, I've got about a half-hour to assess their experience, negotiate limits, and form some sort of connection before I dive in. Inevitably, my demoee informs me that he or she is "an anal slut," a "butt pirate," and "a total exhibitionist." The thing that most people forget is that we are not having sex or doing a scene in the traditional sense: I am teaching a class, in which my focus is constantly split between the person with his or her ass in the air, and the students with their hands in the air (to ask questions, of course). I cannot devote 100 percent of my attention to my bottom, and the audience is always a part of our experience. I've probed some asses that are tighter than *Air Force One* security, and no amount of arousal is going to relax their sphincter muscles, but I am skilled at making the best of less than ideal situations. Overall, few encounters have been mediocre, and most have been incredible.

There's Annie, whom I've done twice; she's sexy and fun, and I nicknamed her Miss Giggles. Both times, when I put a butt plug in her ass to illustrate ways to warm up the butt, she laughed so much that it popped right out, giving me the perfect segue to talk about how to keep a plug in. And then there's Vena, who had been doing lots of anal play with her girlfriend to prepare for my workshop. But nothing could prep me for taking out a thick plug from her ass, lubing up my gloved hand, and finding myself slipping all the way inside her so quickly. The audience was flabbergasted, and I tried to play it cool, like, yeah, this happens all the time, but secretly I was thinking, "Damn, she's making me look good!"

At one event, I was scheduled to teach two classes in one day. I became so smitten with my demoee, John, in my "Anal Sex 101" class in the morning that I put a butt plug in him and told him to leave it in through lunch and return for my advanced class in the afternoon. He was sweetly submissive, looked me directly in the eyes, and communicated well about what he needed to make it happen. When I got my whole hand in his ass, I was transported. I looked up at the crowd of people watching, and for a moment I was speechless. There are no words to describe the feeling of having your entire hand inside someone's ass. It can be simply magical when our bodies are joined in that moment. (To top it off, after the workshop, John sent me a "thank you so much for fisting my ass" note on cream-colored embossed stationery that would've made Miss Manners proud.)

Of the ten people I've recently anally fisted, only one had been anally fisted before me; likewise, only one of my demonstration volunteers had ever been fisted; the rest of them volunteered to let me plow them for a crowd. How gutsy! To know that a stranger could be the one to pop your anal-fisting cherry! I have very small hands, seven inches from the tip of my middle finger to my wrist and seven and a half inches around (yes, that was a blatant advertisement), and size *does* matter.

I have such tremendous respect for these people who give me their butts so willingly. I am in awe of their ability to put their asses on display for friends, community, and complete strangers. It amazes me that we can both do this scary, intense, deeply intimate thing with someone we barely know; I automatically feel closer to the person after the experience. I feel proud of my demoees for their accomplishment and humbled by their ability to achieve it. Through giving workshops on anal fisting, I have honed my techniques, learned different tricks, and even made some new friends. Although I tease about striving to be Anal-Fisting Cherry Popper, the truth is I am not really into goal-oriented sex, and I am easier to please than you might think. It's not about quantity for me, it's about making someone squirm and squeal with some good, old-fashioned anal penetration. It's about giving someone a rectum rush, where the sensation begins in the ass and then resonates throughout the entire body. If I only get four fingers—hell, if I get my little pinky—in your ass, I am a pretty happy camper.

And Bears, Oh My!

A few years ago, I met my friend Mario at a Union Square restaurant for brunch. Since it was packed with hungry shoppers and locals, there was a long wait, but the hostess informed us that there was a table free in the back room, which was reserved for one large group. Starving, we decided that if the gathering didn't mind our crashing, we were happy to join them. There was no banner or sign announcing exactly who was meeting, so Mario and I agreed it would be fun to guess what might have brought these people together: Were they recovering gambling addicts, self-help cult members, visiting cosmetic surgeons?

Our speculation immediately narrowed once people began to arrive, greet one another, and sit down. They were all men. The hostess was correct, this was one large group: Most were big, burly types with bellies and bulging bodies. There was an abundance of hair: Hairy chests sprouted out of the tops of their shirts, and they all seemed to have beards or other facial hair. A common uniform was apparent: flannel shirts, jeans, boots, leather vests, as if they had just come off a construction site. Their tough appearances contradicted their observable warmth and playfulness with one another, lots of hugging, affection, giggling, smiling. Sexual tension was in the air.

"We're in the middle of a meeting of bears," I said, and Mario thought a minute, then nodded his head and boasted, "So in other words, if anyone's gonna get hit on, it's gonna be me!" Although he's heterosexual, no one else's sexual preferences or proclivities seem to faze him. He's just that kind of guy. In fact, he's genuinely fascinated by people's kinks, which is one of the things I love about him. How many straight guys do you know who'd brunch with bears?

Bears are a subculture, within the gay community, consisting mostly of big, mature, hairy, manly men. Think Grizzly Adams, *Little House on the Prairie's* Mr. Edwards, John Goodman—even Santa Claus can be claimed as a bear icon. Some bears like other bears; some like younger bears-to-be, called cubs; some like nonbears; many have tastes that vary. Many bears are working-class, some adopt a working-class aesthetic, and others eroticize rural or working-class archetypes as part of their sexual play.

Our brunch with the bears wasn't my first exposure to this unique slice of gay male life; I can remember over a decade ago, I saw my first copy of *Bear* magazine, with its beefcake pictorials and rough-and-tumble jerk-off stories. What has always struck me about bears is their ingenuity: how a bunch of fat, hairy gay guys found each other and formed a niche.

I first met bear-about-town Ron Jackson Suresha last year at an all-night erotica reading during the Lambda Literary Festival in San Francisco. It was the kind of evening that seemed to go on forever until I thought maybe I never wanted to hear another piece of erotica again. Ron stepped on stage and announced that he'd be reading a piece from his forthcoming anthology, *Bearotica: Hot, Hairy, Heavy Fiction*. The story was indeed hot and raunchy, grabbing my attention and keeping it till the end. After reading, he announced that the author was in the audience, but too shy to read the story *herself*. A woman stood as he said her name, and I was surprised and intrigued; I wondered how a nonbear could write about such dirty bear sex, and what bear fag was willing to publish it. I grabbed Ron at the end of the reading, and he told me about his new book of interviews and discussions called *Bears on Bears*. This hair-raising, bare-all collection covers everything from bear history, terminology, and customs to Gen X bears, transbears, "lesbears," even post-bears and ex-bears.

One way bears shake things up, especially typical heterosexual assumptions, is by presenting the radical notion that a bearded Brawny-paper-towel guy could be—or is—gay. Because of his masculinity, he is assumed to be straight, and so the "straight-looking" gay man has tremendous subversive potential. See this hunky, furry stud? Well, paws off, ladies, he digs dudes. The bear is yet another example of the performance of gender, of drag, of how masculinity is not necessarily only the terrain of hetero men. Just as some bears have a class consciousness and others do not, some of this performance is self-aware and deliberate, whereas some bears believe they were simply born cuddly homo creatures. Bears also embody beautiful contradictions: macho toughness with a warm nurturing side that makes you want to get wrapped up in their never-ending hugs. Ultimately, bear culture is about a lot of things, including claiming masculinity, size, hirsuteness, and maturity; validating and celebrating identity; and connecting with others for friendship, sex, and relationships.

Bears are the butchest of boys, so, as a butch-dyke lover, I'm attracted to their hypermasculinity in an intellectual and theoretical way. I knew Ron's book would be a fun and interesting read, but bears didn't seem that relevant to my life as a pansexual, polyamorous, kinky girl. I mean, I know some bears, but I am not a "lesbear," and I am not particularly attracted to bears, so I wasn't expecting *Bears on Bears* to touch me at such a deep level. My personal connection to bears never occurred to me until I read this book. In fact, I think it should be required reading for anyone interested in gender studies because it's about bears, and then it is about so much more than bears.

As a femme dyke fond of expressing hyperfemininity (you know, channeling my inner drag queen) and into exploring the complexities and power of gender identity, I found myself relating to the stories, connecting with their subjects, being moved and challenged by conversations between and about bears. Femmes and bears have more in common than you may think at first glance. We've both carved out a niche within queer subculture, and our identities are tied tightly to both gender and sex. On the surface, we may appear to be "straight-looking" and gender-conforming, but many of us couldn't be farther from fitting in. Our gender expression may look "normal" to mainstream culture—a bear may look like a lumberjack and a femme may look like the girl next door—but our queer desires automatically problematize such normalcy. Eric Rofes says that bears "simultaneously affirm and undercut traditional masculinities," and I believe femmes do the same thing with femininity.

While many forms of female masculinities are celebrated as cutting edge—butch, boi, drag king—female femininities are seen as obvious, incapable of being conscious or performative. Just as masculinity can be performed by men or women, so can femininity, and femmes call attention to femininity as another form of drag. Just as bears create queer masculinity, femmes forge new forms of queer femininities. No wonder Goldilocks was so interested in those three bears.

This Girl is Different

1. I learned what it was like to be queer even before I was queer in the summer streets of Provincetown from my gay father and Marilyn Monroe

A typical child of divorced parents, I lived with my mom and saw my dad for holidays and school vacations. When I was fifteen, I got to spend the whole summer living at my dad's, and my dad happened to live in Provincetown. I got my first job that summer working at a leather shop, and spent my free time hanging out with drag queens and being crushed out on a dyke bike messenger named Nina. I remember grinning a lot whenever she made deliveries to our store. She had jet black hair, muscles, looked like a tough tomboy all grown up. It never occurred to me that all my friends back home on Long Island weren't having a summer like I was having. The summer when I wore perfume for the first time, and a transvestite named Lola helped me choose it—it was her scent and I loved the way she smelled. Like spiced apples and vanilla. It was a summer of lesbian potluck dinners and five o' clock tea dances at the Boatslip. A summer of watching my dad cruise other men on Commercial Street. A summer to remember.

My father was close friends with a performer named Jimmy James, who impersonated Marilyn Monroe. They called it "female impersonation," but it was really more than that. He was the most exciting, most glamorous person I knew. Unlike the tired queens with cheap shiny dresses who couldn't even lip sync very well, Jimmy sang Marilyn's songs and talked to the audience in Marilyn's voice. And his nightly transformation was magical. When I saw him during the day, he was always cute and perky and witty. When he got himself in that peach-pink sequined dress and blond wig and diamond bracelets, he *embodied* her. She was gorgeous and sexy and naughty and brash, and I wanted to be her. Not the Marilyn I'd seen in *All About Eve* with my dad, not the Marilyn on posters and T-shirts everywhere. I wanted to be the Marilyn Jimmy was.

2. *I learned what it was like to be a lesbian in ivy-covered brick buildings from a girljock and a rabble-rouser named Jen I learned what it was like to be a dyke from 100 percent pre-shrunk cotton T-shirts that said READ MY LIPS I LIKE GIRLS CLITLICKER; I'LL BE DAMNED BUTTFUCKER; TOTAL CONDOM NATION and fluorescent crack-n-peel stickers that read I learned what it was like to be a femme from Mother Camp and Joan Nestle and girls who look like boys*

During the first week of college freshmen orientation, I met Jessie, a shy soccer player from a small town in upstate New York who lived in my dorm. We sat together in calculus class. Neither of us understood our crazy professor's handwriting on the blackboard, but we understood the scribbled notes we passed back and forth, like best friends in high school. She was sensitive, funny, easy going, and she had the most amazing blue eyes. After one of our weekly dorm meetings, Jessie came out to the entire group as a lesbian. When she told us, we all huddled around her kissing and hugging and encouraging her. I remember returning to my room that night and thinking that she was one of the bravest women I knew. That year, she had a beautiful girlfriend who looked like young Elizabeth Taylor, and I loved seeing them together.

All first year students had to attend a series of awareness seminars, and the Bisexual Lesbian and Gay Awareness Workshop was run by queer students. In the workshop, everyone had to go around the room and say we were gay or lesbian and then talk in the first person about what it was like to be gay or lesbian.

"If you aren't gay or lesbian, we encourage you to consider personal experiences when you felt different or ostracized and relate them to the group," said one of the facilitators, a well-dressed senior with tortoise-shell glasses and chunky black shoes. Some people's stories about being gay were true, but you didn't always know which ones. I knew that Jessie was telling the truth.

It seemed like everyone at Wesleyan was queer or at least wanted to be. Everywhere I looked, there were pink triangle buttons, posters for one of several gay student groups, and same sex couples holding hands. When the gay-lesbian-bisexual alliance threw a party, it was an event not to be missed. The best music, the best outfits, and by the end of the night, shirtless boys and topless girls bumping-and-grinding till dawn.

Jessie and I flirted for a year, and by the time we were sophomores, I told her that I was through flirting and I kissed her. Just like that. Well, I wanted to, so I did. I was terrified once I did it, and scared about what would happen next. What happens when two girls kiss? She became my first girlfriend. Jessie was the first girlfriend of a lot of girls, actually. She was a one-woman recruiting agent, but so genuine and unassuming no one suspected their daughters wouldn't be safe around her. Coming to terms with my sexual identity for myself and acting on my feelings got all squished together. I guess I didn't have tremendous self-doubt because I had the luxury of being in a place where it was okay, even great, to be queer. Once Jessie and I became a couple, I was holding her hand around campus just like anyone else I had dated. So I slipped out of the closet, telling everyone I was bisexual. A lot of my friends were queer, so they said, "Yippee! Welcome to the family!"

The way I told my mom was less than ideal. I was home on a school break and talking to Jessie for about an hour on the telephone. My mom kept knocking on my bedroom door, telling me to get off the phone. I was totally frustrated, came storming into the living room.

She said something snide like, "I don't know who this Jessie is and why you have to be on the phone with her for so long."

"She's my girlfriend! And I'm bisexual!" I shouted angrily.

I don't actually remember what she said after that.

Telling my gay father was a lot less dramatic. He just said something like, "That's great—whatever makes you happy." Interestingly, he wasn't jumping for joy over me joining the team or anything.

Jessie and I didn't last very long; we really were better off as friends. I don't think people, including me, realized how serious I was—this wasn't an experiment or whimsy—until I met Jen. Jen was *the* Big Dyke on Campus. She was a senior, super intelligent, opinionated, really out. Everyone knew who she was because she was a big-time activist, very outspoken about things like sex, S/M, and porn. She also went to class dressed in men's shirts and ties. This was no friendly, sporty lesbian that everyone found charming. She was a butch dyke, brazen in her gender and style, and I was drawn to her. She was frantically finishing her honors thesis when we first met, and so our early encounters were at the library. I remember kissing her for the first time on the library steps and feeling such intense desire like I would explode and shatter into tiny bits of flesh at her feet. She was a brilliant flirt, so self-assured, so deliberate and generous with her words, so powerful at casting a spell on me. Consumed by her, I wanted to surrender, to give her everything. She was the smartest, fiercest lesbian I knew. And then she was *my* girlfriend.

Jen used to read *On Our Backs* and *Susie Bright's Lesbian Sex World* to me at bedtime every night. (She was even in charge of bringing Susie Bright to speak on campus that spring.) We were so connected, so engaged in the relationship. Every single day, there was something new to learn, share, discover. I did so many things for the first time with Jen. Jen was the first girl I ever lived with. I experienced the tremors of my first earthquake in bed with Jen and her yellow Lab. I had my first taste of what now is my favorite all-time food at the hands of Jen: sushi. Jen was the first woman to fuck me with a dildo. Jen was the first woman to tie me up. The first woman to spank me. To fuck my ass. She topped me for the first time, I bottomed to her for the first time, and we switched. We watched fag porn together. She was the first girl I ever fucked with a strap-on. She was the first girl I ever stripped for. Jen was the first girl I ever bought a tie for. Jen brought me to buy my first pair of Doc Martens. She was so articulate about her desires and her politics, so sex positive that I felt like I could tell her anything. She was my lover, my mentor, my dyke teacher, and so much of who I am today came from her.

Before her, I felt closeted not only about my desire for women, but my desire to explore the myriad possibilities of sex. Coming out finally gave me the freedom to do so. I was never tortured or miserable with all the boys I'd been with; in fact, physically, they were pretty satisfying.

I couldn't always connect with them on an intellectual or emotional level, so I always felt like something was missing. While I was sexually precocious with men, I never tried new things, experimented, voiced fantasies—being a dyke totally coincided with my overall sexual liberation, and the two awakenings became intrinsically linked.

My mom met Jen for the first time over brunch when we also broke the news that I was going to Hollywood with her when she graduated.

Between bites of her BLT, my mother said, "Jen has a reason to go—to start her career. You are running away from home."

That was the summer I became a dyke. In L.A., I was immersed in queer culture and finally felt like I'd come home, found my tribe, and myself. We became friends with radical faeries who lived in vegan households. We marched at Gay Pride in San Francisco and L.A. We joined ACT-UP and Queer Nation. It was a swirl of actions and demos, protesting everything from homophobic Governor Pete Wilson to a photo lab at the Beverly Center that wouldn't develop pictures of same-sex couples kissing. I marched down Santa Monica Boulevard in West Hollywood in my Doc Martens hundreds of times, hand-in-hand with pierced and tattooed perverts; on my way to fetish clubs and gay cafés; carrying brightly colored stickers and propaganda for distribution. I stayed all night at Kinkos on Highland making those stickers with Cory, who was copying his zine *Infected Faggot* with a bright yellow cover. Cory was a shaved-head-pierced-septum-dress-wearing-civil-but-disobedient-citizen. His anger, his rage, his spirit, and his infected body knew no bounds, and I loved him. When I returned from L.A., I had such a clearer sense of myself, my identity, my purpose.

It was only after I came out as a dyke that, for the first time in my life, I felt ready to celebrate being a girl, and I did. Actually, I overdid. Armed with Esther Newton's *Mother Camp,* Judith Butler's *Gender Trouble,* and Joan Nestle's *Restricted Country,* I embraced femme. I dressed up in short flowery dresses, push-up bras, satin panties, and lacy stockings. I paid great attention to my long, curly, perfectly coiffed hair, my glamorous makeup and especially pouty lips. I spritzed Lola's smell on my skin—Esteé Lauder's Private Collection—and painted my nails. I wore all of it with black combat boots and a brilliant sense of irony. I reveled in my girliness, went over the top, learned how to tweeze my eyebrows and line my lips with a lip pencil.

My gender presentation was unmistakable—blatant female sexuality. I was a proud, in-your-face, take-no-prisoners, uppity, don't-assume-I'm-straight-because-I-wear-lipstick-and-dresses femme dyke. Because femmes are always assumed to be straight or sleeping with men, and I do sleep with men, I made sure to always have a butch on my arm so that I'd be read as femme. Even though I was sure I'd be mistaken for straight, the boys took one look at me and steered clear. It was as if I was too much of a woman for them to handle, like I was a handful, and I was. But butch girls love a handful—a handful of tits, a handful of ass, a girl who needs to be handled, a girl who can handle herself.

How I figured out I was a femme had a lot to do with the women I was attracted to and the dynamic between us. When I was in junior high, I used to mess around with a friend of mine named Angela. Angela was one of those girls who developed early; I remember she had big breasts in, like, sixth grade. We mostly kissed and touched over clothes, and we played out various boy–girl scenarios. I was always the girl—my early femme roots. My favorite of all our little scenes was the one where she was my male boss and I was the secretary. The boss made me have sex with him and told me if I didn't I would get fired. Now, this was all before Clarence Thomas, Anita Hill, and the media awareness/obsession with sexual harassment. I remember she'd tell me to suck her dick and push my face unmercifully into her crotch, which smelled amazing. The drama of it all—the force, the degradation, the power games—really got me off. After that, there was no going back to simplicity. I was hooked on the power.

Jen really epitomized all the girls I was attracted to then and still am. Being with a butch girl, I was valued for my combination of strength and vulnerability, for dressing up, for wanting an arm to hold onto, hips to wrap my legs around, being able to give my body over to her and say I trust you, I'm yours. My butch loved me in low-cut dresses, appreciated my sexual voraciousness, worshipped my inner slut. I reveled in the fact that I could be strong and submissive all at once. Surrender and still be a feminist. Being a dyke is not just about who I fuck and love, it's about being a girl who doesn't play by the rules.

Butch girls don't play by the rules either, and I love butch girls. Girls with hair so short you can barely slide it between two fingers to hold on. Girls with slick, shiny, barbershop haircuts and shirts that button the other way. Girls that swagger. Girls who have dicks made of flesh and silicone and latex and magic. Girls who get stared at in the ladies room, girls who shop in the boys department, girls who live every moment looking like they weren't supposed to. Girls with hands that touch me like they have been touching my body their entire lives. Girls who have big cocks, love blow jobs, and like to fuck girls hard. Everyday, it is the girls that get called Sir that make me catch my breath, the girls with strong jaws that buckle my knees, the girls who are a different gender that make me want to lie down for them.

Someone else said it about me recently and it's right on target: "She gets off on all different sorts of people sexually, but she falls for butches." Like the poet who bought her first strap-on with me and then wanted to sleep with it on. The shrink-in-training who got harassed every time she drove down South. She did look so much like a fifteen-year-old boy, blue button down shirts, neatly combed blond hair. The ad exec who had names for her dildos, and used to love for me to spit shine her wingtips. The photographer whose face was so mannish, she could pass almost anywhere. The writer who wanted a body like Loren Cameron's. The telephone repair woman who drove a truck. The cook who had a boy's name. The academic who got cruised by gay men on Castro Street. The cornfed farmboy from the Heartland with arms so hard and strong you swear they've been working the land not the iron at the gym.

There's the one who's got the James Dean stare down, and dresses like a clean-cut fag, and looks at me like she could look at me forever and never blink or grow tired or move from the spot she's in. She's a girl who loves girls like me—girls in velvet bras, girls who want to surrender to her mouth. She's a girl who isn't afraid to throw a femme down on the bed and fuck her. Possess her. My kind of girl. This girl is different.

Stone Femme

I lay her on her back so that I can better see her need. Her olive skin looks shockingly pale against the dark plaid bedspread, her boyish frame all lines and angles against it. The sharp suit that caught my eye at the club is resting on the hardwood floor. I've made her strip down to her boxer shorts. Restless, she grabs for me, so I take her hands and cover them with mine. I press her knuckles gently into the bed, and kiss her hard and fast. She's splayed out, and I'm struck by how vulnerable she must feel in her own bed. There are down-filled pillows scattered around her, the kind that give easily when you press into them. She told me when we met that she was sick of women assuming she's a big bad top just because she's a gentleman. She told me that she likes to get fucked. I want to hear it again, she has to repeat herself now that we are alone. I want to give her what she craves, but she must first show me a piece of her desire, preferably laced with a touch of desperation. I want her on the edge. When I'm satisfied she's there, I slip inside. She sucks my fingers into her cunt, eager, open. I love butches who take my hand willingly and without apology. I cup her cheeks with my other hand, then slide a finger in her ass. I want to stick something in her mouth, too, but I'm out of hands.

She's grunting like a pig, but her mind is resisting the sensations, fighting the pleasure. *Give up,* I say, *and beg me for it.* She stalls, doesn't want her need exposed like that. *Come on,* I whisper, turning her over onto her belly. I tell her to touch herself. I fuck her deeper. *May...I...please...*—she's starting to crumble—*come?* I raise my voice, trying not to shock her out of it. *Come,* I command, and the release is brutal, furious, beautiful. After she settles, I turn her back over and lie beside her. She begins stroking my inner thigh, toying with the elastic of my underwear. She wants to slip her fingers under the fabric. My hand stops her. In my world, you have to earn the privilege of fucking me, and once you do, you still have to ask permission. And that's not going to happen in one night. I am the one calling the shots here. I am untouchable. I am a stone femme.

You probably know my counterpart, the stone butch: strong, silent, mysterious, misunderstood. She has told you about days of blue-collar jobs and passing on the street, and nights of pleasing women picked up at bars. Sometimes she doesn't take her clothes off, doesn't show her body to you. Sometimes she's Sir, Top, Daddy, running the fuck and foregoing your generous advances. She knows what gets her off: the howl of an orgasm underneath her, brought on by her touch. Screaming herself is not part of the equation. Maybe she guards herself from her past, from her fear, from her pain. For her to sink into her body and share it with you is tougher than her exterior, harder than her cock. She needs trust, she needs security, she needs the urge to overtake the terror. Getting inside her head, her heart, or her body can be like hunting for buried treasure, chasing down a cunning leopard, waiting for a landslide. Patience is a virtue.

I've had many stone lovers, some easier to melt than others. I always found myself with an unquestionable respect and reverence for their stoneness. I let them set the terms of their pleasure. Some part of me understood their choice to be stone on a very deep level without reservation, ambivalence, or resentment. Their self-preservation didn't seem strange or foreign to me. I gave myself to them, and I let them give to me in whatever ways they wanted, needed, were able to. I didn't shame or punish them, push or prod at their secret places. I let them come to me if and when they wanted more—to shed one layer of clothing, of armor, of skin.

But what about the stone femme? She must be lurking somewhere in a smoky bar, long legs encased in bullet-proof fishnets sliding down into stilettos—her weapon of choice. She is another kind of femme, fierce and gorgeous, stunningly guarded. You may have seen her once and mistaken her for someone else, thinking, Why should a femme be stone? Femmes wear skirts because we want to get fucked. Femmes are do-me queens. Femininity means spreading our legs to lie naked and open for you. You assume all femmes are ready, willing, and able. Femmes don't need to protect our strong and fragile selves, don't need to be the ones in charge. Femmes don't have body dissonance or discomfort. Femmes don't get off on getting you off.

I let my stone butch lovers dictate the terms of their pleasure, but it never occurred to me that I could do the same. It wasn't until my own sexuality shifted that I realized I understood stone butches because I *identified* with them. Stone to me is about setting boundaries, a wrestling match between desire and power, need and protection. I am stone when I am not ready to show myself to you fully. I am not shut off, I am on, on you. It's not about fleeing from connection, but about marking borders in order to experience intimacy comfortably without qualms or regret. It's about knowing what my body and spirit are capable of and honoring both. It's about inching toward vulnerability at my own pace. It's about healing.

Stone femme is control. Stone femme is power. Stone femme is bitch Top. Stone is a way to be sexual on my terms, derive pleasure by my own definitions. I know what makes my pussy wet, and it's feeling a butch body yield to me. For me, an equal exchange is not possible or desirable. I think equality is overrated. When I lie down with someone, her hands above her head speak submission, her trembling flesh says, *Take me.* Short gasps and shallow breaths whisper, *I am yours, do with me what you will.* Your cock doesn't scare me, I know how to take your swollen hardness and make magic. I will have you in the palm of my hand before dawn. I am the one calling the shots here. I am untouchable. I am a stone femme.

Tristan's Favorite Sex Stuff

Introduction: My Adventures in Sex, Porn, and Perversion

Deviant Desires: Incredibly Strange Sex by Katharine Gates (Juno Books, 2000).

My Life as a Pornographer and Other Indecent Acts by John Preston (Masquerade Books, 1993).

On Our Backs, 3415 Cesar Chavez St., #101, San Francisco, CA 94110 www.onourbacksmag.com

The Village Voice, 36 Cooper Square, New York, NY 10002, www.villagevoice.com

The Sexual Is Political

My Date with Howard Stern

Private Parts by Howard Stern (Pocket Books, 1997).

Sex and Silence in D.C.

American Brotherhood Leather Contest, www.americanbrotherhood.com

Two's Too Tough

The Ethical Slut: A Guide to Infinite Sexual Possibilities by Dossie Easton and Catherine A. Liszt (Greenery Press, 1998).

The Lesbian Polyamory Reader: Open Relationships, Non-Monogamy, and Casual Sex ed. by Judith P. Stelboum (Harrington Park Press, 1999).

Loving More magazine, www.lovemore.com

The New Intimacy: Open-Ended Marriage and Alternative Lifestyles by Ronald Mazur (toExcel/iUniverse.com, 2000).

Polyamory: The New Love without Limits by Deborah M. Anapol (iUniverse.com, 1997).

Dallas Dildo Defiance

Forbidden Fruit Sex Toy Store, 512 Neches St., Austin, TX 78701, www.forbiddenfruit.com

Leather by Boots, 2525 Wycliff Ave., #124, Dallas, TX 75219, www.leathernetwork.com/lbbpage

Passion Fruit Video, www.passionfruitvideo.com

Eminem Is My Bitch

Angry Blonde by Eminem (ReganBooks, 2000).

Hustler Hollywood, 8920 Sunset Blvd., Los Angeles, CA 90069

Taboo magazine, 8484 Wilshire Blvd., #900, Beverly Hills, CA 90211, www.hustlertaboo.com

The Name of the Rose

V-Day, www.vday.org

Vagina Monologues by Eve Ensler (Villard, 2000).

My Life as a Feminist Pornographer

On Our Backs, 3415 Cesar Chavez St., #101, San Francisco, CA 94110, www.onourbacksmag.com

True Lust Adventures

Intro to Swingers 101

Grand Opening! Sexuality Boutique, 318 Harvard St., #32, Brookline, MA 02446, www.grandopening.com

The Lifestyle: A Look at the Erotic Rites of Swingers by Terry Gould (Firefly Books, 2000).

The Tourist and the Puppy

International Ms. Leather, www.imsl.org

My Date with Betty Dodson

Betty Dodson Productions, P.O. Box 1933, Murray Hill Station, New York, NY 10156, www.bettydodson.com

Going for the Gold in Michigan

Michigan Womyn's Music Festival, www.michfest.com

My Throbbing Mouse

Nerve, www.nerve.com

Cruising for Girls

Squirt, www.squirt.org

Womanline, www.womanline.com

Throb, http://hometown.aol.com/throbparty/

Lusting for Lingerie

Agent Provocateur, 7961 Melrose Ave., Los Angeles, CA 90046, www.agentprovocateur.com

Sex Outside the City

Old Pioneer Country Garden Inn, 2805 Unionville Rd., Unionville, NV 89418

Kinky Summer Camp

Little Darlings directed by Ronald F. Maxwell (Paramount Pictures, 1980).

Fuck Your Gender

Of Butches, Kings, and Masculinity

The Drag King Book by Del LaGrace Volcano and Judith "Jack" Halberstam (Consortium, 1999).

Dréd's website, www.dredking.com

Female Masculinity by Judith "Jack" Halberstam (Duke University Press, 1998).

Murray Hill's website, www.mrmurrayhill.com

New York Kings' website, www.thekingsnyc.com

Trouble in Utopia

Michigan Womyn's Music Festival, www.michfest.com

Porn Queens and Prom Kings

Living Dolls: The Making of a Child Beauty Queen, www.hbo.com

Tranny Chaser

Gender PAC, www.gpac.org

Drag Kings Make Me Wet

International Drag King Extravaganza, www.idke.com

Building a Better Cock

Body Alchemy: Transexual Portraits by Loren Cameron (Cleis Press, 1996).

FTM International, www.ftm-intl.org

Loren Cameron's website, www.lorencameron.com

Paying for It

My Virgin Lap

Strip City: A Stripper's Farewell Journey Across America by Lily Burana (Talk Miramax Books, 2001).

Tips for Tricks

Sex Work: Writings by Women in the Sex Industry ed. by Frédérique Delacoste and Priscilla Alexander (Cleis Press, 1987).

Tricks and Treats: Sex Workers Write About Their Clients ed. by Matt Bernstein Sycamore (Haworth Press, 2000).

Whores and Other Feminists ed. by Jill Nagle (Routledge, 1997).

Organizing Jizz Joints

Exotic Dancers Union, www.exoticdancersunion.com

Live Nude Girls Unite!, www.livenudegirlsunite.com

Lap Dancing in Queens

Network of Sex Work Projects, www.walnet.org/csis/groups/nswp/index.html

PONY: Prostitutes of New York, http://bayswan.org/PONY.html

Hollywood and Sunset Strippers

Chloe's website, www.chloexxx.com

Hot Potato Sex!

National Potato Council, www.npcspud.com

Calling the Shots in Pornville

On Being Buttgirl

Evil Angel Video, www.evilangel.com

Toys in Babeland, www.babeland.com

I'm a Porn Star

Adult Video News, www.avn.com

Who Does Your Pubic Hair?

Playboy, www.playboy.com

Desperately Seeking Dyke Porn

Fatale Video, 1537 4th St., #193, San Rafael, CA 94901, www.fatalemedia.com

S.I.R. Video, 3288 21st St., PMB #94, San Francisco, CA 94110, www.sirvideo.com

Me and Juli Ashton's Ass

Juli Ashton's website, www.clubjuli.com

There's No Place Like "Oz"

GLAAD, www.glaad.org

Oz, www.hbo.com/oz

Queer As Folk, www.sho.com/queer

Your Wife's Porn

Wicked Pictures, www.wickedweb.com

Panic in Pornville

Adult Video News, www.avn.com

Behind the Money Shot

Money Shot, www.moneyshot-theseries.com

Vivid Video, www.vividvideo.com

Dyke Debauchery

Dyke Debauchery, www.dykedebauchery.com

Why I Love Porn

Candida Royalle, Femme Productions, P.O. Box 268, New York, NY 10012, www.royalle.com

Chloe's website, www.chloexxx.com

Sex Ed 201

Girls Who Squirt

The G Spot and Other Discoveries About Human Sexuality by Alice Kahn Ladas, Beverly Whipple, and John D. Perry (Dell, 1983).

The Good Vibrations Guide: The G-Spot by Cathy Winks (Down There Press, 1998).

How to Female Ejaculate directed by Fanny Fatale (Fatale Video, 1992), www.fatalemedia.com.

Tantric Journey to Female Orgasm directed by Debi Sundahl (Isis Media, 1998), www.isismedia.org.

The Art of Anal Fisting

Living in Leather, www.livinginleather.org

Trust, the Hand Book: A Guide to the Sensual and Spiritual Art of Handballing by Bert Herrman (Alamo Square Press, 1991).

Bend Over, Boys!

Bend Over Boyfriend directed by Shar Rednour (Fatale Video/S.I.R. Video, 1998), www.fatalemedia.com.

Bend Over Boyfriend 2: More Rockin', Less Talkin' directed by Shar Rednour and Jackie Strano (S.I.R. Video, 1999).

S.I.R. Video, 3288 21st St., PMB #94, San Francisco, CA 94110, www.sirvideo.com

The Ultimate Guide to Strap-on Sex: A Complete Resource for Men and Women by Karlyn Lotney, aka Fairy Butch (Cleis Press, 2000).

Vixen Creations, 1004 Revere Ave., #B-49, San Francisco, CA 94124, www.vixencreations.com

Wetter Is Better

Astroglide, www.astroglide.com

Eros, www.erosusa.com

ForPlay, Trimensa Pharmaceuticals, (800) 554-1313

Hydra Smooth, www.peekay.com

ID, Westridge Laboratories, www.idlube.com

Liquid Silk and Maximus, www.blowfish.com/catalog/supplies/lube.html

Probe, Davryan Labs, www.davryan.com

Slippery Stuff, Wal-Med, www.wallace-medical.com

Wet International, www.wetinternational.com

The Five-Finger Club

Elegant Angel Video, www.storeelegantangel.com

A Hand in the Bush: The Fine Art of Vaginal Fisting by Deborah Addington (Greenery Press, 1998).

Seymore Butts Home Movies, www.teamtushy.com

My Tantra Mantra

Barbara Carrellas's website, www.tootallblondes.com

The Complete Kama Sutra trans. by Alain Danielou (Inner Traditions, 1995).

Sexual Energy Ecstasy: A Practical Guide to Lovemaking Secrets of the East and West by David and Ellen Ramsdale (Bantam Doubleday Dell, 1993).

Tantra.com, www.tantra.com

Tantra: The Art of Conscious Loving by Charles and Caroline Muir (Mercury House, 1990).

Tantric Journey to Female Orgasm directed by Debi Sundahl (Isis Media, 1998), www.isismedia.org.

Ass Licker

The Ultimate Guide to Anal Sex for Women by Tristan Taormino (Cleis Press, 1998).

The Female Hard-On

Eros CTD, www.urometrics.com/products/eros

Fairy Butch, www.fairybutch.com

For Women Only: A Revolutionary Guide to Overcoming Sexual Dysfunction and Reclaiming Your Sex Life by Jennifer L. Berman and Laura Berman (Henry Holt, 2001).

Pump Up Your Clit

Clit Pump, www.millenniumpumps.com/clitpumpset.htm

Millennium Pumps, www.millenniumpumps.com

Sex Nerds

NakkidNerds, http://guests.NakkidNerds.com

Society for the Scientific Study of Human Sexuality, www.sexscience.org

Society for the Scientific Study of Human Sexuality–Western Region, www.sssswr.org

Ponies, Puppies, and Perverts

I Was a Pro-Dom Virgin

Pandora's Box, www.punishmentsquare.com/pandorasbox/index.html

Sir, Yes Sir!

Dyke Uniform Corps, http://members.aol.com/ducny/

Pervy Ponygirl

Equus Eroticus, www.equuseroticus.com

The Human Equine, www.thehumanequine.com

John Fluevog, www.fluevog.com

Me, My Panties, and the Mayor

Rhode Island Enforcers, www.mindspring.com/~enforcersri/

Wide World of Water Sports

Holy Smoke directed by Jane Campion (Miramax, 1999), www.holysmokethemovie.com.

The Water Boys, www.waterboys.com

Leather Puppy Love

Leatherdog, www.leatherdog.com

Pierced for Pleasure

Coming to Power: Writings and Graphics on Lesbian S/M by SAMOIS (Alyson, 1983).

Fakir Musafar's website, www.bodyplay.com

Play Piercing FAQ, www.queernet.org/deviant/fsplyprc.htm

Play Piercing How-To, www.sexuality.org/l/bdsm/needle.html

Finding My Inner Dom

The Beauty of Fetish by Steven Diet Goedde (Edition Stemmle, 1998).

Cruel Beauty directed by Ernest Greene (Bizarre Video, 2000).

Dark Paradise directed by Ernest Greene (Bizarre Video, 1998).

FetishDiva Midori's website, www.fetishdiva.com

The Master's Manual: A Handbook of Erotic Dominance by Jack Rinella (Daedalus, 1994).

The Sexually Dominant Woman: A Workbook for Nervous Beginners by Lady Green (Greenery Press, 1998).

The Topping Book: Or, Getting Good at Being Bad by Dossie Easton and Catherine A. Liszt (Greenery Press, 1998).

Looking for Mommy

Bad Boys Get Spanked, www.badboysgetspanked.com

Doing It for Daddy ed. by Pat Califia (Alyson, 1994).

Dress Up for Daddy (Fatale Video, 1991), www.fatalemedia.com.

Every Women I Ever Loved: Lesbian Writers on Their Mothers ed. by Catherine Reid and Holly Iglesias (Cleis Press, 1997).

Hubbies.com, www.hubbies.com.

Loving in the War Years: Lo Que Nunca Pasó por Sus Labios by Cherríe Moraga (South End Press, 1983).

San Francisco Dyke Diva and Dyke Daddy Contest, www.dykedaddydiva-sf.org

Sweet Boy directed by Karen Everett (Karen Everett Films, 2001), www.kareneverettfilms.com.

Whap! Magazine, www.whapmag.com

The Unbearable Queerness of Being

My Gay Boyfriend

Gay Video News, www.gayvn.com

Sister and Brother: Lesbians and Gay Men Write About Their Lives Together ed. by Joan Nestle and John Preston (HarperCollins, 1994).

The State of Lesbian Sex

After School Special (Fatale Video, 2000), www.fatalemedia.com.

Alley of the Tranny Boys directed by Christopher Lee (Christopher Lee, 1998).

TRISTAN TAORMINO'S TRUE LUST

Girl King directed by Ileana Pietrobruno (Ileana Pietrobruno, 2002).

Lesbian Sex Mafia, www.lesbiansexmafia.org

Passion Fruit Video, www.passionfruitvideo.com

Please Don't Stop: Lesbian Tips for Givin' It and Gettin' It directed by Oriana Bolden (Homosexual Chocolate Productions/Sexpositive Productions, 2001).

S.I.R. Video, 3288 21st St., PMB #94, San Francisco, CA 94110, www.sirvideo.com

Sugar Sweet directed by Desiree Lim (Desiree Lim, 2002).

Electric Shocks/Lesbian Cocks

Juice: Electricity for Pleasure and Pain by Uncle Abdul (Greenery Press, 1998).

Real Sex on HBO, www.hbo.com/docs/latenight/realsex.html

The Ultimate Guide to Strap-on Sex: A Complete Resource for Men and Women by Karlyn Lotney, aka Fairy Butch (Cleis Press, 2000).

Queer Co-Ed Lust

Opposite Sex: Gay Men on Lesbians, Lesbians on Gay Men ed. by Sara Miles and Eric Rofes (NYU Press, 1998).

PoMoSexuals: Challenging Assumptions About Gender And Sexuality ed. by Carol Queen and Lawrence Schimel (Cleis Press, 1997).

Switch Hitters: Lesbians Write Gay Male Erotica and Gay Men Write Lesbian Erotica ed. by Carol Queen and Lawrence Schimel (Cleis Press, 1996).

Queering the Swing

The Lifestyle: A Look at the Erotic Rites of Swingers by Terry Gould (Firefly Books, 2000).

I Fucked a Straight Girl

A Hand in the Bush: The Fine Art of Vaginal Fisting by Deborah Addington (Greenery Press, 1998).

Cherry Popper

Trust, the Hand Book: A Guide to the Sensual and Spiritual Art of Handballing by Bert Herrman (Alamo Square Press, 1991).

And Bears, Oh My!

Bearotica ed. by Ron Suresha (Alyson, 2002), www.bearotica.com.

Bears on Bears ed. by Ron Suresha (Alyson, 2002), www.bearsonbears.com.

This Girl Is Different

Gender Trouble by Judith Butler (Routledge, 1999).

Mother Camp by Esther Newton (University of Chicago Press, 1979).

A Restricted Country by Joan Nestle (Firebrand Books, 1987).

Susie Sexpert's Lesbian Sex World by Susie Bright (Cleis Press, 1999).

Stone Femme

The Persistent Desire: A Femme–Butch Reader ed. by Joan Nestle (Alyson, 1992).

Stone Butch Blues by Leslie Feinberg (Firebrand Books, 1993).

www.butch-femme.com

www.stonebutch.com

www.stonefemme.com

About the Author

TRISTAN TAORMINO is the award-winning author of *Pucker Up: A Hands-on Guide to Ecstatic Sex* and *The Ultimate Guide to Anal Sex for Women*. She is director, producer and star of two videos based on her book, *Tristan Taormino's Ultimate Guide to Anal Sex for Women 1 & 2*, which are distributed by Evil Angel Video. She is a columnist for *The Village Voice* and *Taboo* and series editor of *Best Lesbian Erotica*, for which she has edited nine volumes. She has been featured in over 300 publications including *The New York Times*, *Redbook*, *Glamour*, *Cosmopolitan*, *Playboy*, *Penthouse*, *Entertainment Weekly*, *Vibe*, and *Men's Health*. She has appeared on NBC's *The Other Half*, MTV, HBO's *Real Sex*, *The Howard Stern Show*, The Discovery Channel, Oxygen, and *Loveline*. She teaches sexuality workshops around the country and her official web site is www.puckerup.com.